Schuwirth, Erman & Partner

The Design of the City

Preface by/*Vorwort*
Walter Wulf

Introduction by/*Einleitung*
Filippo Beltrami Gadola

Texts by/ *Text*
Heinz Thiel

Photographic Credits
Helmut Claus, H.G. Esch,
Heike Seewald, Jörg Winde

Editorial Director USA
Pierantonio Giacoppo

Chief Editor of Collection
Maurizio Vitta

Publishing Coordinator
Franca Rottola

Graphic Design
Paola Polastri

Editing
Martyn J. Anderson

Colour-separation
Litofilms Italia, Bergamo

Printing
Poligrafiche Bolis, Bergamo

First published March 1999

Copyright 1999
by l'Arca Edizioni

All rights reserved
Printed in Italy

ISBN 88-7838-046-6

Contents
Inhalt

5	Preface by / *Vorwort* Walter Wulf	112	KRUPP EXPO Exhibition Centre / *Ausstellungspavillon*
9	Introduction by / *Einleitung* Filippo Beltrami Gadola	116	DSS The Spree Warehouses / *Die Spree Speicher*
15	Works / *Werke*	122	KTC Technology Centre / *Technologiezentrum*
16	MAZ Office Centre / *Bürohaus*	128	HCH Office Centre and Shopping Mall / *Büro- und Einkaufszentrum*
26	GALERIE LUISE Shopping Mall / *Ladenpassage*	134	RO 30 Commercial Complex with Retail, Offices and Apartments / *Büro-, Geschäfts- und Apartmentkomplex*
36	NORCON Office Building / *Bürohaus*	140	HAUS WULF One-Family-House / *Einfamilienhaus*
46	MAI-NI2-NI3 Office Complex / *Bürohaus*	148	HEMME- HOF House-Ensemble / *Wohnhausgruppe*
56	HFS Military Pilot School / *Heeresfliegerwaffenschule*	154	HAUS KÖRNER One-Family-House / *Einfamilienhaus*
62	EXPO 2000 German Expo Pavilion / *Deutscher Expo Pavillon*	158	PLOT 176 Hotel and Shopping Mall / *Hotel- und Einkaufspassage*
66	KW 2 Office Building for German Rail / *Bürogebäude der DB AG*	162	G 38 Commercial Building / *Büro- und Geschäftshaus*
70	PITTLER Headquarters / *Hauptverwaltung*	170	KS 23-25 Commercial Building / *Büro- und Geschäftshaus*
74	MPC Medical Park Hotel and Office Centre / *Medical Park Hotel-und Bürozentrum*	176	LS 4 Commercial Building / *Büro- und Geschäftshaus*
78	BOCO Laundry / *Wäscherei*	184	AGID Freight Centre / *Frachtzentrum*
86	DH 1 Dental Store / *Dentallager*	193	List of works / *Liste der Werke*
94	AF 16 B Office Building / *Bürohaus*	199	Biography / *Biographie*
104	BSHG Bosch- Siemens Service Centre / *Bosch- Siemens- Kundendienstzentrum*		

Preface
Vorwort
by Walter Wulf

"It is accordingly the task of architects to bring themselves into line with the salient facts of the day and the principal goals of the society of which they form part and also to design their works on the basis of these. They will as a result refrain from transferring the design principles of previous epochs and bygone social structures to their works, but will instead foster a fresh approach in each case to the task in hand as well as creative fulfilment of all objective and spiritual calls on them."

Drafted by a high proportion of major European architects of the day, this statement in the declaration of the Congrès Internationaux d'Architecture Moderne (CIAM I) held at La Sarraz in June 1928 succinctly and precisely proclaims the credo of the traditional modernists. This should continue to apply without restriction in today's post-modern society, however much it seeks to modishly categorize dialogue between architects and society as a process of so-called visual communication.

Klaus Schuwirth and Erol Erman as architects working in tandem have obviously felt obliged to observe this credo right from the start of their output, all the more so since they belong to a generation which received a training entirely in the spirit of the traditional modernists. Hailing from different cultural groups and initially moulded by the traditions and impressions received from these, in 1977 they became independent so as to be able to directly realize their own ideas. In doing so they were obviously following Martin Gropius's call "to break through the barriers of erroneous academic wisdom" and to build "in the imagination", applying only the most rigorous yardsticks to their work and its implementation. Here again - if perhaps not aware of this - they were observing the dictum in Gropius's flyer for a 1919 exhibition by unknown architects that ideas perish "as soon as they become compromises."

The two architects may be in the tradition of classic modernists in pursuing such ideas; yet they equally and directly square up to the challenges of the present, which with the exploitation of new technologies also opens up fresh opportunities for design. A synthesis of aesthetics and technology thus becomes a crucial and continually applied principle in their output.

Although such idioms of current architectural language as reflecting facades, sharply angled corners, tent roofs, massive cylinders, light structural frameworks and indeed even the pyramid are not absent from their work, Schuwirth and Erman do not simply pursue fashionable trends. Of central importance is the fact that while they may apply the elements of modern architecture - quoted often enough and everywhere - they do so only when these conform with the basic concept behind a building and sensibly underline and highlight its function. Their architecture remains honest, since its ideas do not merely become mannerisms, instead being exploited in surprising fashion and in the process becoming characteristic of the architects as well as

„Die Aufgabe der Architekten ist es deshalb, sich in Übereinstimmung zu bringen mit den großen Tatsachen der Zeit und den großen Zielen der Gesellschaft, der sie angehören, und ihre Werke danach zu gestalten. Sie lehnen es infolgedessen ab, gestalterische Prinzipien früherer Epochen und vergangener Gesellschaftsstrukturen auf ihre Werke zu übertragen, sondern fordern eine jeweils neue Erfassung einer Bauaufgabe und eine schöpferische Erfüllung aller sachlichen und geistigen Ansprüche an sie."

Dieses Postulat aus der Erklärung des Congrès Internationaux d'Architecture Moderne (CIAM I), abgefaßt im Juni 1928 in La Sarraz von einem großen Teil der seiner Zeit bedeutendsten europäischen Architekten, manifestiert knapp und präzise den Anspruch der klassischen Moderne. Es sollte uneingeschränkt auch heute noch in der postmodernen Gesellschaft gelten, die den Dialog zwischen Architekten und Gesellschaft jedoch modisch als sogenannte visuelle Kommunikation artikulieren möchte.

Das Architektenpaar Klaus Schuwirth und Erol Erman hat sich diesem Anspruch offenbar von Anfang seines Schaffens verpflichtet gefühlt, zumal es einer Generation angehört, die ihre Ausbildung noch ganz im Geiste der klassischen Moderne erhalten hat. Aus unterschiedlichen Kulturkreisen kommend und zunächst geprägt von den dort empfangenen Traditionen und Eindrücken finden sie 1977 zur Selbständigkeit, um ihre eigenen Vorstellungen unmittelbarer verwirklichen zu können. Dabei folgen sie offenbar einem Aufruf von Martin Gropius, „die Schranken verbildender Schulweisheit zu durchbrechen" und „in der Phantasie", zu bauen, und lassen im Anspruch an ihre Arbeit und ihre Realisierung von Beginn an nur höchste Maßstäbe zu, wieder – wenn auch vielleicht nicht bewußt – Gropius' Flugblatt zur Ausstellung für unbekannte Architekten aus dem Jahre 1919 folgend, der die Ideen sterben sieht, „sobald sie Kompromisse werden".

Mit diesen Grundideen stehen die beiden Architekten zwar in der Tradition der klassischen Moderne; doch öffnen sie sich ebenso und unmittelbar den Herausforderungen der Gegenwart, die insbesondere mit der Nutzung neuer Techniken auch neue Möglichkeiten der Gestaltung erschließt. So wird die Synthese von Ästhetik und Technik zu einem entscheidenden und durchgängigen Prinzip in ihrem Schaffen.

Dabei folgen sie nicht modischen Trends, obwohl die Zitate der aktuellen Architektursprache – verspiegelte Fassaden, scharfkantige Gebäudeecken, Zeltdächer, großvolumige Zylinder, leichte Tragwerke, ja sogar die Pyramide – nicht fehlen. Entscheidend ist jedoch, daß die Elemente moderner Architektur, oft genug und überall zitiert, von Schuwirth und Erman dann genutzt werden, wenn sie in Einheit mit der Grundkonzeption stehen und sinnhaft die jeweilige Funktion des Baues verdeutlichen und hervorheben. Die Architektur bleibt ehrlich; die Ideen werden nicht zur Manier, sondern sind in überraschender Weise genutzt, wobei sie charakterisierend für die Architekten und identifikationsstiftend für Bauherrn und Nutzer werden.

conferring identity on clients and users. This directly involves yet another characteristic: the buildings conform to their surroundings wherever appropriate, yet without becoming subservient. Insofar as their task requires this, their design and dimensions set yardsticks for the neighbourhood, emphasize these and open up fresh areas in town planning.

The ideas and intentions of the two architects became evident at an early stage in their few purely residential buildings. The "Hemme-Hof" development pursues the idea of integrating an ensemble of modern architecture in an established village centre. "Haus Wulf" achieves the adaptation of a "technical" object to an unspoiled natural environment.

Like the BOSCH-SIEMENS distribution and office centre (BSHG), the warehousing and industrial complex at Hannover airport (AGID) becomes almost a piece of traditional modern architecture, the core and the forerunner for subsequent buildings.

The office and exhibition complex (MAZ) represents a convincing example of the mastery of surface and space as well as of individual structural design. This is complemented by the nearby NORCON-HAUS office block, which throws doubt on the maxim "function follows form" by convincingly demonstrating that the one does not exclude the other, while the dental warehouse (DH 1) erected with such ease and skill for flexible usage sets a visual accent for a newly built area of the city. It is most desirable that the design for the planned medical park hotel and office centre (MPC) nearby, with its flowing, thin-skinned tent roof offsetting the solidity of the flanking blocks, can yet be realized. This also applied to the office building for German Rail (KW 2) whose dynamic form emulates the speed of advanced trains and embodies a strong identity. The design of the MAI – NI 2 – NI 3 office ensemble is also notable for excitingly composed and imposing blocks as well as its mastery of space.

Galerie Luise provides a convincing example of successful adaptation to an existing urban environment. Its svelte elegance - providing spaciousness and transparency between two different arched entrances - bids fair to add a fresh attraction to this central location in Hannover.

For all the differing character of their buildings and the sometimes surprising architectural solutions, any consideration of Schuwirth and Erman's work so far will reveal certain constant features which convey a specific identity and, for all due caution, permit a reference to one style. Irrespective of whether these consist of solitary buildings, large or small, or buildings (ensembles) making an impact on the whole vicinity, these are characterized by an all-round view and accessibility from all sides. In traditional fashion the aim has been holistic architecture both within and without - and the high degree to which aesthetics and serviceability, form and usefulness, have been reconciled remains astonishing. The utilization of novel materials and techniques, with interesting ideas and convincing solutions culminating in a synthesis of technology and design, again and again seems to pose a special challenge.

Damit ist unmittelbar ein weiteres Charakteristikum verbunden: Die Bauten passen sich dort, wo es geboten ist, ihrem Umfeld an, doch sie unterwerfen sich nicht. Soweit die Aufgabe es erfordert, setzen sie Maßstäbe in Gestaltung und Dimension für ihre Umgebung, akzentuieren sie und eröffnen neue städtebauliche Räume.

Die Vorstellungen und Absichten der beiden Architekten werden bereits frühzeitig deutlich bei den wenigen reinen Wohnbauten. Die Bebauung „Hemme-Hof" setzt die Idee der Integration eines Ensembles neuer Architektur in ein gewachsenes Dorfzentrum um. Das „Haus Wulf" realisiert die Einpassung eines „technischen" Objekts in Kontrast zu einer ursprünglich belassenen, naturräumlichen Umgebung.

Der Lager- und Industriekomplex Flughafen Hannover (AGID), fast ein Stück Architektur der klassischen Moderne, wird zum Kern und Vorbild nachfolgender Bauten, ebenso wie das BOSCH-SIEMENS Vertriebs- und Verwaltungszentrum (BSHG).

Für die Beherrschung von Fläche und Raum bei gleichzeitiger Durchbildung im einzelnen steht der Büro- und Ausstellungskomplex (MAZ) als überzeugendes Beispiel; ergänzt durch das nahe Bürogebäude NORCON-HAUS, dessen filigrane Konstruktion die Devise, die Funktion bestimme die Form, in Frage stellt, indem es überzeugend verdeutlicht, daß das eine das andere nicht ausschließt, und das in spielerischer Leichtigkeit für flexible Nutzung errichtete Dentallager (DH 1), wurde hier der optische Akzent für einen neu erschlossenen Stadtbereich gesetzt. Es wäre zu wünschen, daß der Entwurf des nahebei geplanten Medical Park Hotel- und Bürozentrum (MPC), dessen schwingende, dünnhäutige Zeltdachmembranen gegen die Festigkeit der flankierenden Blöcke gesetzt sind, noch realisiert werden könnte. Letzteres gilt auch für das Bürogebäude der Deutschen Bahn (KW 2), dessen die Schnelligkeit moderner Züge umsetzende dynamische Gestalt ein hohes Identifikationsmodell darstellt. Spannungsreich komponierte, sich durchdringende Baukörper und beherrschter Raum charakterisieren auch die Gestaltung des Büroensembles MAI – NI 2 – NI 3.

Für die gelungene Einpassung in eine gewachsene stadträumliche Umgebung zeugt in überzeugender Weise die Galerie Luise, deren elegante Urbanität – großzügige Weite und Transparenz zwischen zwei unterschiedlichen Torarchitekturen – der Zentrumssituation Hannovers eine neue Attraktion zu geben vermochte.

Betrachtet man das bisherige Werk der Architekten Schuwirth und Erman, so werden bei aller Unterschiedlichkeit der Objekte und ihrer zum Teil überraschenden architektonischen Lösungen bestimmte Konstanten deutlich, die eine spezifische Identität vermitteln und es bei aller gebotenen Vorsicht erlauben, von einem Stil zu sprechen. Gleich, ob es sich um kleine oder große Solitärbauten handelt oder um stadträumlich wirksame Gebäude(gruppen), kennzeichnend sind dabei Rundumsichtigkeit und allseitige Zugänglichkeit. In traditioneller Weise wird noch ganzheitliche Architektur von Äußerem und Inneren angestrebt, wobei es erstaunlich ist, in welch hohem Maß Ästhetik und Nutzung, Gestalt und Gebrauchswert miteinander in Einklang gebracht werden können. Eine besondere Herausforderung scheint auch

Yet creative ideas and visions could not be successfully and convincingly realized without setting a high standard - extending to the smallest detail - in their application. Schuwirth and Erman impose this on themselves and their partners. They aim to uphold it in a society increasingly questioning its own values. It remains desirable that in future too they should find clients whose requirements of architecture are not solely determined by considerations of investment and profit but also by the fact that good architecture itself represents something of value which can also find splendid commercial fulfilment in pursuit of corporate identity. That this idea is by no means new is proved by such developments as the Woolworth and Lever buildings in New York, the Thyssen high-rise in Düsseldorf and BMW's head office in Munich, to mention only a few.

One can only wish for a wide circulation for this brief monograph as a testimony - less with its text than in the superb illustrations - to fine architecture.

immer wieder darin zu liegen, neuartige Materialien und Techniken zu nutzen, wobei interessante Ideen und überzeugende Lösungen einer Synthese von Technik und Gestaltung gelingen.

Die kreativen Ideen und Vorstellungen wären jedoch nicht erfolgreich und überzeugend zu realisieren ohne einen hohen Anspruch an die Qualität bei ihrer Umsetzung, auch bis ins Detail. Schuwirth und Erman haben diesen Anspruch an sich selbst und an ihre Partner. Sie sollten sich ihn erhalten in einer Gesellschaft, die ihre Werte selbst zunehmend in Frage stellt. Man möchte wünschen, daß sie auch in Zukunft Partner finden, deren Ansprüche an Architektur nicht allein von Investitionen und Profit bestimmt werden, sondern auch von der Tatsache, daß gute Architektur einen Wert an sich darstellt und sich auch kommerziell hervorragend im Sinne einer modernen Corporate Identity einsetzen läßt. Daß dieser Gedanke nicht neu ist, bezeugen Objekte, wie das Woolworth und das Lever Building in New York, das Thyssen Hochhaus in Düsseldorf oder das BMW-Verwaltungsgebäude in München, um nur einige zu nennen.

Man möchte dieser kleinen Werkmonographie eine weite Verbreitung wünschen, damit sie von guter Architektur zeugen kann, mehr durch die hervorragenden Abbildungen als durch das Wort.

Introduction
Einleitung
by Filippo Beltrami Gadola

The idea of a possible context cannot possibly be overlooked when describing or commenting on Schuwirth and Erman's works of architecture and designs. Nothing could be more difficult: in a certain sense, the artistic-stylistic development of these German architects, whose work is grounded in and focuses around building technology and engineering, constitutes in itself a sort of context.

The chance to take a closer look at some of the most recent and perhaps most successful buildings on the German architectural scene also provides us with the opportunity to focus on the image of a German mega-city, on its interaction with the environment, and on the most notable transformations it has undergone. As in France, strenuous efforts to reinforce and reform its built structures provide a sort of benchmark for other European cities: take, for instance, the work carried out to create the first pedestrian areas in Hamburg and Frankfurt or to construct the Sbahn railway link in Munich, Bavaria, a number of years ago. German technology, in all its various guises, deserves credit for being the first to recognise, in a modern key, the importance of transport and communications in creating and knitting together metropolitan areas other than those already historically forming part of the great nineteenth-century network of capital cities. Herein, perhaps, lies Germany's proverbial supremacy in the fields of manufacturing and technology, a notion of modernity that strives to represent itself in its own stylistic forms and whose underlying historical-cultural roots always seem to be just out of reach.

In some respects, Schuwirth and Erman's works of architecture represent a world in search of its own identity, a totally different world from the hypertechnological downtown neighbourhoods of the American built landscape, quite alien to any form of pseudo-vernacular stylistic re-reading. Their work is, however, pushed along by the financial thrust of one of the planet's most stable economies that never stops modernising its own structures, tools, facilities, and scenarios. But this certainly is not a brutal world geared exclusively to profit to the detriment of the widescale quality of life, quite the contrary: Germany is now one of the nations most concerned about environmental issues, energy saving, and the real possibility of reconciling economic growth with the need to safeguard its cultural-environmental heritage. Careful planning capable of detecting large portions of the country to be governed by landscape protection measures and, in some respects, public opinion which has always been concerned about environmental issues make Germany one of the nations at the real cutting-edge of compatible growth.

This means there are good reasons for suspecting that Schuwirth and Erman's city is a city of both public and private agencies, of large real-estate and financial companies, that is looking for its own room to grown and new models to work on, often well way from traditional city centres. Attention is focused on creating and identifying new scenarios compatible with industrial and technological growth rates and with the desire to create an effective and efficient corporate image, free from even

Beschreibt oder kommentiert man die Architektur und Entwürfe von Schuwirth und Erman ist die Idee des Kontextes nicht zu übersehen. Nichts aber könnte schwieriger sein: Denn in gewissem Sinne begründet die künstlerisch-stilistische Entwicklung dieser deutschen Architekten, deren Arbeit sich auf Bau- und Ingenieurtechnik konzentriert, bereits in sich eine Art Kontext. Die Möglichkeit, sich intensiver mit einigen der neuesten und vielleicht sogar erfolgreichsten Gebäude der deutschen Architektur-Szene auseinanderzusetzen, gibt uns die Gelegenheit, sich mit dem Bild der deutschen Großstädte zu beschäftigen, ihrem Zusammenspiel mit dem Umland und den bedeutendsten Veränderungen, denen sie ausgesetzt gewesen ist. Wie auch in Frankreich tragen die rastlosen Versuche, die gegebenen Strukturen zu verstärken und zu verbessern, Vorbildcharakter für andere europäische Städte: Nehmen wir beispielsweise die Anstrengungen, vor einigen Jahren erste Fußgängerzonen in Hamburg und Frankfurt einzurichten oder das S-Bahn-Netz in München. In all ihren Erscheinungen verdient deutsche Technologie Anerkennung dafür, daß sie als erste die Bedeutung von Transport- und Kommunikationsmitteln erkannt hat, um andere städtische Gebiete zu schaffen und miteinander zu verknüpfen als jene historischen, die bereits im 19. Jahrhundert Bestandteil des großen Netzwerkes von Hauptstädten bildeten. Vermutlich liegt genau hier die sprichwörtliche deutsche Vormachtstellung auf dem Gebiet der Produktion und Technik, die Vorstellung einer Moderne, die danach strebt, sich selbst in ihrer eigenen stilistischen Formensprache zu repräsentieren und deren zugrundeliegende historisch-kulturellen Wurzeln immer ein wenig außer acht zu lassen.

In mancher Beziehung spiegelt die Architektur von Schuwirth und Erman eine Welt auf der Suche nach der eigenen Identität, eine gänzlich andere Welt als jene der hypertechnischen Innenstadtgebiete amerikanischer Machart, fern allen pseudo-idiomatischen stilistischen Lesarten. Dennoch wird ihre Arbeit durch die finanzielle Schubkraft einer der stabilsten Wirtschaften dieses Planeten angetrieben, welche niemals aufhört, ihre eigenen Strukturen, Instrumente, Einrichtungen und Szenarien zu modernisieren. Doch es handelt sich sicherlich nicht um eine brutale Welt, deren einziges Ziel es ist, Profit auf Kosten der Lebensqualität zu erzielen. Im Gegenteil: Deutschland ist heute eine der Nationen, die sich am intensivsten mit Umweltfragen, Energieproblemen und den gegebenen Möglichkeiten, wirtschaftliches Wachstum mit dem Schutz kulturellen Erbes in Einklang zu bringen, auseinandersetzt. Sorgfältige Planungen, die es erlauben, große Teile des Landes unter Landschaftsschutz zu stellen, wie auch, in mancher Hinsicht, eine für Umweltfragen sensibilisierte Öffentlichkeit, machen Deutschland zu einer der Vorreiternationen in Bezug auf umweltverträgliches Wachstum.

Das bedeutet, daß es gute Gründe gibt zu vermuten, daß die Stadt in der Vorstellung von Schuwirth und Erman eine Stadt sowohl mit öffentlichen als auch privaten Institutionen, mit großen Immobilien- und Finanzunternehmen ist, die nach Expansionsraum und neuen Arbeitsmodellen sucht, häufig jenseits der traditionellen Stadtzentren. Volle Aufmerksamkeit gilt der Suche nach neuen

the slightest trace of rhetoric. The sheer scale of the phenomenon and the results that have been achieved in quantitative terms are such as to allow real experimentation, to continually play with the geometric patterns of forms, to come up with new solutions of quite conflicting types, to produce new materials, to revert to some of the boldest aspects of building science and statics, and then to test all this out on the concrete grounds of project design. Unusually for Europe, this has been a successful, low-key, anti-theoretical attempt to construct large-scale projects, paying great attention to and showing a genuine sense of responsibility towards real issues. The architecture is never designed to astound at all costs, drawing exclusively on the latest marvels of advanced technology; on the contrary, it merely exploits these technological developments to produce its own architectural idiom, to create signs of a possible new collective identity, mingling together the combined skills of both engineers and architects. The busy work and successful careers of this team are brought out in this essay which, with the exception of the EXPO pavilions, focuses exclusively on buildings that have actually been constructed.

Over the last twenty years, Schuwirth and Erman seem to have set themselves the task of inventing and then actually making use of an architectural vocabulary which is less geared to "grand design" than to what they call "minuscule consideration" and "precise formulation", in which versatility and the ability to adapt design play an important role; variability is not simply a means of expression, it is substance in its own right.

In some respects this is the case with the headquarters of the NORCON Real Estate Agency, whose offices are equipped with technological innovations - requested by both the client and required by certain financial considerations - that combine to create an architectural complex with a design flair all of its own. The technical-structural shell partly encloses the building, redesigning its main fronts in what might be described as almost classical patterns and rhythms: the contrast between the dark, compact glass facades and the gleaming whiteness of the layout of metal columns makes the building even a visual landmark for its nearby surroundings, as part of a successful attempt to instil new parts of the city with their own *genius loci*.

The headquarters of the mechanical engineering company, Pittler, is quite similar in its own peculiar way. This ten-storey office block in Frankfurt is located in the vicinity of an urban crossroads, making it possible to construct an entrance of distinctly heroic proportions based around a huge arch culminating in a massive reticular frame of beams crowning the roof. The interplay of masses and position of the building fronts draws our gaze towards the centre of the design where the main entrance is located; the fact that the building is constructed at a certain distance from the roads and the interplay of geometric forms, based on the construction of a triangular-shaped complex, gives a definite sense of identity to this predominantly industrial context with no real stylistic connotations and creates a circular plaza inside a rather rigid road grid big enough, from the right distance, to offer a perspective view of the entire structure. The

Szenarien, die sich mit industriellen und technologischen Wachstumsraten und dem Wunsch nach einem effektiven Firmenimage beschäftigen, frei von allen rhetorischen Worthüllen. Die tatsächliche Bandbreite dieses Phänomens und die bisher erreichten Ergebnisse auf quantitativer Basis erlauben es, zu experimentieren, fortwährend mit geometrischen Formen zu spielen, Lösungen unterschiedlichster Art einzubringen, neue Materialien zu entwickeln, zu den mutigsten Aspekten des Bauens und der Statik zurückzukehren und dann all dieses in Form konkreter Projektentwürfe auszuprobieren. So ungewöhnlich dieses für Europa sein mag, es stellt einen erfolgreichen, zurückhaltenden und anti-theoretischen Ansatz dar, große Projekte auszuführen, und dabei zentrale Fragen mit Respekt zu berücksichtigen.

Diese Architektur dient niemals dazu, unter allen Umständen zu beeindrucken und dabei ausschließlich die neuesten Wunder fortschrittlicher Technik vorzuführen; im Gegenteil, sie schöpft lediglich diese technischen Entwicklungen aus, um ihr eigenes architektonisches Vokabular zu entwickeln, Zeichen einer möglichen neuen kollektiven Identität zu setzen, die Fähigkeiten von Ingenieuren und Architekten zu verbinden und gemeinsam zu nutzen. Dieser Essay widmet sich der rastlosen Arbeit und dem erfolgreichen Weg dieses Teams; im Vordergrund stehen dabei, mit Ausnahme des EXPO-Pavillons, ausschließlich Gebäude, die tatsächlich gebaut worden sind.

Über die letzten 20 Jahre scheinen Schuwirth und Erman sich das Ziel gesetzt zu haben, eine neue Architektursprache zu entwickeln und zu nutzen. Sie setzen dabei weniger auf „große Entwürfe" als auf das, was sie selbst „minutiöse Erwägung" und „ präzise Formulierung" nennen, wobei Vielseitigkeit und die Fähigkeit, Entwürfe anzupassen, eine wichtige Rolle spielen; dabei ist Variabilität nicht einfach als ein Mittel des Ausdrucks zu betrachten, sondern eine Qualität eigenen Rechtes.

Dies ist in mancher Hinsicht der Fall bei dem Hauptquartier der NORCON Immobilien-Agentur, deren Büros mit technischen Innovationen – sowohl auf Wunsch des Kundens als auch aus finanziellen Erwägungen – ausgestattet sind, die sich zu einem architektonischen Komplex mit singulärem Flair verbinden. Die technisch-strukturelle Schale umschließt teilweise das Gebäude und prägt die Hauptfassaden mit fast klassischen Mustern und Rhythmen: Der Kontrast zwischen den dunklen, kompakten Glasfassaden und der gleißenden Weiße der Metallträger läßt das Gebäude zu einem optischen Wahrzeichen für die nähere Umgebung werden - Teil des erfolgreichen Versuches, neue Areale der Stadt mit ihrem spezifischen genius loci *auszustatten.*

Das Hauptquartier der Maschinenbaufirma Pittler funktioniert auf ähnliche, wenn auch eigene Art und Weise. Dieses zehnstöckige Bürogebäude in Frankfurt liegt in der unmittelbaren Nähe einer städtischen Kreuzung. Hier war die Konstruktion eines Eingangsbereiches mit großartigen Proportionen möglich, basierend auf einem großen Bogen, der, in einem massiven netzartigen Rahmen von Trägern kulminierend, das Dach bekrönt. Das Zusammenspiel der Massen und der Position der Gebäudefassaden zieht unseren Blick in das Zentrum des Entwurfes, auf den

context also favours the construction of a building capable of changing appearance according to the angle from which it is viewed: seen from the square, it is the representational nature of the project that catches the eye, but viewed from the inside of the building block the fronts feature a more classical office-block design.

Identity and identification provided ideal foundations on which to construct the HFS, a new training centre for helicopter pilots in the German Federal Armed Forces in Bückeburg, where the exposed brick architectural masses suspended several metres in the air are held in place by light columns culminating in a vaulted roof: a clear allusion to those old airships and Germany's great tradition in aviation.

The projects bearing Schuwirth and Erman's signature are, by their very nature, all quite different from each other, responding to the specific needs of a rapidly evolving society: upon closer scrutiny it can almost always be seen how economic growth and alterations to the urban (or suburban) fabric have been geared to the creation of social, entertainment, cultural, leisure or just plain relaxation facilities, regardless of whether these spaces are designed for the community or small groups of individuals.

One of the main leitmotifs, as in most major Western cities, is the proper, functional re-use of urban spaces and the creation of new works of architecture capable of knitting together different parts of the city: a form of architecture apparently designed to generate new, functional "gap sites" resolving the contradictions deriving from the history and growth of the cities in question. Compactness and openness, density and transparency, these are the pairs of expressions Schuwirth and Erman now use to describe their own work; in actual fact, the works of these two German architects can be read on two different levels: on one hand, their ability to keep on creating architectural complexes capable of forming powerful urban connections; on the other, the capacity to create products that stand up on their own, emerging with great force from their surroundings, as in the case of the Alter Flughafen Office Block.

The GLJO project - Gallery Luise Shopping Mall - seems to work on various levels: maximum exploitation of its urban lot, which is penetrated in-depth through the creation of an indoor shopping arcade, close physical interaction between shopping and service facilities, the complicated issue of how the mall entrances create a series of different urban facades, the construction of a vaulted central space injecting a definite sense of identity, and, last but not least, the need to create an effective pedestrian area that respects the unwritten rules of the retail industry. Schuwirth and Erman's approach to reforming and reconverting parts of the old city is based on clear-cut transformation: this is the case with the BSHG - Kundendienstzentrum Bosch-Siemens-Hausgeräte in Hannover - where a services-style complex has been built on an old shopping site. It was decided to design a sort of permeable building block, bordered and terminated on the outside by the building structures; the heart of this urban lot, filled with trees, is connected to the outside by a series of pedestrian entrances, whose

Haupteingang. Die Tatsache, daß der Komplex in einem gewissen Abstand zu den Straßen steht, wie auch das Zusammenspiel der geometrischen Formen, die auf dem dreieckigen Grundriß des Gebäudes basieren, geben diesem hauptsächlich industriellen Kontext ohne wirkliche stilistische Eigenschaften eine eigene Identität und schaffen einen kreisförmigen Platz innerhalb eines eher strengen Straßenrasters – groß genug, um aus der richtigen Entfernung einen perspektivischen Blick auf die gesamte Anlage zu ermöglichen. Der Kontext begünstigt auch die Konstruktion eines Gebäudes, das, je nach Standort des Betrachters, sein Aussehen verändert: Es ist die repräsentative Natur des Projektes, die, vom Platz aus gesehen, ins Auge fällt; steht man jedoch innerhalb des Komplexes, erscheinen die Fassaden eher in der Gestalt eines klassischen Bürohausblocks.

Identität und Identifikation boten ideale Grundlagen für die Konstruktion des HFS, eines neuen Trainingszentrums für Hubschrauberpiloten der Bundeswehr in Bückeburg. Hier wird eine massive Ziegelarchitektur von leichten Säulen, die in einem gewölbtem Dach kulminieren, mehrere Meter hoch in der Schwebe gehalten: Eine deutliche Anspielung auf Zeppeline und Deutschlands große Tradition in der Luftfahrt.

Von Natur aus unterscheiden sich die Projekte, die Handschrift von Schuwirth und Erman tragen, deutlich voneinander, sie reagieren auf die speziellen Anforderungen einer sich rasch verändernden Gesellschaft: Bei näherer Betrachtung wird beinahe immer sichtbar, wie wirtschaftliches Wachstum und Wandlungen der urbanen (oder suburbanen) Struktur mit der Schaffung von Sozial-, Unterhaltungs- und Kultureinrichtungen verbunden worden sind, unabhängig davon, ob diese für die Gemeinschaft oder für kleine Gruppen von Individuen entworfen wurden. Eines der Leitmotive, wie in den meisten größeren westlichen Städten, ist die angemessene und funktionale Wiederbelebung urbaner Räume und die Schaffung neuer architektonischer Werke, die die verschiedenen Teile einer Stadt miteinander verbinden: Eine scheinbar zu dem Zweck entworfene Architekturform, neue, funktionale „Lücken" entstehen zu lassen, die die Widersprüche auflösen, die sich aus Geschichte und Wachstum einer jeden Stadt ergeben. Kompaktheit und Offenheit, Dichte und Transparenz sind die Ausdruckspaare, die Schuwirth und Erman jetzt zur Beschreibung ihrer eigenen Arbeit heranziehen; tatsächlich können die Arbeiten dieser beiden deutschen Architekten auf zwei verschiedene Ebenen verstanden werden: Auf der einen Seite steht ihre Fähigkeit, mit architektonischen Lösungen kraftvolle urbane Verbindungen herzustellen; auf der anderen Seite ihr Können, eigenständige Bauten zu entwerfen, die mit großer Kraft aus ihrer Umgebung herausragen, wie beispielsweise der Büroblock auf dem Alten Flughafen.

Die Galerie Luise; eine Einkaufspassage in Hannover, scheint auf verschiedenen Ebenen zu funktionieren: Maximale Ausnutzung der urbanen Parzelle durch eine die gesamte Tiefe eines Häuserblockes durchdringende Einkaufspassage sowie das enge Zusammenspiel von Einkaufs- und Dienstleistungseinrichtungen. Weiterhin die Art, wie die Eingänge der Passage eine Reihe verschiedener urbaner Fassaden entstehen lassen, dazu die Konstruktion eines überwölbten, zentralen Raumes, der eine ganz bestimmte Identität evoziert. Und, letztlich,

heroic proportions are brought out by a sturdy central column cleverly concealing the stairwells. There is a huge block at the foot of the entire complex with metal columns freely rising up into sort of unusual upturned capital to set the rhythm of the curtain facades. The juxtaposition of different building materials, the use of glass and metal and the way these materials react to sunlight, combine to inject the whole system with a certain dynamism that conflicts and contrasts with the simplicity of the site plan.

To grasp the sense and significance of Schuwirth and Erman's architecture, there is no need, and indeed it would probably be detrimental, to refer to their major business and real-estate operations connected with projects designed to create the future capital of united Germany (towards which the entire continental architectural scene has provided its own contribution). It would be more advisable to focus on projects and developments linked with their much more local, distinctly German architecture mainly related to development work for the various federal states and important cities, historically blessed with considerable economic and political autonomy.

The most important projects designed by these German architects include the MPC - Medical Park Center Hotel - part of an ambitious project to create a new centre of gravity for the city of Hannover's communications network and capable of drawing together and connecting up major scientific-educational facilities like the local university and hospital with the biomedical industry and research centres. Schuwirth and Erman's design is so instantly striking that it creates a real landmark for this newly developed urban area, featuring a vast covered plaza, and a multi-purpose hall confined in height by a tensile structure, whose geometrical signs derive from a metal grid whose position and functions make it the backbone of the entire system. The covered plaza is actually the hub of a multi-purpose mechanism hosting a wide variety of activities. Not far away, in close vicinity to Hannover Medical School, we come across the MAZ - Medical Exhibition and Marketing Centre - which, in some respects, is stylistically more advanced than the rest of the BSHG designs - Kundendienstzentrum Bosch-Siemens-Hausgeräte; the project area extends around a pedestrian plaza with car parks hidden beneath it and terminating in three buildings which, except for the glass pyramid that marks a possible way up to the building, draw on a theme that Schuwirth and Erman are most fond of: a complicated web of metal columns, connected together but also quite separate, that hold up what is here a quite novel element, big glass grilles protecting the facades which, due to their form, form a sort of ideal waterfall running down to the foot of the plaza.

This complicated-looking system attracts the onlooker's attention through a dynamic interplay of transparent materials and opaque/translucent columns, involving straight facades and soft angular curves.

The KW2 project - Office Complex with Computer Center for the German Rail - is part of a general redevelopment programme for the new German city and, at the same time, designed to use the forms and intuitions of architectural design to create a sense of

das Bedürfnis nach einer effektiven Fußgängerzone, die die ungeschriebenen Gesetze des Einzelhandels respektiert.

Schuwirth und Ermans Herangehen an die Verbesserung und Verwandlung alter städtischer Substanz basiert auf entschiedener Veränderung: So zum Beispiel beim Kundendienstzentrum Bosch-Siemens Hausgeräte in Hannover (BSHG). Hier wurde ein Kundendienst-Komplex auf einem ehemaligen Industriegelände errichtet. Man entschied sich für eine durchlässige Blockbebauung, außen begrenzt und bestimmt durch die Gebäudestrukturen; das Herz dieser urbanen Parzelle, mit Bäumen bepflanzt, ist mit der Außenseite durch eine Reihe von Fußgängereingängen verbunden, deren großartige Proportionen durch eine kräftige Säule, die geschickt die Treppenaufgänge verdeckt, betont werden. Am Fuß des gesamten Komplexes befindet sich ein großer Block mit frei aufsteigenden Metallsäulen, die durch ungewöhnliche, nach oben gebogene Kapitele den Rhythmus der Vorhangfassaden bestimmen. Die Nebeneinanderstellung der verschiedenen Baumaterialien, die Verwendung von Glas und Metall und die Art und Weise, wie diese auf Sonnenlicht reagieren, verleihen in ihrer Kombination dem gesamten System eine Dynamik, die im Gegensatz zu der Einfachheit des Lageplans steht.

Es ist unnötig, womöglich nachteilig, auf die Bau- und Immobilientätigkeit von Schuwirth und Erman in Verbindung mit den Projekten für die künftige Hauptstadt des vereinigten Deutschlands (die gesamte kontinentale Architektur-Szene hat hierzu eigene Beiträge beigesteuert) hinzuweisen, um Sinn und Besonderheit ihrer Architektur zu verstehen. Es wäre daher eher ratsam, sich auf Projekte und Entwicklungen zu konzentrieren, die sich durch ihre eher lokale, spezifisch deutsche Architektur auszeichnen und die in Zusammenhang mit der Entwicklungsarbeit für die verschiedenen Bundesländer und wichtigen Städte zu sehen sind, die von jeher beachtliche wirtschaftliche und politische Autonomie besitzen. Die wichtigsten Projekte dieser Architekten beinhalten das MPC – das Medical Park Hotel- und Bürozentrum – als Teil eines ehrgeizigen Projektes, Hannovers Kommunikationsnetz ein Zentrum zu verleihen, das in der Lage ist, wichtige Ausbildungseinrichtungen der Wissenschaft, wie die lokale Universität und das Krankenhaus, mit der biomedizinischen Industrie und Forschungszentren eng miteinander zu verknüpfen. Der Entwurf von Schuwirth und Erman ist so unvermittelt auffällig, daß er ein wirkliches Wahrzeichen bedeutet für dieses neu entwickelte urbane Gebiet. Der große überdachte Platz und die Mehrzweckhalle mit ihrer zugfesten Dachstruktur, deren geometrische Muster sich von einem Metallraster herleiten, werden durch Position und Funktion zum Rückgrat der gesamten Anlage. Tatsächlich ist der überdachte Platz Mittelpunkt eines komplizierten Gefüges für eine große Bandbreite von Aktivitäten. Nicht weit davon entfernt, nahe der Medizinischen Hochschule Hannover, nähern wir uns dem Medizinischen Ausstellungs- und Vertriebszentrum (MAZ), das, in gewisser Hinsicht, stilistisch weiter entwickelt ist als der oben genannte BSHG-Entwurf. Das Projektgebiet breitet sich um einen Fußgängern vorbehaltenen Platz mit darunterliegenden Parkplätzen aus und mündet in drei Gebäude, die, abgesehen von der gläsernen Pyramide,

identity and belonging. The resulting work of architecture is a clever architectural complex brimming with ideal and symbolic allusions to the activities going on inside and to railways in general: a sort of metal super-train negotiating a curve in the track runs along the entrance way to the building which terminates at both ends in a dynamic dip in the roof, whose openings and choice of materials create a sort of twin locomotive like those in the projects designed in Germany and the rest of Europe in 1930s, as part of the wider issue of aerodynamics related to developments in high-speed international communications.

The pictures in the following pages show how a human scale landscape incorporates Schuwirth and Erman's works of architecture in a carefully designed grid of communications links, landscaping, town-planning measures, and metropolitan public services. Nevertheless, it would be wrong to think that this powerful pragmatism and keen attention to the concrete needs of clients, mainly interested in manufacturing structures, in any way cramped Schuwirth and Erman's poetic vision and artistic force: the intricate machinery of the pavilion for Expo 2000, constructed out of reticular components and huge, brightly shining, circular, metal containers, hides a complicated exhibition system designed in the form of an engine concealing conference, meeting and socialising facilities. Architectural design turns into an exploratory model, a means of experimenting with different building styles. This is the case with Krupp Two - the Hannover Expo Center - in which form does not follow from function, but function from form. Forms become icons of opportunities lying in the future. These are not symbols appealing to the senses, but visible sensations; there has been an attempt to show how it might be possible to envisage new kinds of exhibition spaces in terms of their geometric forms, stylistic designs, and objectives: a large vaulted space, whose forms are reminiscent of airport designs and whose rhythm is set by the broad structural ribbing of the roof, is reflected along its entire length in two symmetrical pools of water; the space encloses an entrance platform hosting exhibitions, meetings and conventions over a number of overlapping levels.

The wide range of different projects carried out and conceptual differences in the designs clearly illustrate the great architectural expertise of these German architects, whose stylistic artistry has its roots in the intriguing world of science and technology: the large metal frames, that often conclude the covered spaces of these metropolitan works of architecture, inject these structures designed to structurally renovate and reform the polycentric city with an unusual sort of monumentalism.

An example of this is the DH ONE - Warehouse and Distribution Center for Dental Products - a goods storage and distribution warehouse shaped like a small metal box: a perfect square rising up into a compact, translucent office/warehouse block held in place by a system of metal cables and columns for supporting the roof. Colour differences point to and underline the function of the columns, which, by serving the exquisitely technical purpose of creating wide open spaces on the inside, are topped by a new sort of structural capital.

die einem die Eingänge in das Gebäude weist, sich auf ein Thema bezieben, das zu den Favoriten von Schuwirth und Erman gehört: ein kompliziertes Netz von Metallsäulen, die, miteinander verbunden und doch getrennt voneinander, hier ein ganz neues Element stützen, nämlich große, die Fassade schützende, gläserne Gitter, die entsprechend ihrer Form so etwas wie einen ideellen Wasserfall bilden, der auf die Ebene des Platzes herunterstürzt. Dieses kompliziert wirkende System fesselt die Aufmerksamkeit des Betrachters durch ein dynamisches Zusammenspiel durchscheinender Materialien und opak/transparenter Säulen unter Einbeziehung der geraden Fassaden und leicht gewinkelter Rundungen. Das KW2-Projekt – ein Bürokomplex mit Computerzentrum der Deutschen Bahn – ist Teil eines generellen Neuentwicklungsprogramms für die deutsche Stadt und dient gleichzeitig der Schaffung von Identität und Zugehörigkeit mit den Mitteln architektonischer Form und Intuition. Das Ergebnis ist ein intelligenter architektonischer Komplex mit einer Überfülle ideeller und symbolischer Anspielungen auf die Aktivitäten innerhalb des Gebäudes und auf Eisenbahnen im Allgemeinen: Vor dem Eingangsbereich des Gebäudes liegt in einer Schienenkurve ein metallener Superzug. Das Gebäude selbst endet an beiden Seiten mit einer dynamischen Senkung im Dach, dessen Öffnungen und Materialwahl im Rahmen eines übergeordneten Stichworts von Aerodynamik in Verbindung mit den Entwicklungen der schnellen internationalen Kommunikation an Zwillingslokomotiven denken lassen, ähnlich derer in deutschen und europäischen Projekten der 30er Jahre. Die Bilder auf den folgenden Seiten zeigen wie die Architektur von Schuwirth und Erman sich durch ein sorgfältig entworfenes Netz von Kommunikation, Landschafts- und Stadtplanungsmaßnahmen und metropolitanen öffentlichen Dienstleistungen in die Kulturlandschaft einfügt. Nichtsdestotrotz wäre es falsch anzunehmen, daß dieser kraftvolle Pragmatismus und der scharfe Blick für den konkreten Bedarf der hauptsächlich aus der Industrie stammenden Kunden, Schuwirth und Ermans poetische Vision und künstlerische Gestaltungskraft hemmten: die komplizierte Mechanik des Pavillons für die EXPO 2000, gebaut aus netzartigen Komponenten und riesigen, hell scheinenden, runden Metallcontainern, versteckt ein komplexes, in Form einer Maschine entworfenes Ausstellungssystem mit Konferenz- und Begegnungseinrichtungen. Der architektonische Entwurf verwandelt sich in eine Versuchsanordnung, in ein Mittel, um mit verschiedenen Baustilen zu experimentieren. So im Fall von Krupp Zwei – dem EXPO-Center für Hannover – in welchem Form nicht der Funktion folgt, sondern Funktion der Form. Formgebungen werden zu Zeichen von Möglichkeiten, die in der Zukunft liegen. Sie sind nicht Symbole, die die Sinne ansprechen, sondern sichtbare Eindrücke. Sie entstehen aus dem Versuch zu zeigen, wie man sich neue Arten von Ausstellungsräumen in Bezug auf ihre geometrischen Formen, ihre stilistische Prägung und ihre angestrebten Ziele vorstellen könnte: Ein großer überwölbter Raum, dessen Erscheinung an Flughafengebäude erinnert und dessen Rhythmus sich durch die breiten, strukturierenden Rippen des Daches bestimmt, wird in seiner gesamten Länge in zwei symmetrischen Flächen von Wasser gespiegelt; der Raum umschließt eine Eingangsebene, die auf

The square-shaped base marks the main entrance and layout of offices on the first floor above grade level.

The idea of creating a metal building frame to serve structural purposes is also a key design feature in the construction of AF 16 B - Hoseg Office Complex, one of the most unusual of all Schuwirth and Erman's numerous works of architecture. The construction of a standard building type, a hospital facility designed for third-world countries and easy to transport, features a base element, which could theoretically be repeated indefinitely, constructed on the outside of a glass wall held up by two vertical steel cables. The metal frame gently sets the rhythm of the entire building, determining its size, and completing the spatial layout near the outside. The sequence of metal stanchions is interrupted near the entrance, where the uniform facade screen breaks up to carefully create areas of shade in parts of the building set back in relation to the perimeter of the base.

Colour differences between the metal support frame and main building block are also a key design feature in the BOCO Central Laundry Factory that draws heavily on engineering: working on technical guidelines of an industrial nature, the challenge was to make a low-cost manufacturing plant look like a dynamic construction designed with great stylistic innovation. The clarity and rhythm created by the beams of four large bridges cast across the main building structure also determine the layout of the main building front, whose glass windows call to mind (by their colour) the water used in the industrial plants inside.

Schuwirth and Erman's architectural designs combine to form an urban-territorial system capable of changing shape and growing based on the kind of technical and technological developments which, in Germany, are part of the national heritage. This great tradition is part of a legacy which, in certain respects, instils a sort of soul in German cities, as they seek images and scenarios to represent their own identities projected towards the future in a completely rhetoric-free way.

mehreren Etagen Ausstellungen, Kongresse und Treffen beherbergt.

Die große Bandbreite der verschiedenen ausgeführten Projekte und die konzeptionelle Differenziertheit der Entwürfe illustrieren deutlich die große architektonische Professionalität dieser Architekten, deren stilistische Kunst ihre Wurzeln in der faszinierenden Welt der Wissenschaft und Technik besitzt: Die großen metallenen Rahmen, die häufig die überdeckten Räume dieser urbanen Bauten umfangen, verleihen diesen für die strukturelle Erneuerung und Reform der polyzentrischen Stadt entworfenen Konstruktionen eine ungewöhnliche Art von Monumentalität. Ein Beispiel dafür ist das DH ONE Lager- und Verkaufszentrum für Dentalprodukte – geformt wie eine kleine metallene Box: Ein perfektes Quadrat, das sich zu einem kompakten, transparenten Büro- und Lagerblock erhebt, umfaßt durch ein System von Metallbändern und das Dach tragender Säulen. Farbabstufungen unterstreichen die Funktion der Säulen, welche, während sie dem rein technischen Zweck dienen, weite und offene Innenräume zu schaffen, von einer neuen Art struktureller Kapitelle bekrönt werden. Die quadratisch geformte Basis kennzeichnet den Haupteingang und gibt das Layout der Büroräume des ersten Stockwerkes vor.

Die Idee einer Metallhülle für ein Gebäude, die strukturellen Zwecken dient, ist auch das Hauptkennzeichen der Konstruktion des AF 16 B Hoseg-Bürokomplexes, eines der ungewöhnlichsten von Schuwirth und Ermans zahlreichen Bauwerken. Die Konstruktion eines standardisierten, einfach zu transportierenden Bautyps eines Krankenhauses für Länder der dritten Welt besteht aus einem Basiselement aus gläsernen Fassaden, die von zwei vertikalen Stahltrossen zusammengehalten werden und theoretisch unendlich oft wiederholt werden könnten. Der Metallrahmen gibt sanft den Rhythmus für das gesamte Gebäude vor, bestimmt seine Größe und vollendet es an der Außenseite. Die Abfolge der Metallträger wird nahe des Einganges aufgebrochen und die uniforme Außenwand durchdrungen, um sorgfältig verschattete Nischen in den im Verhältnis zum Umfang des Sockels zurückgesetzten Teilen des Baues zu schaffen. Farbunterschiede zwischen dem tragenden Stahlrahmen und dem Block des Hauptgebäudes sind auch ein Schlüsselelement der BOCO Großwäschereianlage, die stark auf die Ingenieurtechnik zurückgreift: Während die technischen Richtlinien für eine solche Anlage zu berücksichtigen waren, bestand die Herausforderung darin, ein kostengünstiges Industriegebäude mit einer dynamischen Konstruktion völlig neuen Stils zu verbinden. Die von den Bögen der vier über das Hauptgebäude gespannten Brücken geschaffene Klarheit und deren Rhythmus prägen auch das Aussehen der Hauptfassade, deren Fenster (durch ihre Farbe) an das Wasser erinnern, das in der Anlage im Inneren benutzt wird. Die architektonischen Entwürfe von Schuwirth und Erman verbinden sich zu einem System urbaner Flächen, das zu Wandlungen der Gestalt und Wachstum fähig ist. Beide basieren auf jener Art von technischen Entwicklungen, die in Deutschland Teil des nationalen Erbes darstellen. Diese große Tradition ist etwas, das in mancher Hinsicht deutschen Städten so etwas wie eine Seele einhaucht, in dem sie nach identitätsstiftenden Bildern und Szenarien suchen und diese ohne Rhetorik in die Zukunft projizieren.

Works / *Werke*

MAZ
Office Centre
Bürohaus

In its use of space the Medical Exhibition and Sales Centre (MAZ) is reminiscent of block developments at the turn of the century, whose inner courtyards permitted truly intimate and undisturbed neighbourliness. The MAZ is also a block around a centre. An inner yard of accentuated length may open on to the street but very largely relates to the "inner life" of the whole complex. The variety of forms used to banish boredom from the facade represent an essential difference to traditional forerunners. The glass pyramid to the right of the entrance to the inner courtyard is however crucial for drawing attention and providing an aesthetic point of reference.

The complex as a whole consists of three sections of the building. Two of these sections cling in a right angle to the L-shaped centre, while the third appears like the stroke in an exclamation mark for which the glass pyramid supplies the dot.

The separate buildings are structured into smaller parts by extracting space elements with rounded expanses of glass. This produces the impression of a complex which is extensive but not bulky. Elements recurring in series, such as floor frameworks and steel girders, underline the favourable impression of a volume constructed with a light hand. A comparison with the ingenious termite heaps of Africa seems almost appropriate although this bears no relation to the aesthetics here - and is simply an impression caused by the delicacy of the facade of being confronted by something "weighty". The pyramid provides emphatic confirmation of this, but also a constant potential distraction for the eye. This was intended as a restaurant for MAZ users and visitors and also to make an impact on the neighbourhood, but just a few years after construction of the MAZ the pyramid had already become a feature whose attractiveness extended right into downtown Hanover.

Das Medizinische Ausstellungs- und Vertriebszentrum Hannover (MAZ) erinnert in seiner Flächennutzung an die Blockbebauungen der Jahrhundertwende, in denen die Innenhöfe ein recht ungestörtes intimes Nachbarschaftsleben zuließen. Auch das MAZ ist als Block um eine Mitte gebaut. Ein in der Länge akzentuierter Innenhof öffnet sich zwar zur Straße, ist aber doch weitgehend auf das 'Innenleben' des Gesamtkomplexes bezogen. Die vielfältigen Formen, mit denen der Fassade die Langeweile ausgetrieben wurde, sind ein wesentlicher Unterschied zum historischen Vorgänger. Entscheidend ist aber für die Aufmerksamkeit und die ästhetische Einordnung die gläserne Pyramide zur Rechten der Innenhofzufahrt.

Der Gesamtkomplex besteht aus drei Gebäudeteilen. Zwei dieser Teile schmiegen sich rechtwinklig um die L-förmige Mitte, der dritte Teile erscheint wie die Linie eines Ausrufezeichens, dessen Punkt von der Glaspyramide gebildet wird.

Die einzelnen Baukörper sind durch vorgezogene Raumelemente mit abgerundeten Glasflächen kleinteilig strukturiert. Es entsteht dadurch zwar der Eindruck eines volumenreichen, aber nicht der eines massigen Komplexes. Seriell sich wiederholende Elemente, wie die Stockwerksrahmen und die Stahlträger, unterstreichen den positiven Eindruck eines spielerisch aufgebauten Volumens. Der Vergleich mit den kunstvollen afrikanischen Termiten-Haufen drängt sich fast auf, obwohl er keinerlei Anhaltspunkt in der Ästhetik findet - es ist nur der durch die Feingliedrigkeit der Fassade hervorgerufene Eindruck, etwas 'Gewichtiges' vor sich zu haben.

Als akzentuierende Bestätigung, aber zugleich auch als stetige potentielle Ablenkung für das Auge erweist sich die Pyramide. Sie war als Restaurant für die MAZ-Nutzer und -Besucher gedacht und sollte auch in die Nachbarschaft ausstrahlen, aber schon wenige Jahre seit der Errichtung des MAZ hat die Pyramide eine bis in die Innenstadt reichende Attraktivität entwickelt.

Model and, bottom of page, plans of the ground floor and first floor.
Modell und auf der Seite unten: Grundriß des Erd- und ersten Obergeschosses.

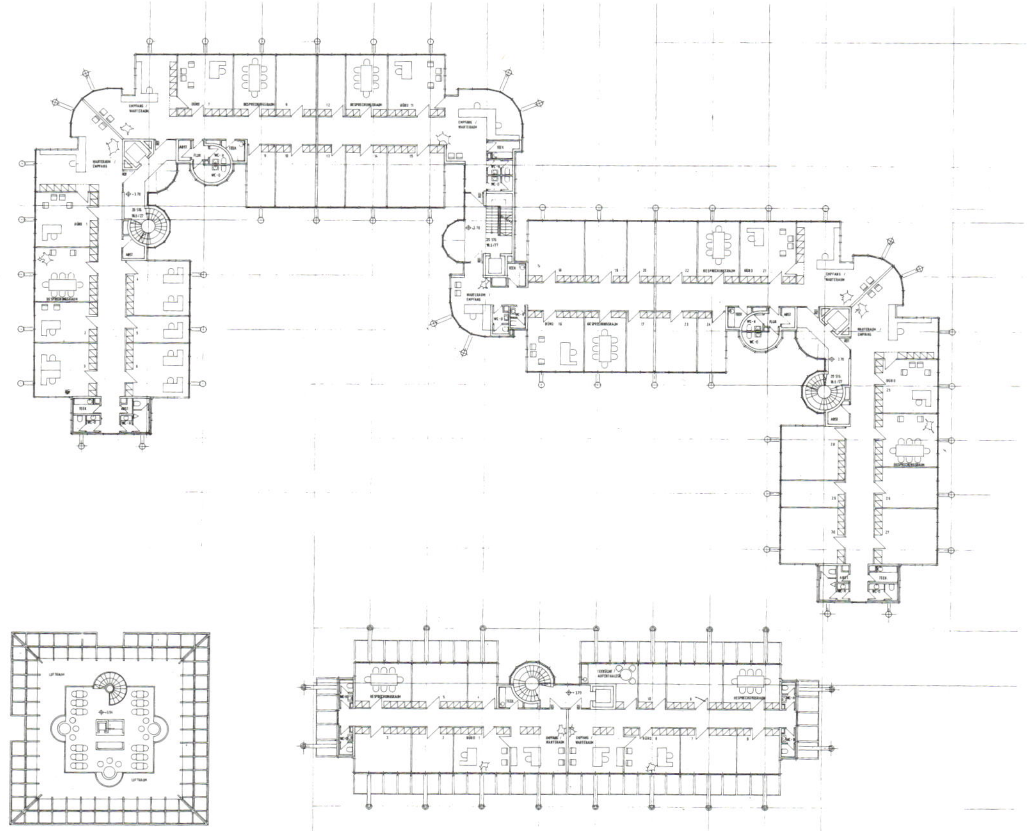

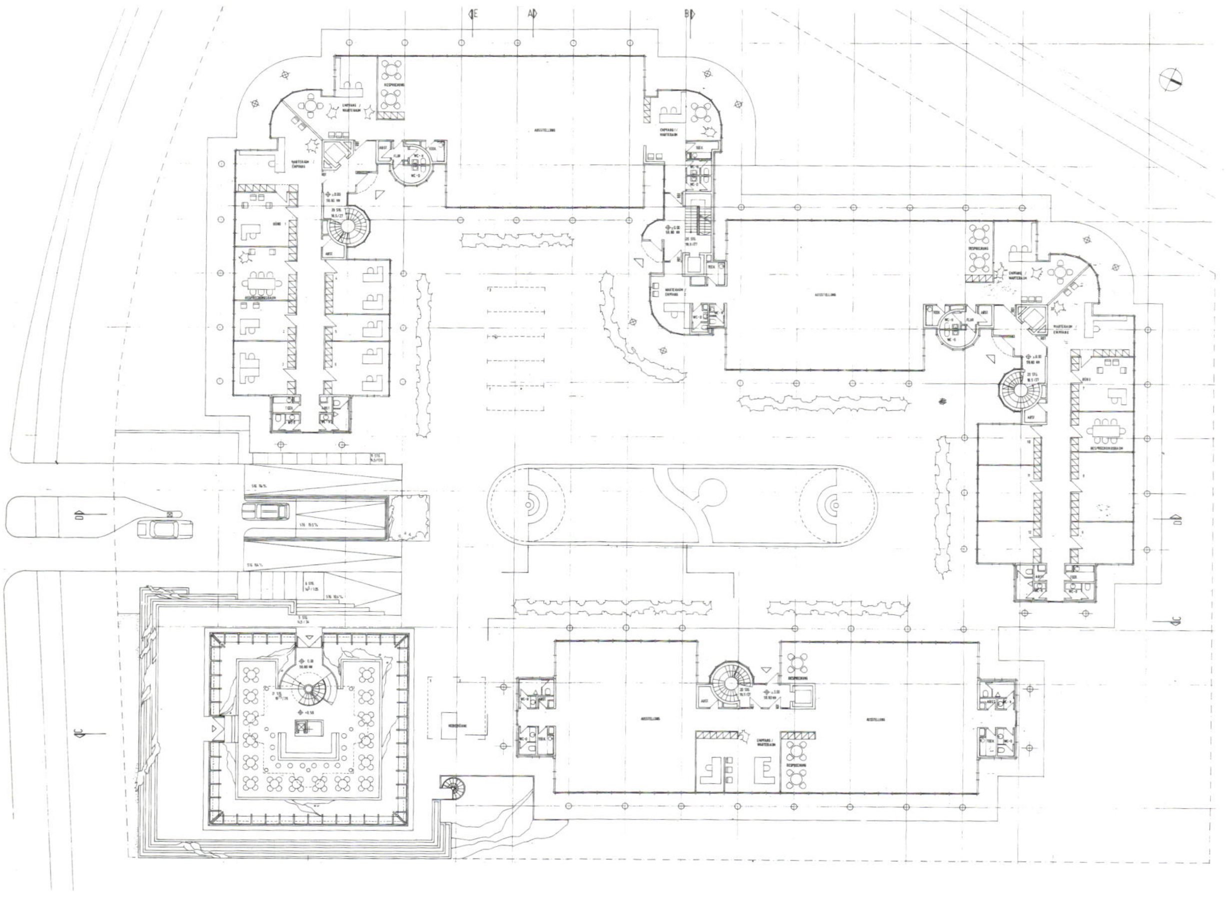

Detail of the south-west corner. The exposed structure of the centre combines steel, glass, and ceramics.
Detail der südwestlichen Gebäudeecke. Die nach außen gestellte Konstruktion des Gebäudekomplexes verbindet Stahl mit Glas und Keramik.

View of the inner courtyard and, below, axonometry of the complex of three buildings constructed around a central platform above a large car park.
Blick auf den Innenhof, darunter die Isometrie des Gesamtkomplexes, der aus drei Gebäuden besteht, die sich über einem pleateaubildenden Untergeschoß, das einer geräumigen Tiefgarage Platz bietet, gruppiert.

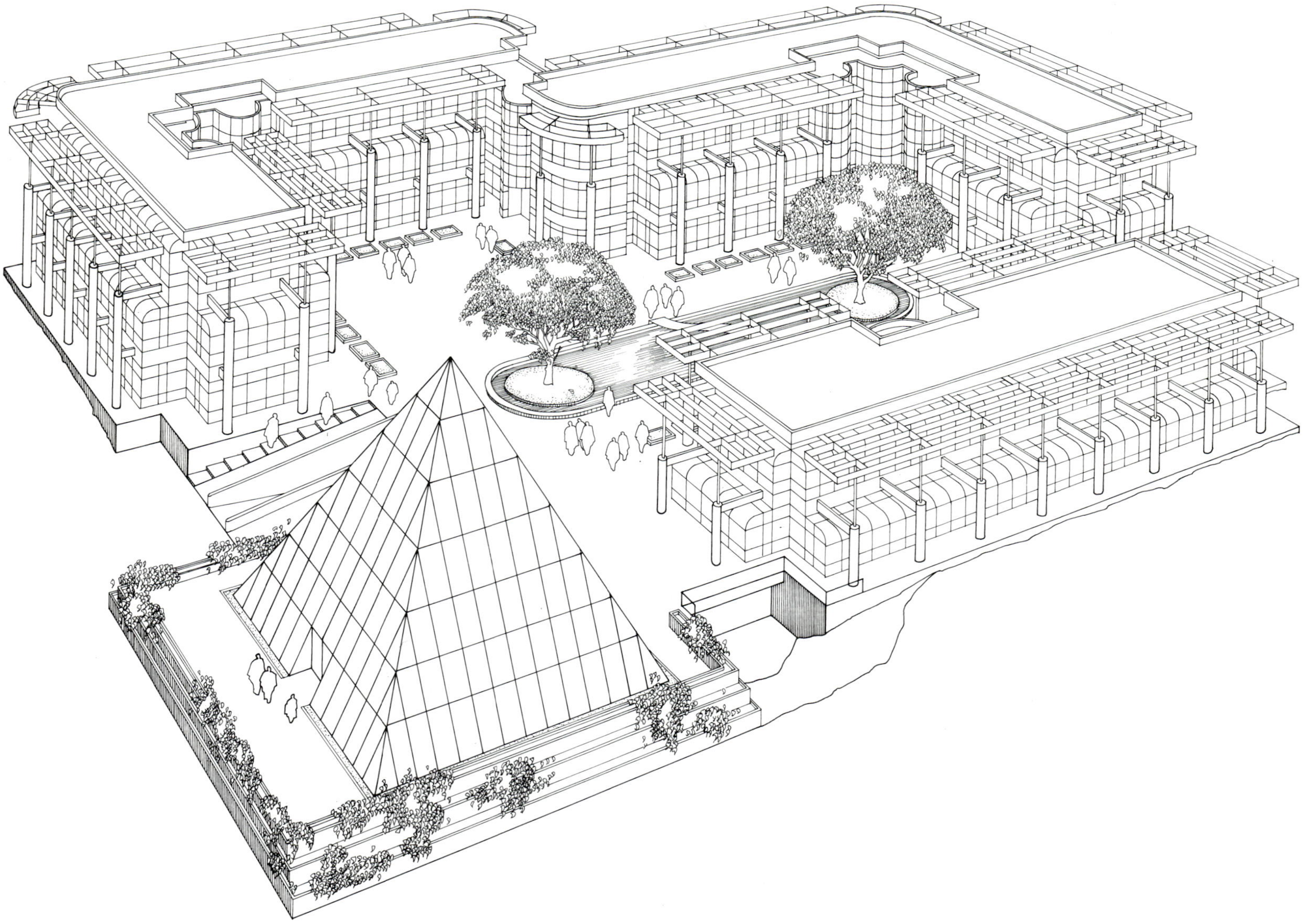

The glass pyramid at the south-east corner of the complex houses a two-level restaurant catering for firms in the other two buildings and in the neighbourhood.
Die Glaspyramide an der süd-östlichen Peripherie der Anlage beherbergt unter ihrem Glasdach auf zwei Ebenen ein Restaurant, das der Versorgung der im MAZ angesiedelten Firmen und der Nachbarschaft dient.

21

Perspective views of the curtain wall facade made of self-supporting aluminium sections with reflecting-insulating glazing and thermal insulating Policolor panel units in the wall area.
Ansicht der Vorhangfassade, die aus selbsttragenden Aluminiumprofilen mit Reflexions-Isolierverglasung und wärmegedämmten Policolor-Paneelelementen im geschlossenen Wandbereich besteht.

Detail of the entrance and staircase area.
Detail der Eingangs- und Treppenhauszone.

The externally located steel frames and beams leave plenty of flexible space on the inside.
Feststehende Stockwerksrahmen aus Stahlstützen und Stahlträgern ergeben eine große Flexibilität der inneren Raumnutzung.

Detail of the beams with 15 m spans and ceramic-clad columns supporting the curtain facade constructed around a basic grid of 1.25 m.
Detail der Stahlträger mit einer maximalen Spannweite von 15 m und Detail der Pfeiler, die mit Keramik verkleidet sind und die das Gebäude und die Fassade tragen. Das Fassadenraster von 1,25 m bildet das Entwurfsmodul für die variable Nutzungsflächenaufteilung des Gebäudes.

GALERIE LUISE
Shopping Mall
Ladenpassage

The shopping passage and commercial complex form the heart of Galerie Luise but not by any means the sum of its architecture. 155 metres of "architecture for strollers" so captivate passers-by that they quite fail to notice the two office blocks on Luisenstrasse in the context of the gallery.

The three entrances to Galerie Luise each lie only a few metres away from some of the city centre's focal points. The main train station, the opera house and Kröpke are between 100 and 250 metres from the Luisenstrasse, Joachimstrasse and Theaterstrasse entrances.

The shopping gallery leads into normally inaccessible areas behind the blocks near the station. The tunnels leading down into the yards at the back form a "Y". At its central junction the shopping streets paved in natural stone give way to a square which is part atrium, part piazza. A glass cupola, 18 metres high and 14 metres in diameter, gives the ensemble a majestic stamp.

Only the passage from the Luisenstrasse has been given a glass barrel roof. This is faceted with bright panels of identical size. Violet-brown rows of grid ceilings provide an optical lead. They form the framework. This holds together what otherwise threatens to float and become blurred. The glass vaulting and the two-storey glass fronts of over 40 shops here convey a bright, floating and transparent quality in a cluster virtually impossible to unravel. Although the architecture embodies precise structures, the passer-by is aware only of the variety of sensual stimulants emanating from the interiors of the shops. The glass causes the emphatic divisions produced by projecting partitions and right-angle steel elements to become an imaginary structure. The passage's individuality is largely determined by the wares on display. The strength of this architecture resides in the fact that it makes a happening of what is customarily overshadowed as "backyard building".

Die Ladenpassage und der wirtschaftliche Komplex sind das Herzstück der Galerie Luise, aber sie sind längst nicht die ganze Architektur. 155 m „Schlender-Architektur" nehmen den Passanten so gefangen, daß er die beiden Bürohäuser an der Luisenstraße im Kontext der Galerie gar nicht wahrnimmt.

Die drei Eingänge der Galerie Luise liegen jeweils nur wenige Meter von den Zentralpunkten der Innenstadt entfernt: zwischen 100 m und 250 m sind es nur vom Hauptbahnhof, vom Opernhaus oder vom Kröpke zu den Eingängen Luisenstraße, Joachimstraße und Theaterstraße.

Die Einkaufsgalerie führt in die normalerweise unzugänglichen Bereiche hinter der bahnhofsnahen Blockbebauung. Die in die Tiefe der Hinterhöfe führenden „Tunnel" bilden ein Y. In ihrem Gabelpunkt weiten sich die natursteinbelegten Einkaufsstraßen zu einem Platz, der teils Atrium teils Piazza ist. Eine 18 m hohe Glaskuppel mit einem Durchmesser von über 14 m gibt dem ganzen ein majestätisches Gepräge. Nur die von der Luisenstraße kommende Passage trägt eine tonnenförmige Glasdecke. Sie ist durch gleichgroße helle Scheiben facettiert. Als optische Führungsleiste finden sich violett-braune Bandrasterdecken. Sie geben den Rahmen ab. Er hält zusammen, was sonst zu verschweben und verschwimmen drohte. Denn das Glasgewölbe und die zweistöckigen Glasfronten der über 40 Läden vermitteln als nahezu unentwirrbares Knäuel Durchsichtigkeit, Schweben und Leichtigkeit. Obwohl die Architektur exakte Gliederungen aufweist, nimmt der Passant nur die Vielfalt der sinnlichen Anregungen wahr, die ihm aus dem Inneren der Läden entgegentritt. Das Glas läßt die klaren Gliederungen durch vorkragende Ausfachungen und rechtwinklige Stahlkonstruktionen zu einer imaginären Struktur werden. Die Individualität der Passage wird weitgehend von den Auslagen geprägt. Die Stärke dieser Architektur ist es, daß sie den Teil zum Erlebnis macht, der meistens als „Hinterhofbebauung" im Schatten liegt.

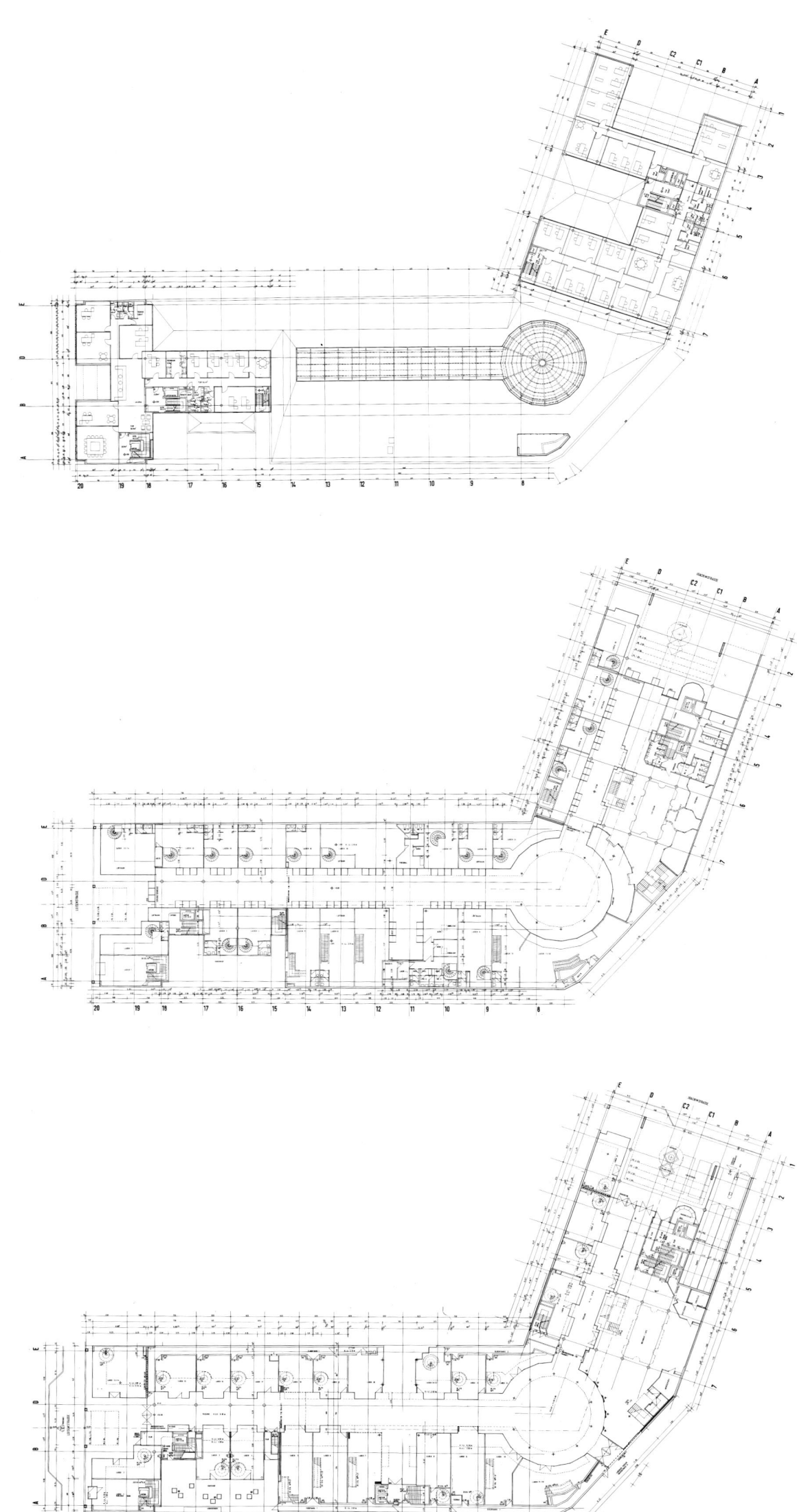

From bottom of page up: plans of the ground floor, mezzanine and first floor.
Opposite page: entrance along Luisenstraße.
Von unten nach oben: Grundrisse des Erdgeschosses, des Mezzanins und des ersten Obergeschosses. Auf der Seite nebenan: Eingang Luisenstraße.

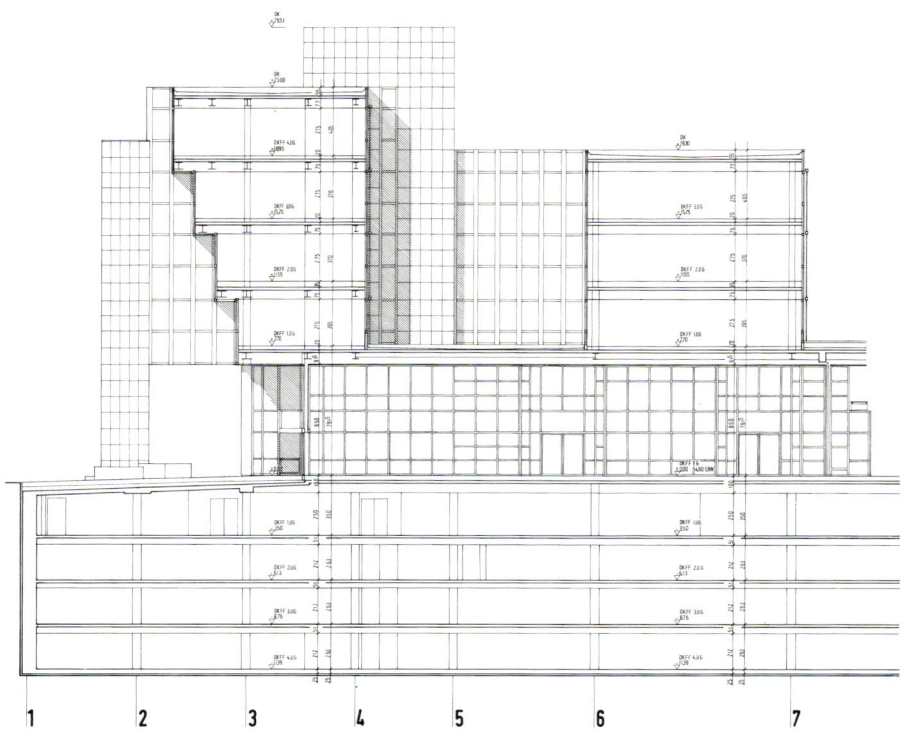
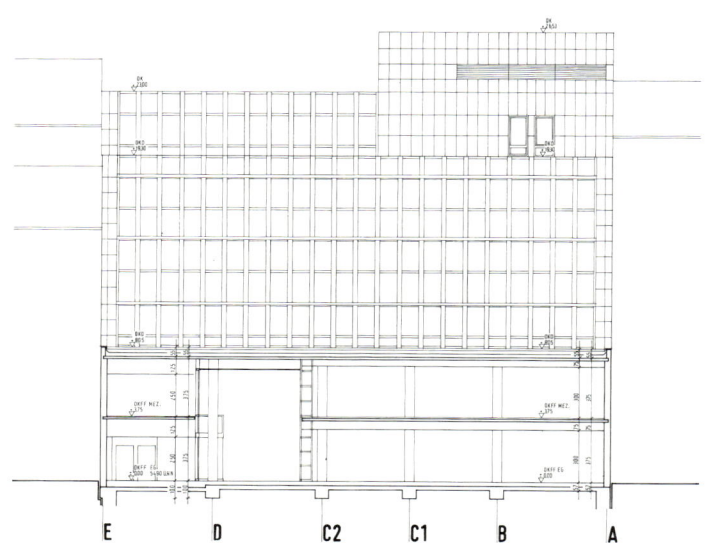
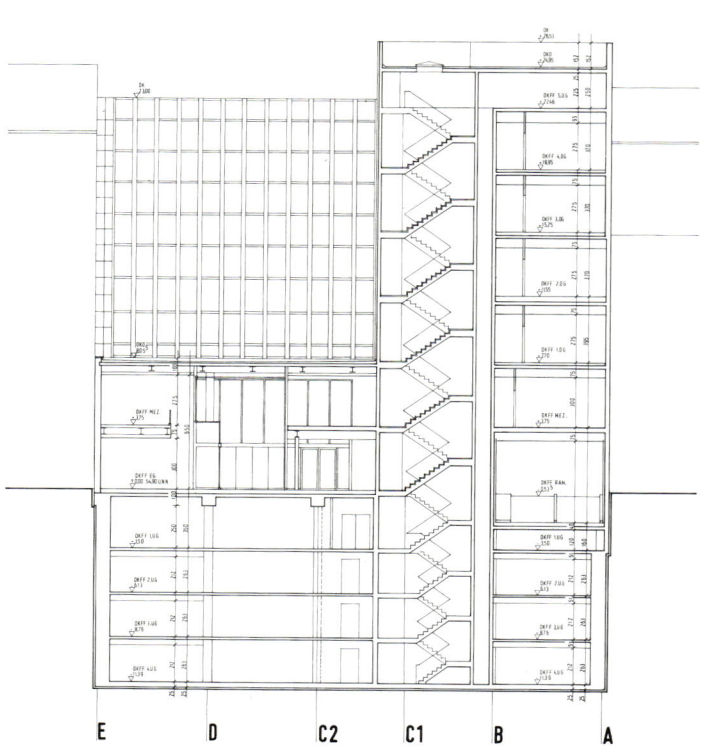

Several cross sections. Below: entrance along Joachimstraße. Opposite page: longitudinal section.

Diverse Querschnitte. Unten: Eingang Joachimstraße. Auf der Seite nebenan: Längsschnitt.

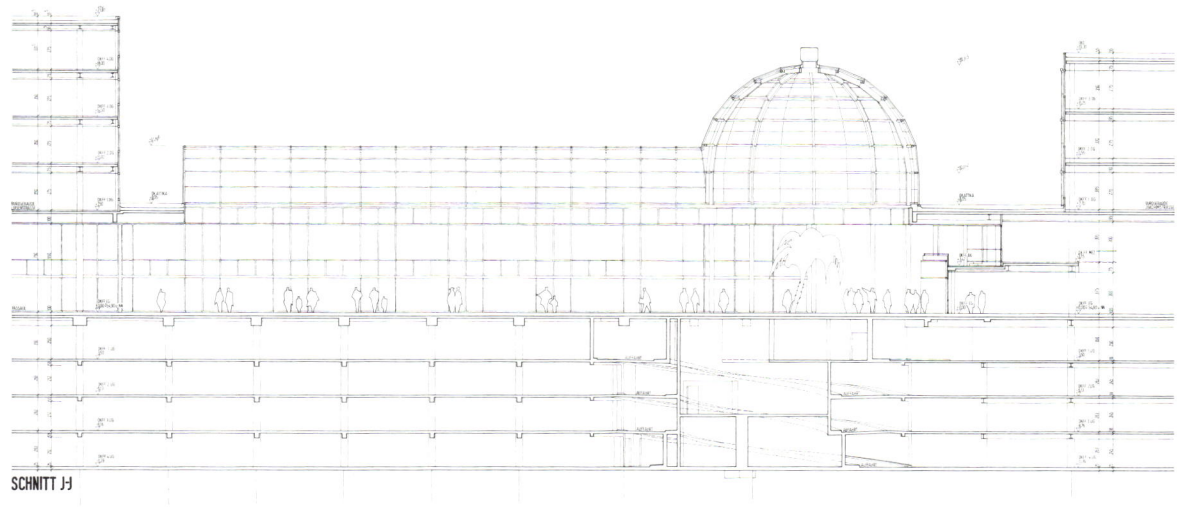

SCHNITT J-J

Partial views of the shopping gallery.
Teilansichten der Einkaufspassage.

The central rotunda, where the three paths meet.
Die zentrale Rotunde, wo die drei Flügel sich treffen.

Partial views of the inside of the mall measuring 155 m in length.

Teilansichten des Inneren der Galerie Luise, die sich über eine Länge von 155 Metern erstreckt.

NORCON
Office Building
Bürohaus

The client wished to cater for the spirit of the age with an office and administration building of unconventional stamp. One "interior" requirement for it consisted of large floor areas free of supports. This guarantees a high degree of flexibility for forthcoming usage, possibly of another type. The idea was to produce a functional industrial building capturing the attention.

The significance of avantgarde was "suspended" unambiguously from the tubular steel structure. A suspended structure offered the only possibility for keeping the interior spaces free of support pillars. The steel/glass facade of all floors is undramatic. The serial alignment of the window elements drives the volume of the building into the background.

The main section consists of two rectangular ground floor areas. The four-storey office section has thus been made to appear smaller.

Tubular steel structures with a multi-storey building suspended quite often look clumsy. Fire protection regulations are to blame that a slender structure cannot be conferred on the aesthetic as a whole. Implementing this particular design called for the conduct beforehand of intensive research in the fire protection field.

Instead of conventional sheathing of the steel tubes which would conceal and distort the impact of the materials used for supports and suspended elements, it was decided to cool the steel tubes as preferred. Inside each of the bearer tubes is a second one through which a cooling liquid flows downwards if it is heated should a fire occur and then ascends along the outer surfaces of the tubes. Heat exchange between the steel and the coolant creates a suction enabling the circulation to function "naturally". This novel system has been used for the first time in this building.

Dem Zeitgeist Rechnung tragen wollte der Bauherr mit einem Büro- und Verwaltungsgebäude unkonventioneller Prägung. Ein 'inneres' Kriterium für das Gebäude waren große stützungsfreie Geschoßflächen. Dadurch ist auch für kommende und möglicherweise anders geartete Nutzung ein hohes Maß an Flexibilität gewährleistet. Es sollte ein industrieller Zweckbau mit hohem Aufmerksamkeitswert erstellt werden.

Die Signifikanz von Avantgarde wurde unzweideutig an der Stahlrohrkonstruktion 'aufgehängt'. Nur durch eine Hängekonstruktion konnten die Innenflächen frei von Stützpfeilern gehalten werden. Die Stahl-Glas-Fassade aller Geschosse ist ruhig. Die serielle Reihung der Fensterelemente läßt das Gebäude-Volumen zurücktreten.

Der Haupttrakt ist in zwei rechteckige Erdgeschoß-Flächen gesetzt. Dadurch wird der viergeschossige Bürotrakt nochmals optisch verkleinert.

Stahlrohrkonstruktionen mit einer eingehängten Geschoßbauweise haben nicht selten ein plumpes Aussehen. Brandschutzvorschriften sind daran Schuld, daß in solchen Fällen die Schlankheit der Konstruktion nicht auf die Gesamtästhetik übertragen werden kann. Um diese Gestaltung umsetzen zu können, mußten erst intensive Forschungen im Bereich des Brandschutzes durchgeführt werden.

Statt einer konventionellen Ummantelung der Stahlrohre, die die Materialwirkung der Stützen und Hänger verdeckt und verfremdet hätte, wählte man eine Kühlung der Stahlrohre. Im Inneren eines jeden tragenden Rohres steckt ein zweites, durch das eine kühlende Flüssigkeit im Falle einer Erhitzung durch Brand nach unten strömt und an den Außenwänden des Rohres wieder nach oben steigt. Der Wärmeaustausch zwischen Stahl und Kühlflüssigkeit erzeugt einen Sog, so daß die Zirkulation 'natürlich' funktioniert.

Dieses neuartige System ist an diesem Gebäude erstmalig eingesetzt worden.

Aerial view of the office development.
Below, from bottom of page up: plans of the ground floor and upper floors.

Vogelperspektive des Bürokomplexes. Darunter, von unten nach oben: Grundrisse des Erdgeschosses, und der Obergeschosse.

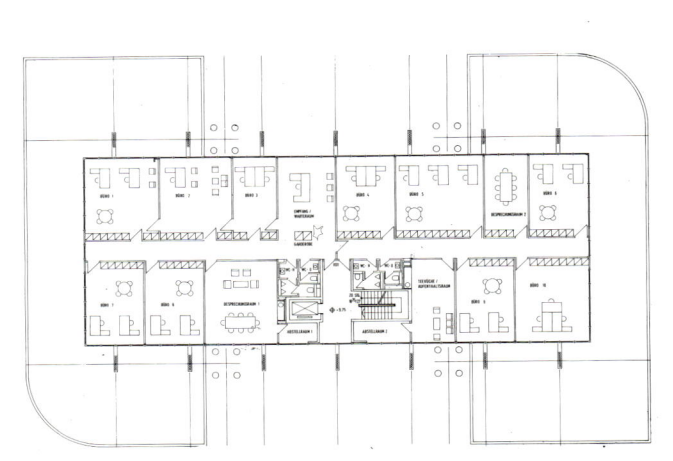

2. OBERGESCHOSS

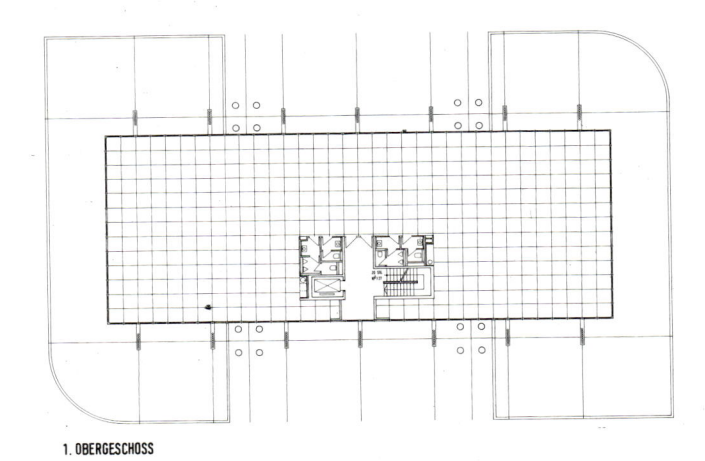

1. OBERGESCHOSS

ERDGESCHOSS

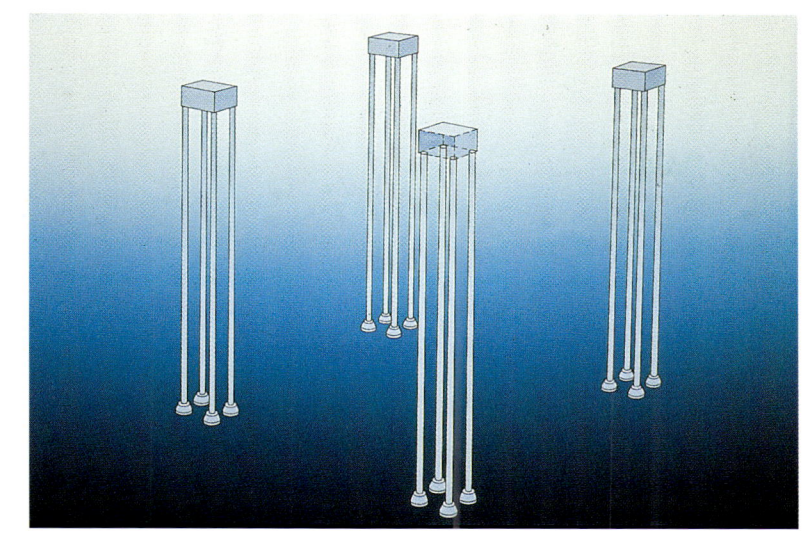

Left: structural layout of the building.
Below: detail of the exposed frame.

*Links: das konstruktive Konzept des Bauwerks.
Unten: Detail der sichtbaren Stahlstruktur.*

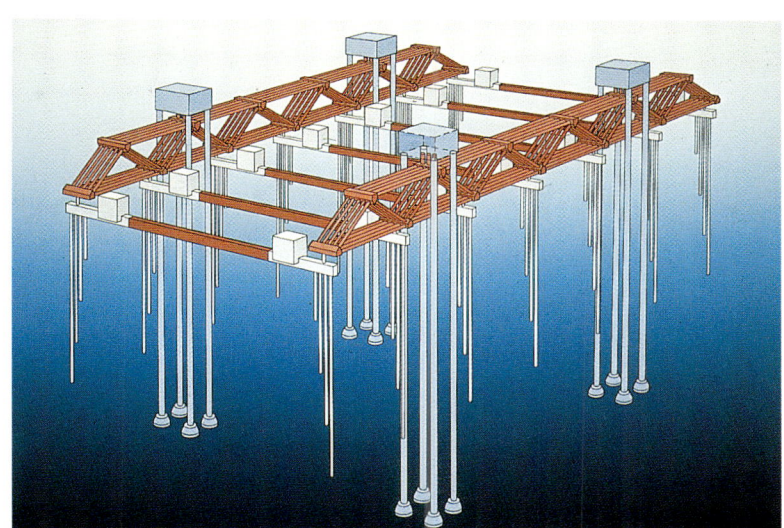

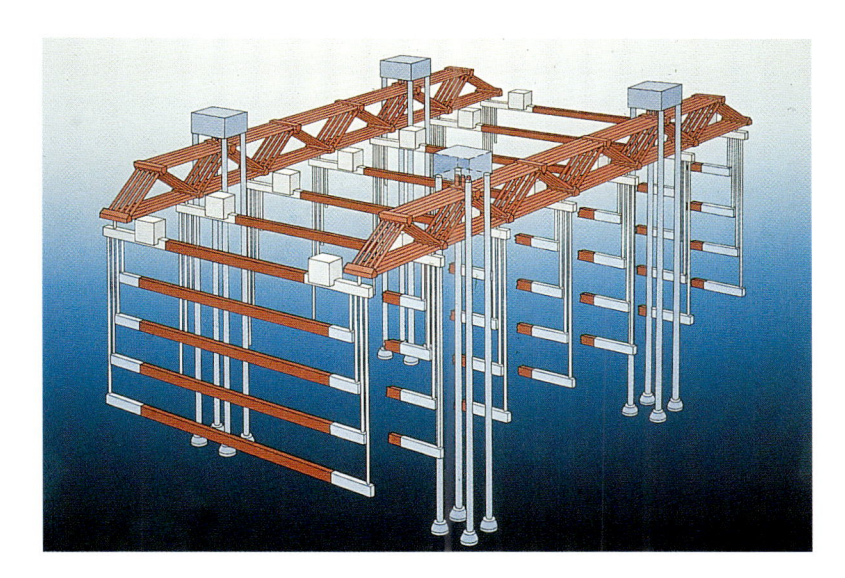

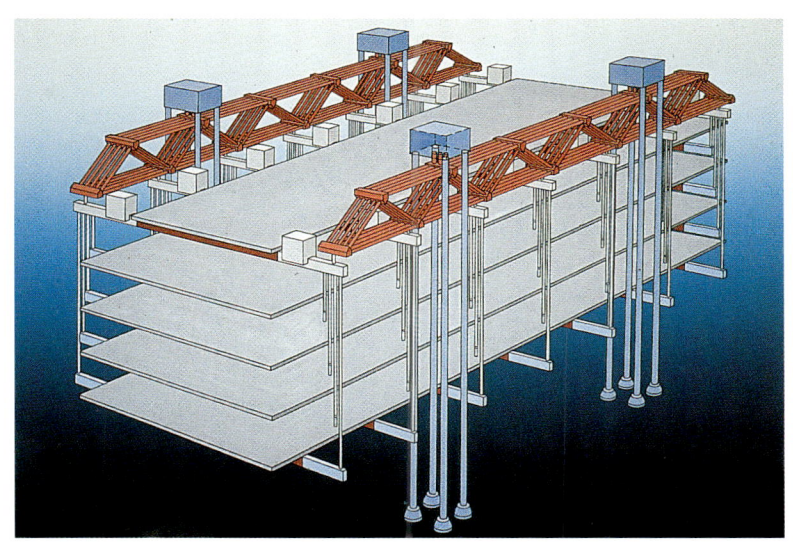

39

Detail of the top of the tubular steel frame supporting the complete building. Below: axonometry.
Details des Kopfs eines der Stahlpylone, welche das gesamte Gebäude tragen. Unten: Isometrie.

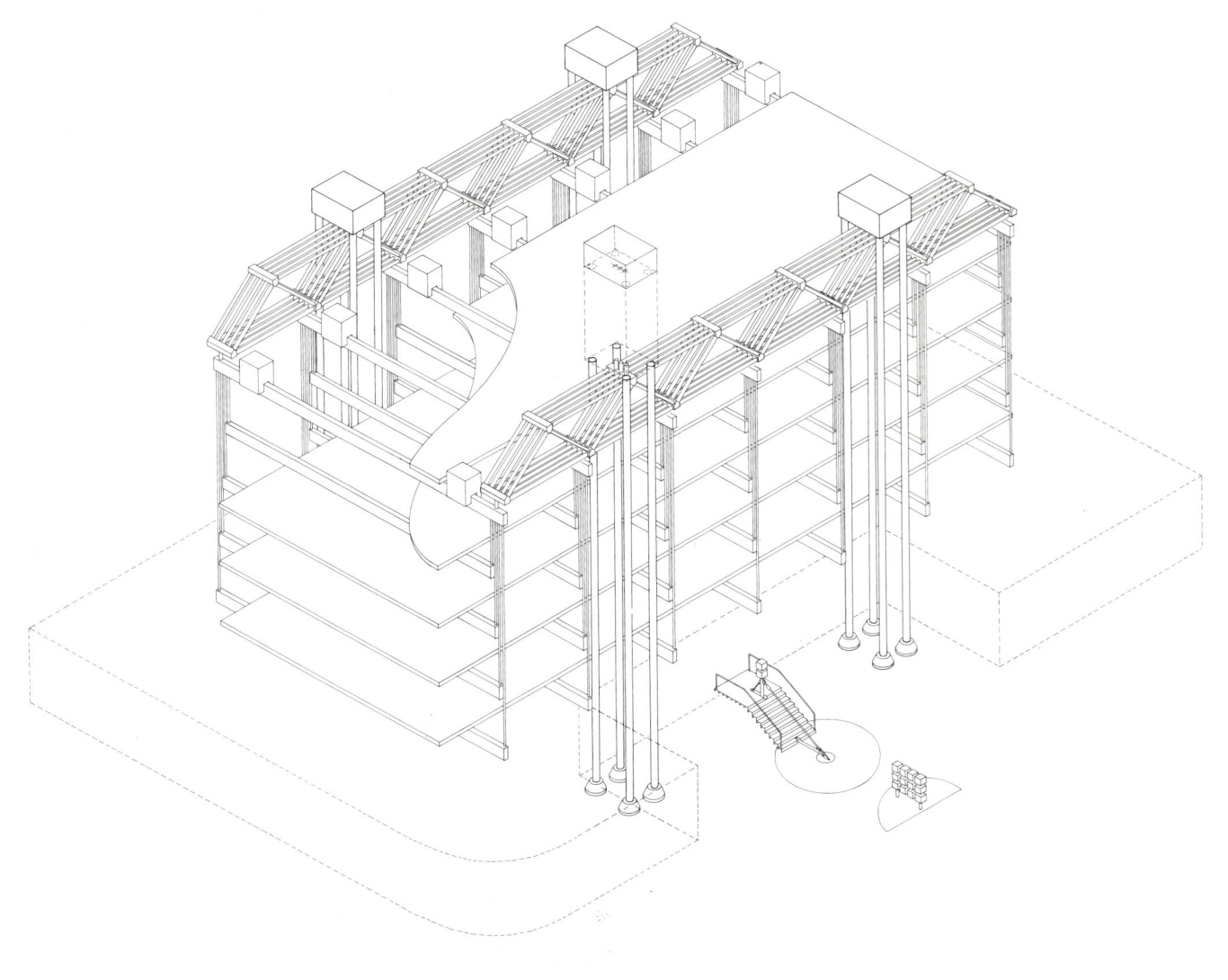

Details of the suspended tube construction specially designed to contain an internal fire-extinguishing liquid.
Detail des Stahlgitterträgers, dessen Konstruktion im Inneren, die Flüssigkeit zur Kühlung im Brandfall aufnimmt.

41

Longitudinal and cross sections. Right: main facade.
Längs- und Querschnitt. Rechts: Gebäudeansicht.

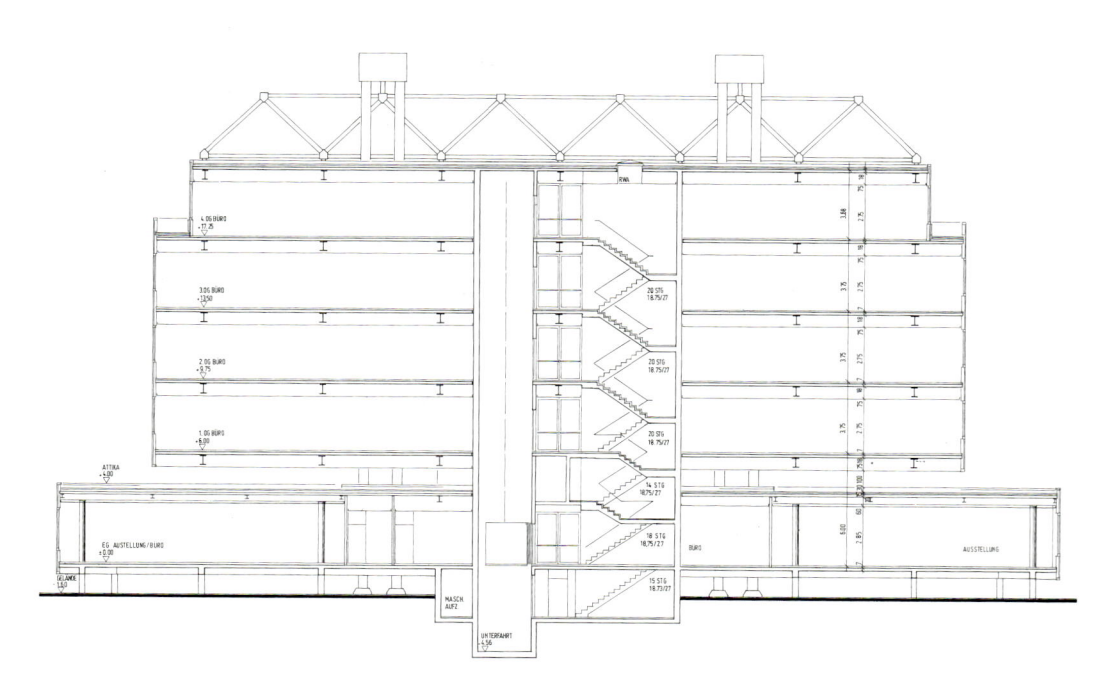

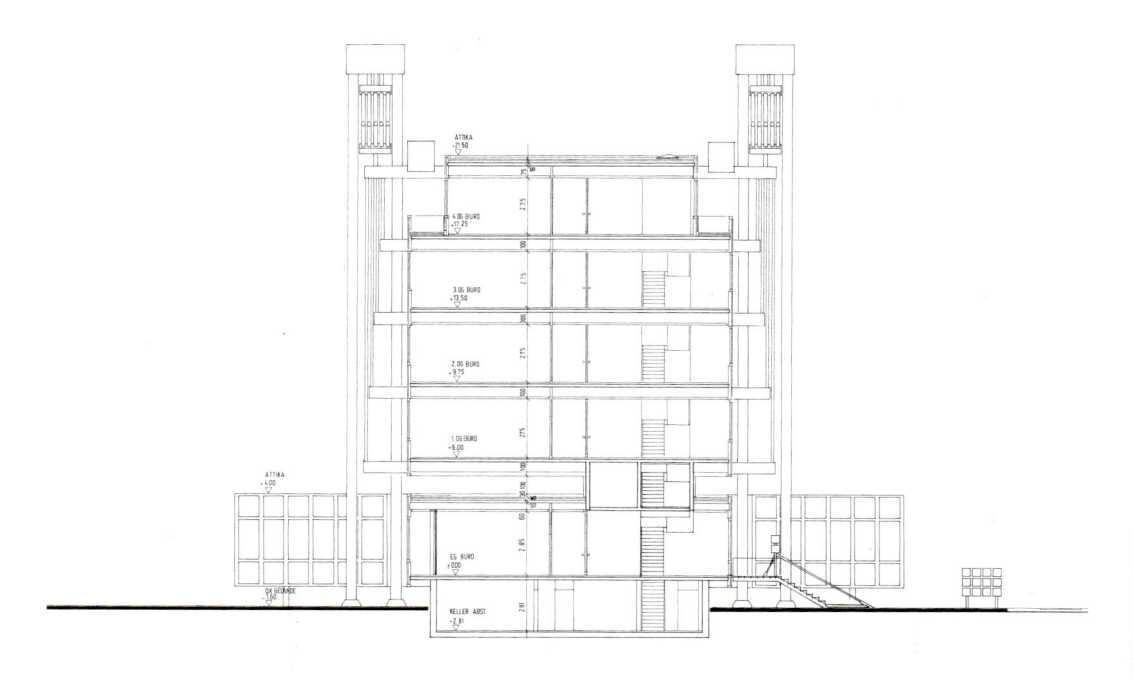

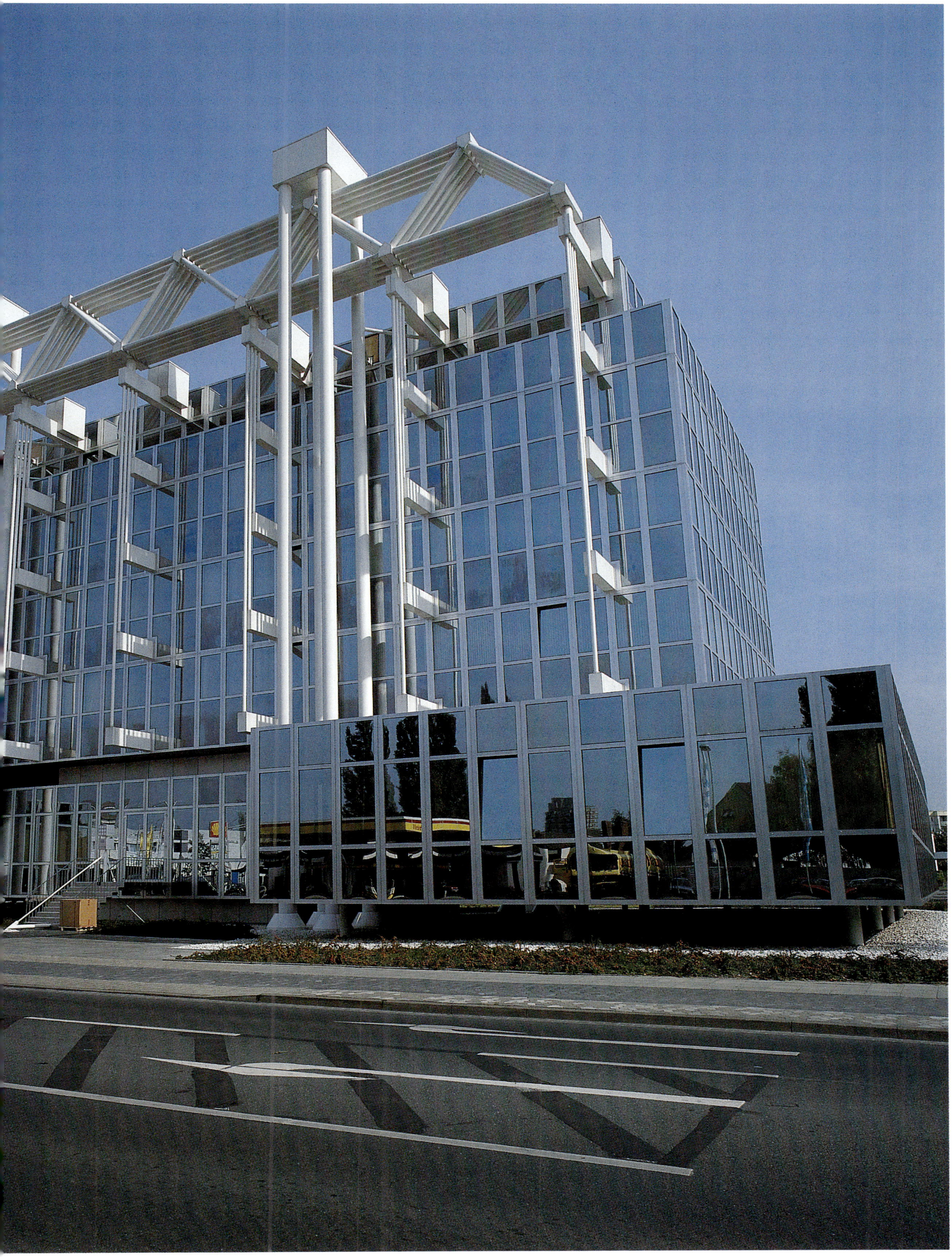

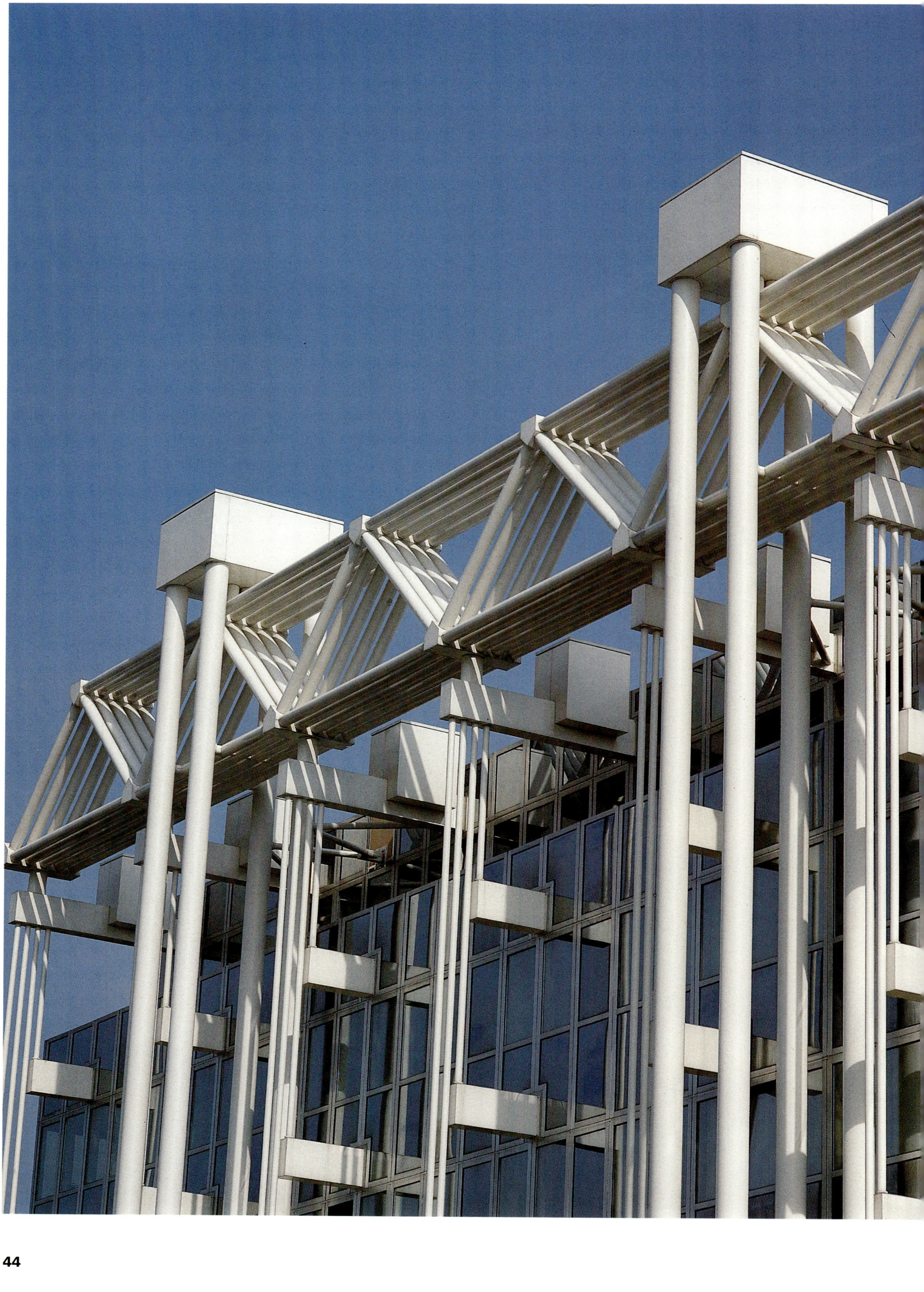

Details of the suspended steel structure and glass facades.
Details der abgehängten Stahlkonstruktion und Glasfassaden.

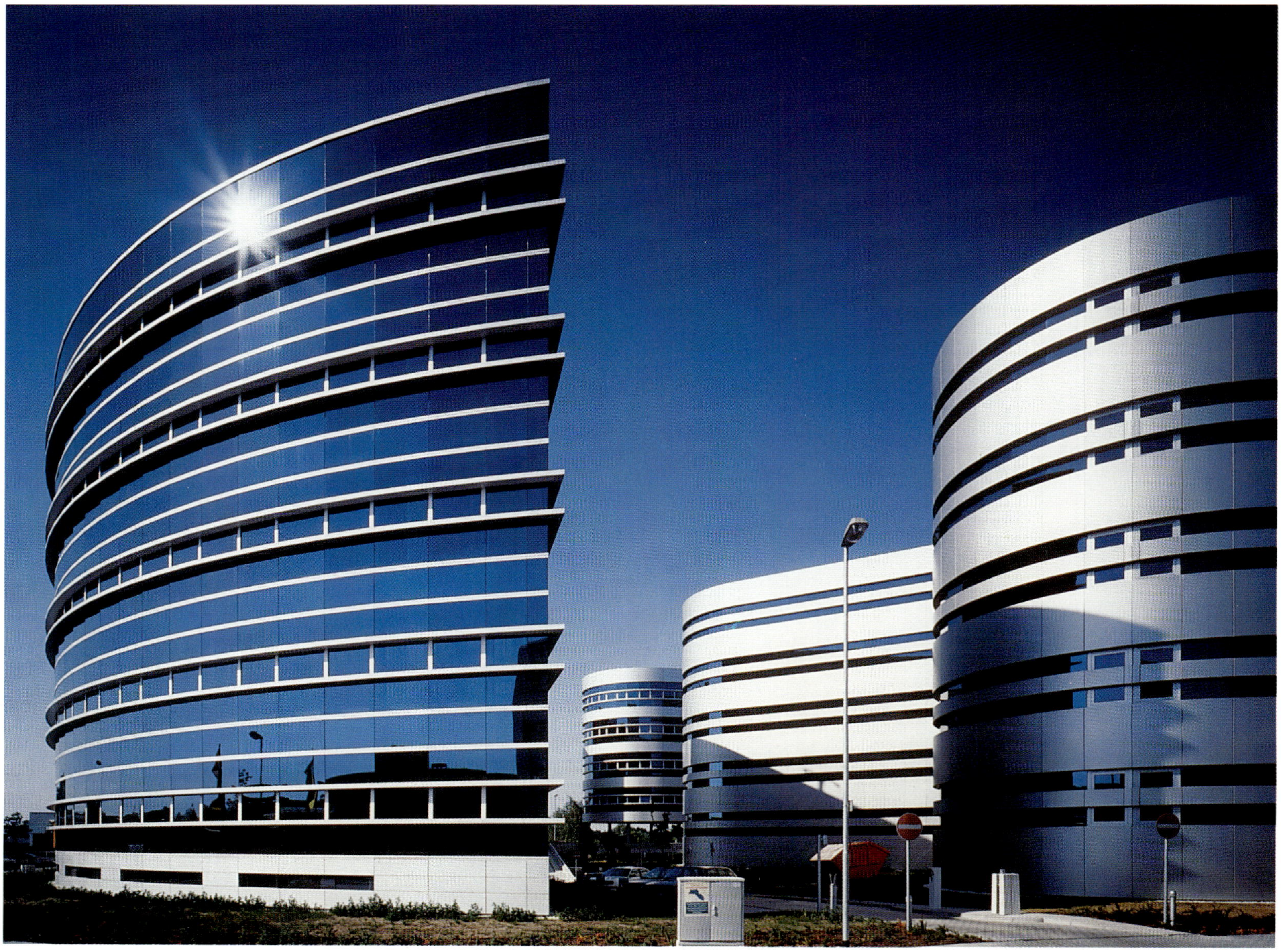

MAI-NI2-NI3
Office Complex
Bürohaus

In an unusual manner, a three-section complex of office and administrative buildings here fills a plot of entirely normal shape. A lengthy six-storey block, a rounded triangle of the same height and a five-section building reminiscent of a wing screw or the foliage beneath a blossom.

The ground plan of these three buildings possesses no harmony. Being based on the ground plan sketch and only discernible from the air, that would in reality barely be visible. Harmony resides solely at the sight level of visitors or passers-by. Driving around the plot or walking across it, they encounter a dense landscape of shapes rich in associations. One spontaneously feels reminded of the relaxing yet solid elegance of the Pullman trains of the 1940s. The two compact buildings and the space-embracing four-wing building on the boundary of the site convey a deep feeling of gentle yet purposeful movement. Associations are aroused of Italian futurism in its glorification of technology and speed. Yet the great quality of the design of blocks and facades lies primarily in the fact that all associations constitute no more than a mental reminiscence. Nothing is blatantly clear. The elegance of this architecture is like the original picture of elegance, not tied to any contemporary taste yet the essence of contemporaneity.

The entire complex offers visitor and onlookers a changing view from all corners, ever at once severe and relaxed. Each of the three buildings possesses its own roundings and these express their own meaning through the delicate treatment of the facades.

All three buildings have a glass-aluminium facade divided strictly horizontally. The "wing building" makes the most compact impression thanks to narrow rows of windows which broaden out from one building to another to become a virtually all-glass facade.

The technical-floral character of the whole designs corresponds to a dialectical play between transparency and compactness.

Ein dreiteiliger Komplex von Büro- und Verwaltungsgebäuden füllt auf ungewöhnliche Weise ein Grundstück durchaus üblichen Zuschnitts. Auf einer gedrungen rechteckigen Fläche stehen ein langgestreckter sechsstöckiger Baukörper, ein gleich hohes einseitig abgerundeten Dreieck und ein fünfteiliges Gebäude, dessen Form in der Aufsicht an eine Flügelschraube oder an den Fruchtstempel einer Blüte erinnert.

Für diese drei Gebäude gibt es keine Grundrißharmonie. Die wäre in der Realität auch kaum einsehbar, da sie auf der Grundriß-Zeichnung basiert und nur aus der Luft zu erkennen ist. Die Harmonie ist einzig in die Sichtebene von Besuchern oder Passanten gelegt. Ihnen eröffnet sich beim Umfahren oder Durchschreiten des Grundstücks eine dichte und assoziationsreiche Formenlandschaft. Man fühlt sich spontan an die spielerisch-massive Eleganz der Pullmann-Züge aus den 40er Jahren erinnert. Die beiden kompakten Gebäude und besonders das raumgreifende, die Grenze des Grundstücks tangierende vierflügelige Gebäude vermitteln ein intensives Gefühl von sanfter, zielstrebiger Bewegung. Gedankliche Verbindungen zum italienischen Futurismus in seiner Verherrlichung von Technik und Geschwindigkeit klingen hier an. Und doch liegt die große Qualität der Baukörper- und Fassadengestaltung vor allem darin, daß alle Assoziationen nicht mehr als eine geistige Reminiszenz sind. Nichts ist eindeutig. Die Eleganz dieser Architektur ist wie das Urbild der Eleganz, nicht gebunden an einen Zeitgeschmack und doch der Inbegriff von Zeitgenossenschaft.

Der gesamte Baukomplex bietet dem Besucher und Betrachter von allen Ecken eine andere, immer zugleich strenge und verspielte Ansicht. Jedes der drei Gebäude hat eigene Rundungen und die entfalten ihre Prägnanz durch eine delikate Fassadengestaltung.

Alle drei Gebäude haben eine Glas-Aluminium Fassade, die streng horizontal gegliedert ist. Das „Flügelgebäude" vermittelt den kompaktesten Eindruck durch schmale Glas-Lichtbänder, die sich dann von Gebäude zu Gebäude verbreitern bis fast zur Nur-Glas-Fassade.

Der technisch-florale Charakter der Gesamtgestaltung korrespondiert mit einem dialektischen Spiel von Transparenz und Geschlossenheit.

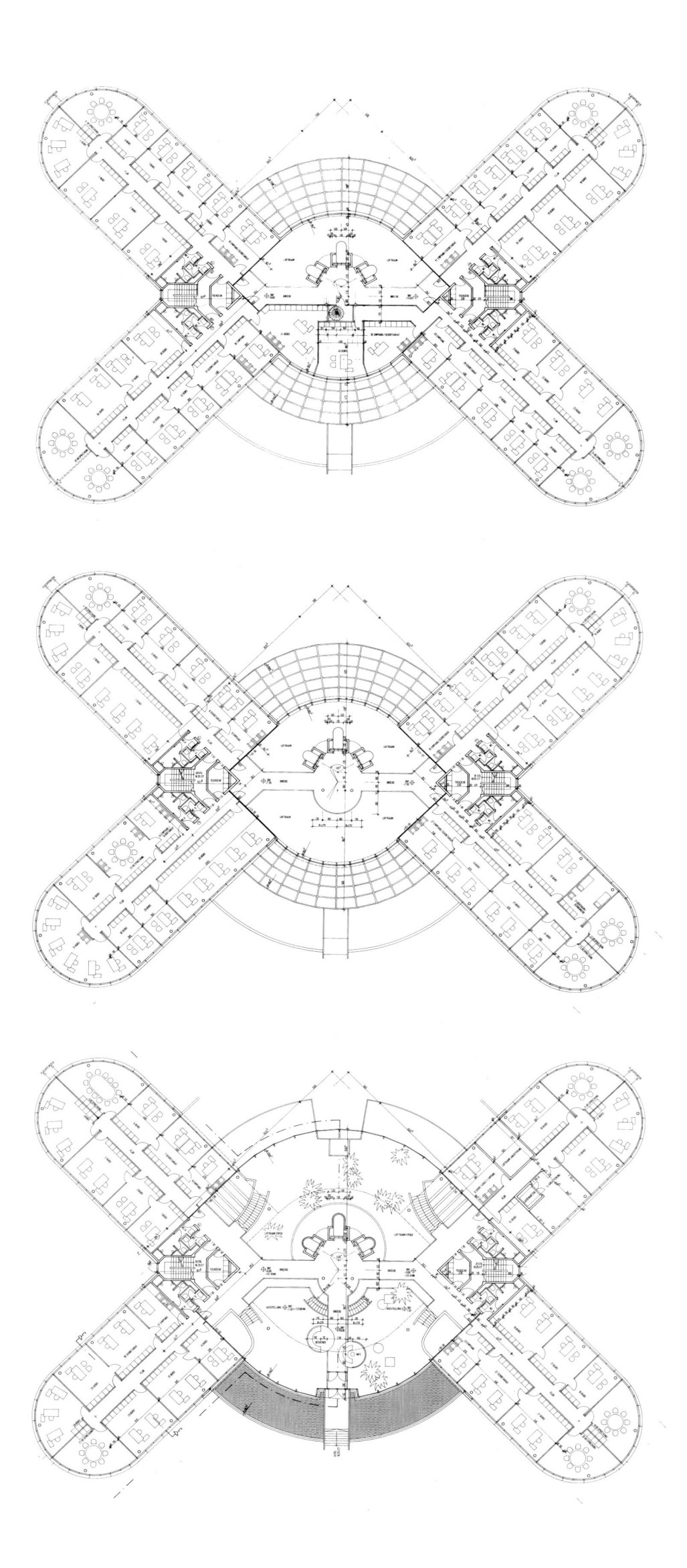

From bottom of page up: plans of the ground floor, first floor and fourth floor.
Von unten nach oben: Grundrisse des Erdgeschosses, des ersten Obergeschosses und des vierten Obergeschosses.

Model of the centre and below three sections.
Model des Komplexes und darunter drei Schnitte.

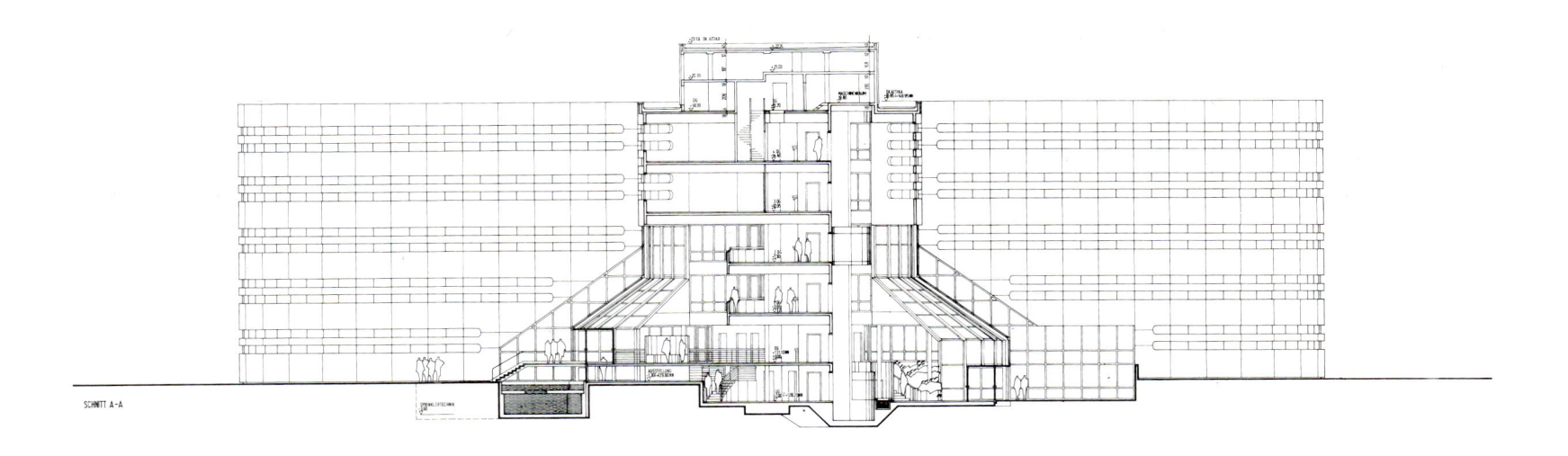

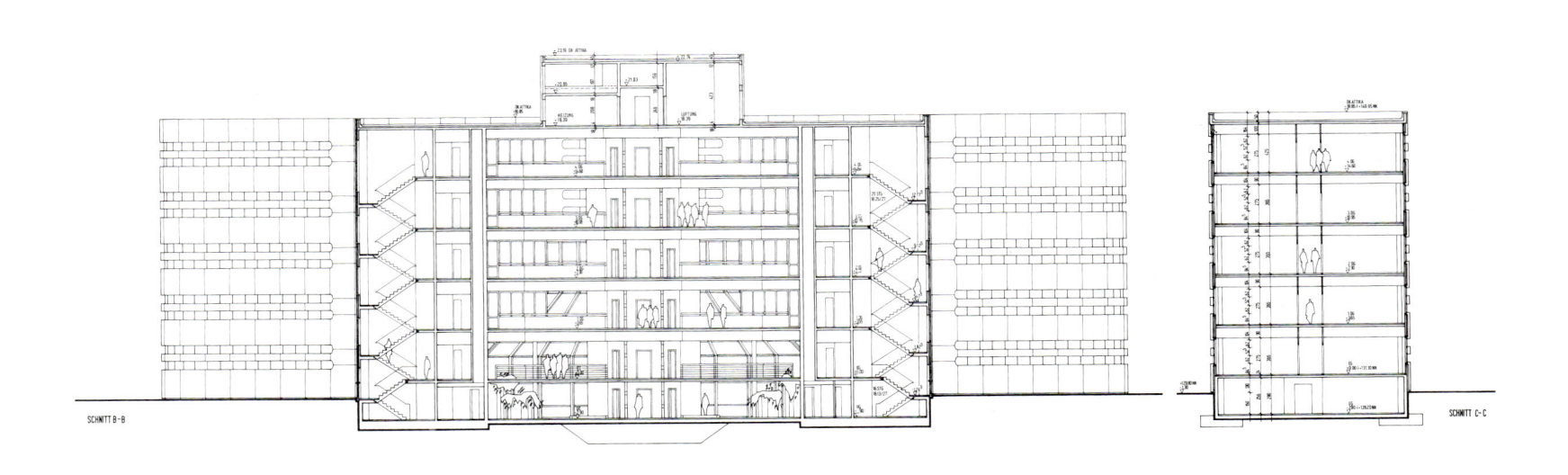

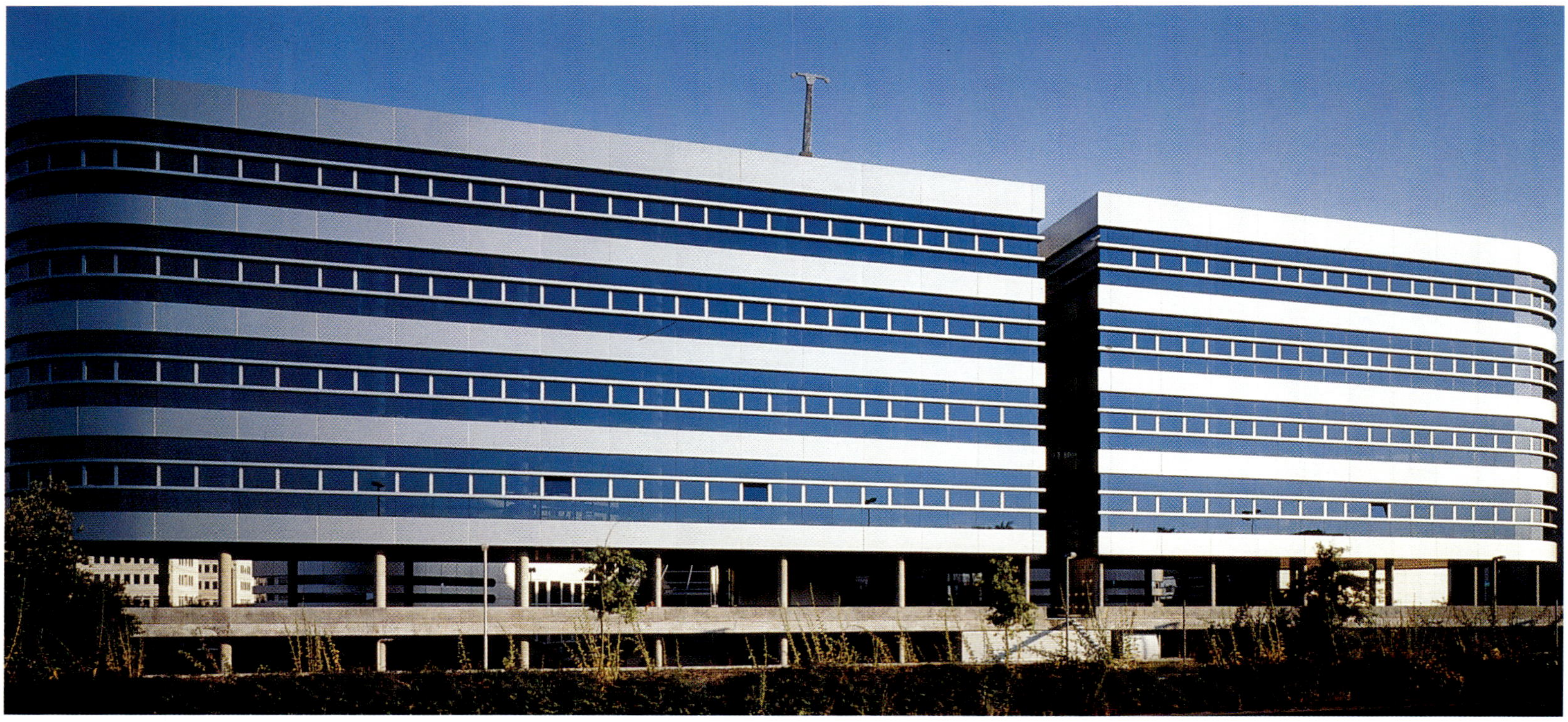

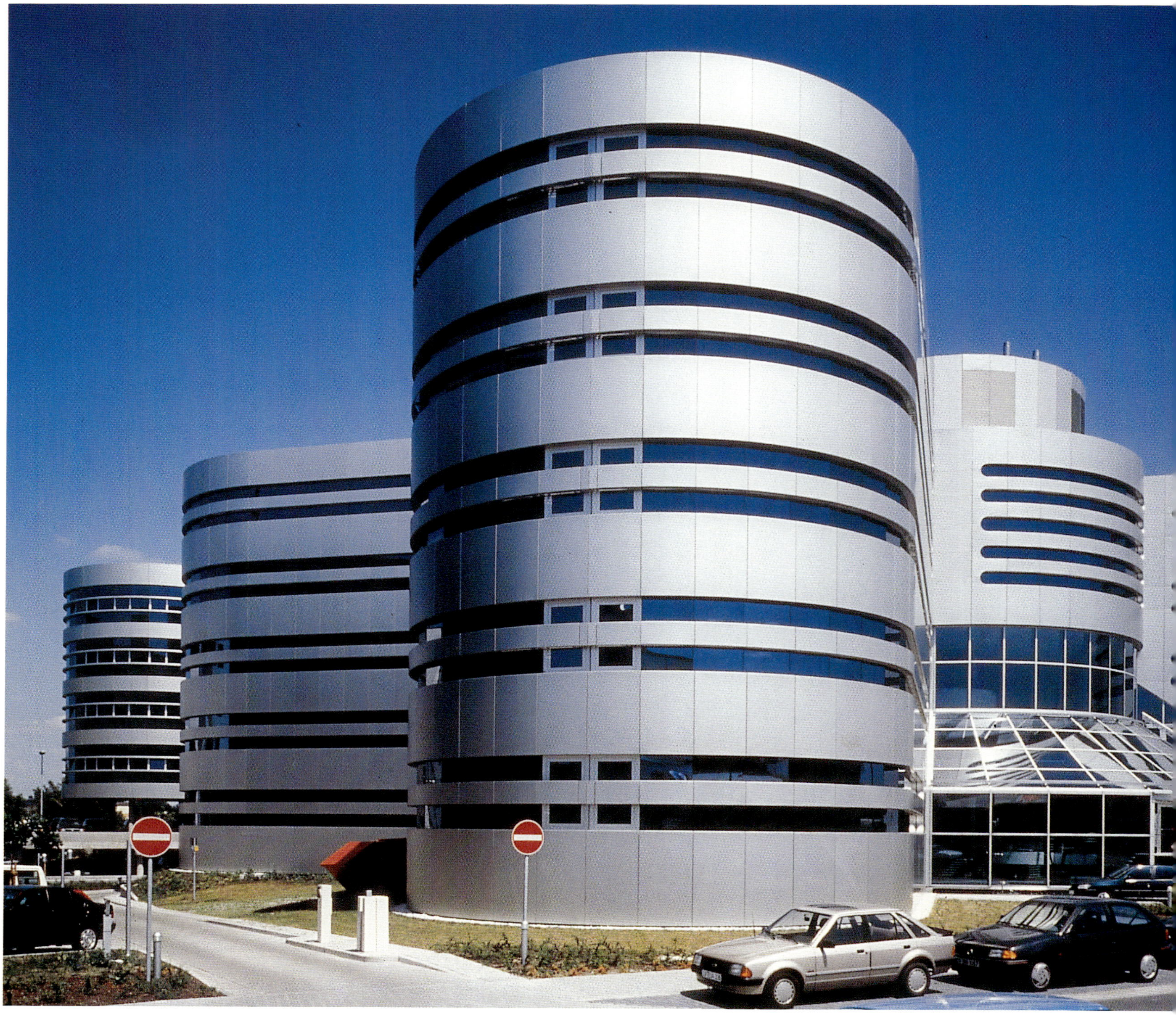

Views of the various building facades. The three buildings all feature curved forms and curtain facades made of various combinations of aluminium and glass.

Ansichten der verschiedenen Gebäudefassaden. Die drei Gebäude sind alle mit Vorhangfassaden versehen, die rund geformt sind und aus einer Variation von differenzierten Kombinationen aus Aluminium und Glas entwickelt sind.

Left, below and opposite page: the star-shaped building's glass central lobby (the first to be built), which is the real hub of the entire complex in both visual and spatial terms. Rising up through all six floors of the building, it holds the stairways and lift shafts and is connected to the four office wings.

*Links, darunter und auf der Seite nebenan: die zentrale Halle des sternförmigen Gebäudes, die als erste errichtet wurde.
Die Halle ist das Herzstück des Hauses. Sie ist gleichermaßen repräsentativer Mittelpunkt wie auch äußerst wirtschaftliches Erschließungssystem. Die 6-geschossige Halle enthält die Treppenkerne und die Aufzüge und ist mit den anderen vier Büroflügeln vereint.*

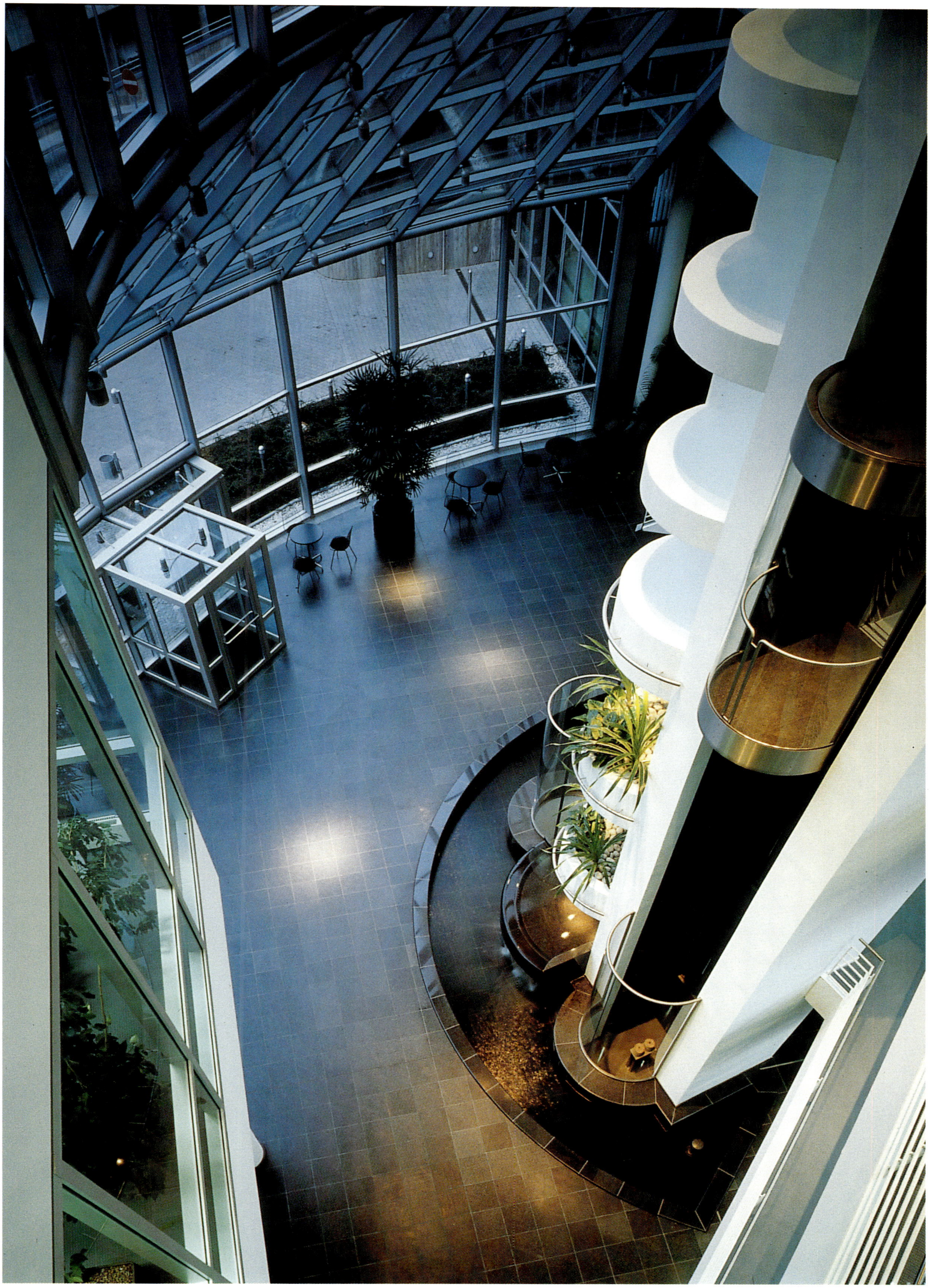

The interior and opposite page: exterior of the central lobby accessable across a stainless steel bridge.
Das Innere und auf der gegenüberliegenden Seite: das Äußere der Halle, die man über eine Brücke aus Edelstahl erreicht.

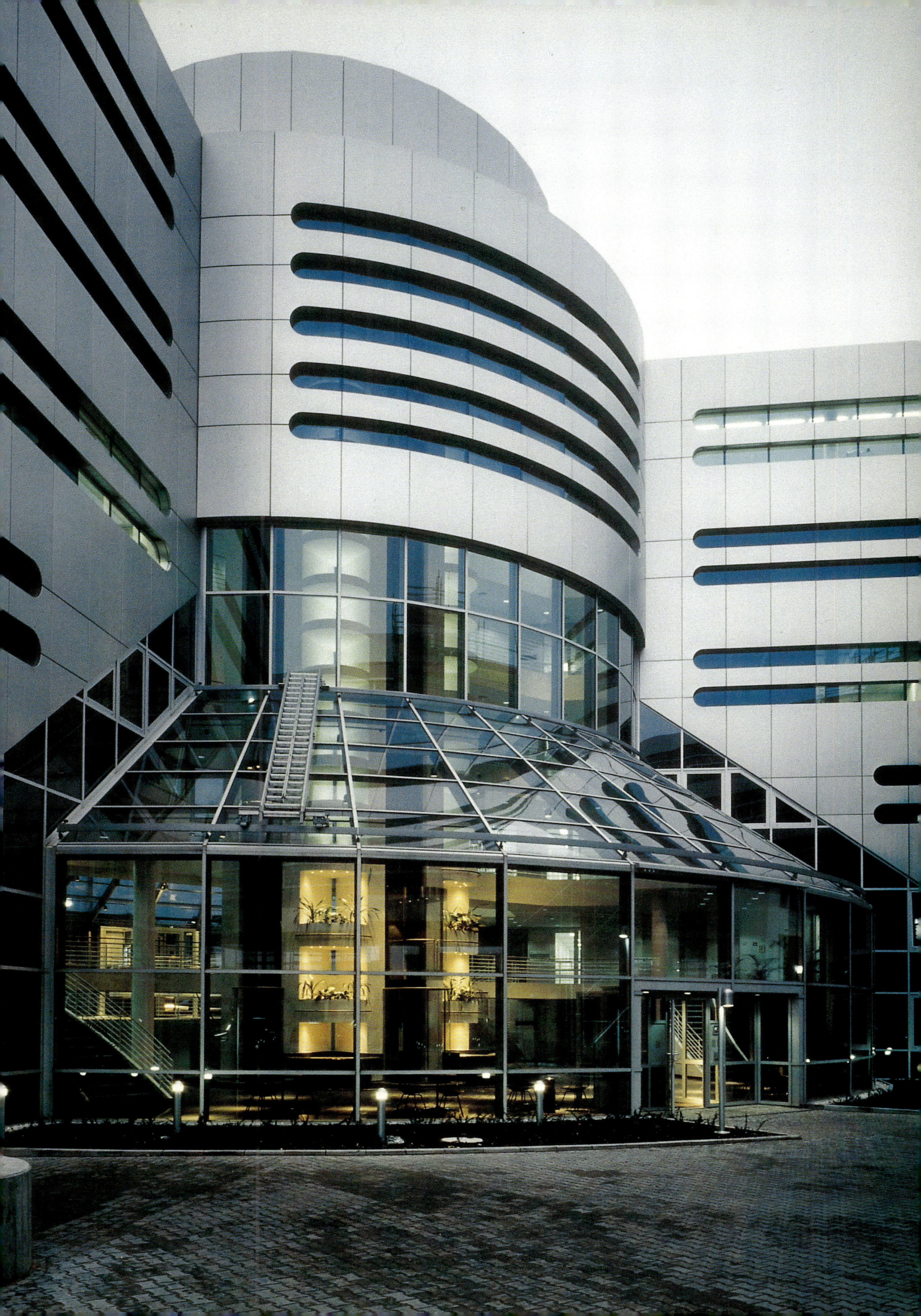

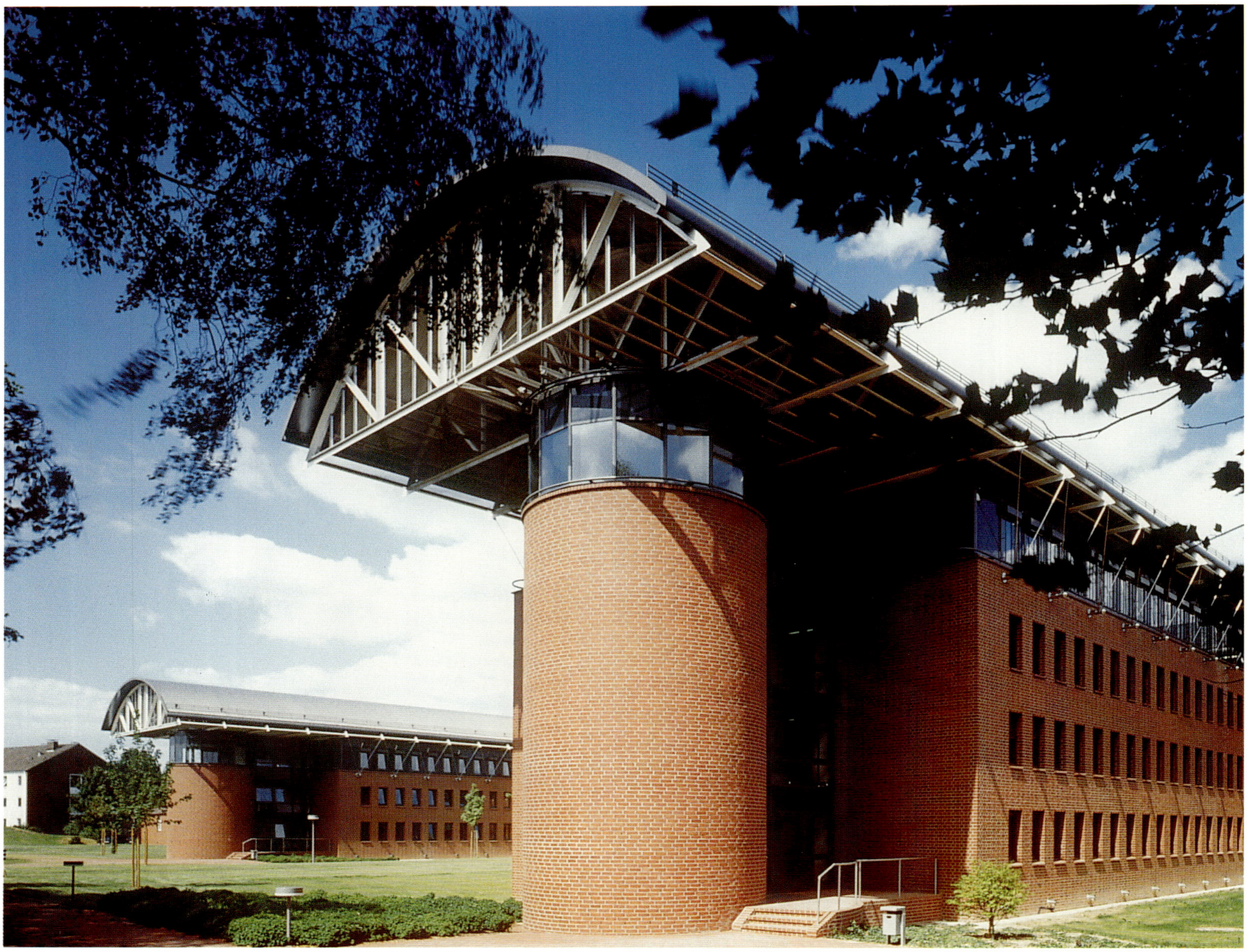

HFS
Military Pilot School
Heeresfliegerwaffenschule

Aircraft and airfields conjure up the idea of a hangar. This fuses our notions of what is at once monumental and light. The new buildings of the military pilot school appropriately provide a play on all that we associate with hangars. Three complexes have been created for the instructional and staff areas. The planning enabled an existing lecture building to be incorporated into a clearly defined scheme. Two large L-shapes and the architectural substance form an integrated complex providing two open courtyards. Open green spaces and paving add a lighter, almost labyrinthine note to the strict geometry of the axes of the buildings.

The L-shaped blocks for the staff area and the instructional area are three and four storeys high, respectively, and finished in brick facing. These are topped by a light steel structure which almost appears to be floating. The open and thus so filigree barrel roof makes the entire complex seem slender. Stout round pillars at the ends of the four rectangular subsidiary blocks seem to carry the roof alone. This impression of lightness is stressed by the glass-aluminum facade structure of each of the upper floors. Visually, the rows of window detach the roof from a solid block rendered positively sturdy by its brickwork.

Compactness, monumentality and lightness blend into a single aesthetic whole.

Mit Flugzeugen und Flugplätzen verbindet man einen Hangar. Er verschmilzt unser Verständnis von Monumentalität und Leichtigkeit. Die neuen Gebäude der Heeresfliegerwaffenschule spielen aus gegebenem Anlaß mit Hangar-Assoziationen. Drei Gebäudekomplexe wurden für den Lehrbereich und den Stabsbereich geschaffen. Vorhanden war ein Hörsaalgebäude, das durch die Planung in ein klar gegliedertes Konzept einbezogen wurde. Zwei große L-Formen bilden mit dem architektonischen Bestand einen zusammenhängenden Komplex, der zwei offene Innenhöfe bildet. Die Grünzonen und die Pflasterungen geben der strengen Geometrie der Gebäudeachsen ein spielerisches und ansatzweise labyrinthisches Gepräge.

Die L-förmigen Baukörper für den Stabsbereich und den Lehrbereich sind in rotem Ziegelverblendmauerwerk einmal drei und einmal vier Stockwerke hochgezogen worden. Gekrönt werden sie von einer leicht und fast schwebend wirkenden Stahlkonstruktion. Das offene und deshalb so filigrane Tonnendach läßt den gesamten Komplex schlank erscheinen. Stämmige Rundpfeiler an den Enden der vier rechteckigen Teilkörper scheinen das Dach allein zu tragen. Unterstrichen wird dieser Eindruck von Leichtigkeit durch die Glas-Alu-Fassadenkonstruktion des jeweils oberen Stockwerks. Die Fensterbänder heben das Dach optisch vom soliden, durch seine Mauerung stämmigen Baukörper ab.

Kompaktheit, Monumentalität und Leichtigkeit verbinden sich zu einem ästhetischen Ganzen.

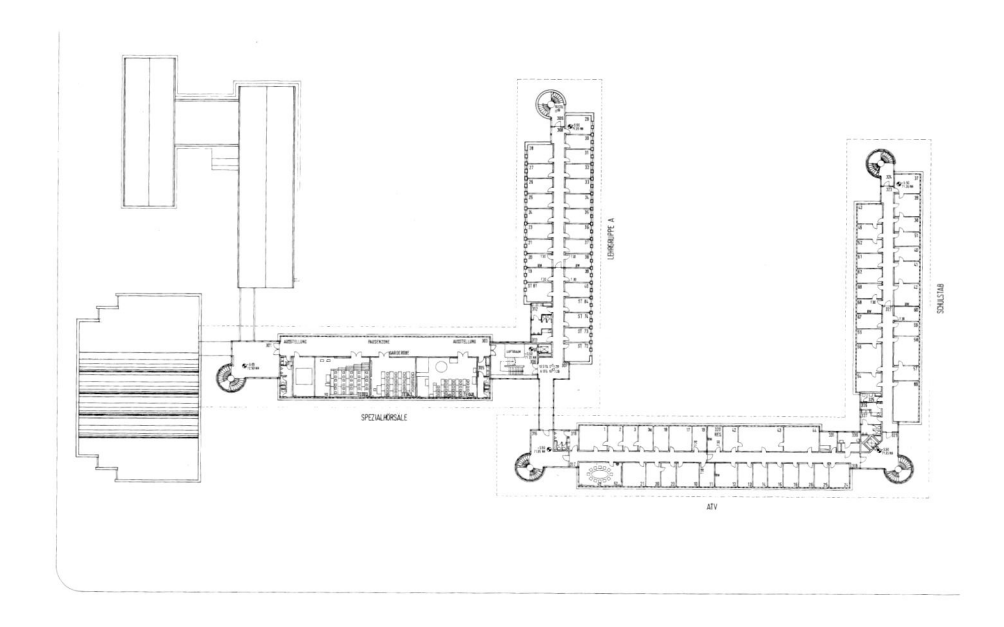

From bottom up: plans of the ground floor, first floor and second floor.
Von unten nach oben: Grundrisse des Erdgeschosses, des 1. Obergeschosses und des 2. Obergeschosses.

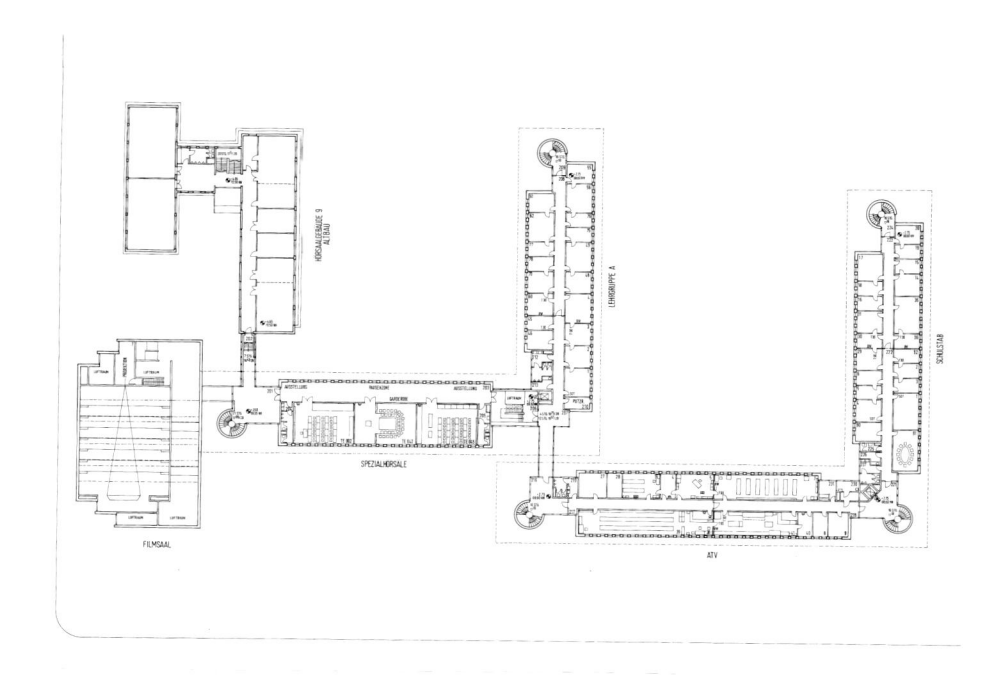

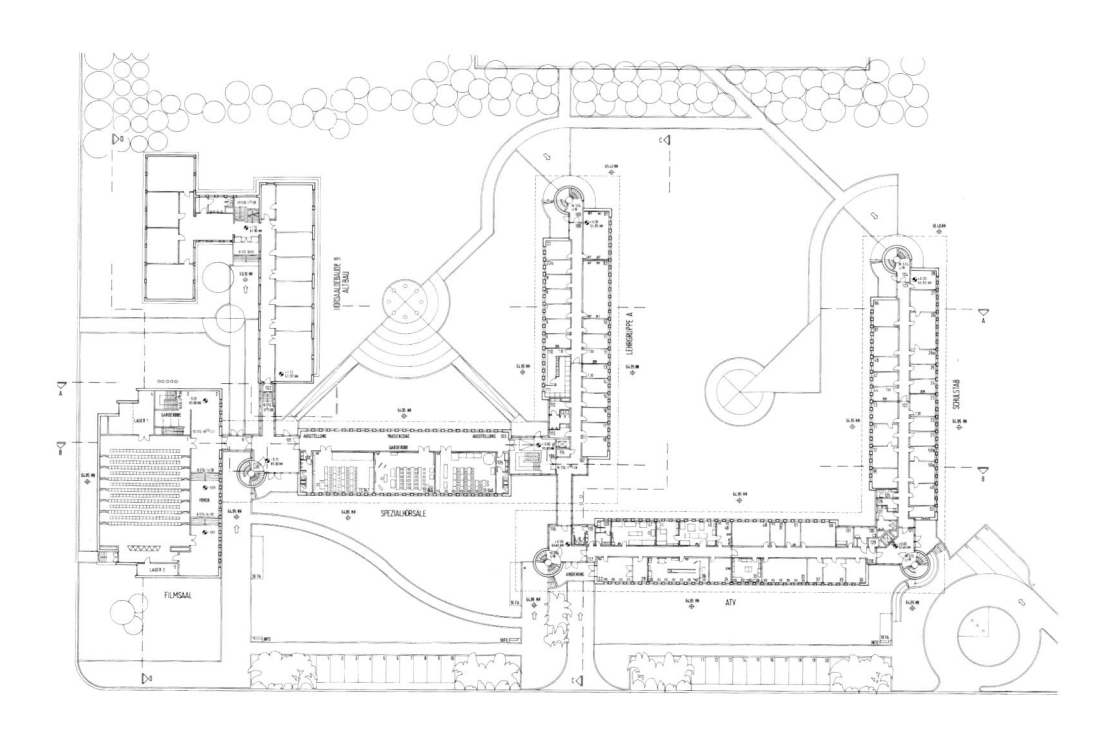

Left: the internal courtyard opening up on the south side.
Below: north facade of the training centre.
*Links: der innere Hof, der sich südlich öffnet.
Unten: die Nordfassade des Ausbildungszentrums.*

From bottom of page up the centre, viewed from the north, several sections.
Opposite page: views of the inside of the centre, which in addition to the lecture halls and training area, also holds a 300-seat-projection room and administration offices.

Von unten nach oben: der Komplex von Norden gesehen: diverse Schnitte. Auf der Seite nebenan: Ansichten des Inneren des Zentrums, das neben Hörsälen, Ausbildungszonen auch einen Vortragssaal für 300 Personen und den Verwaltungs-Stabsbereich aufnimmt.

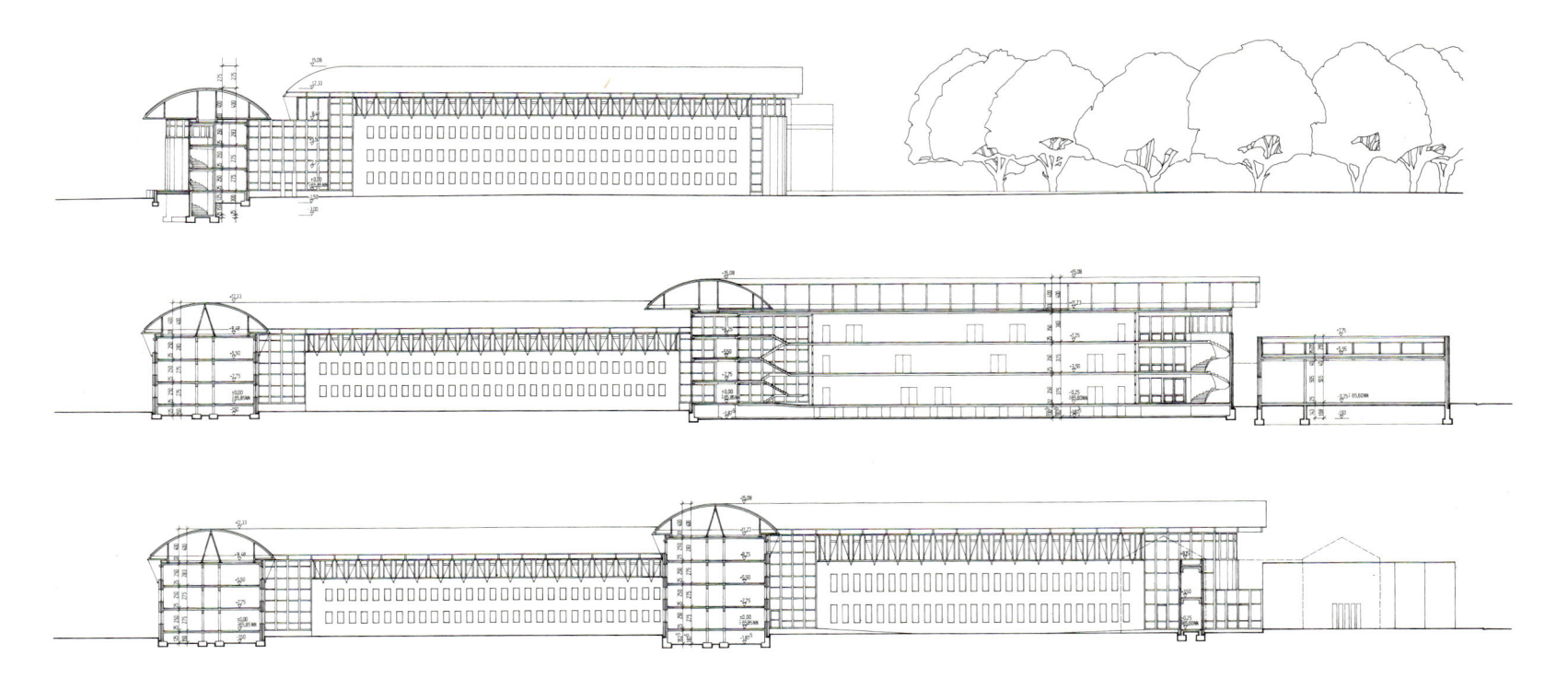

61

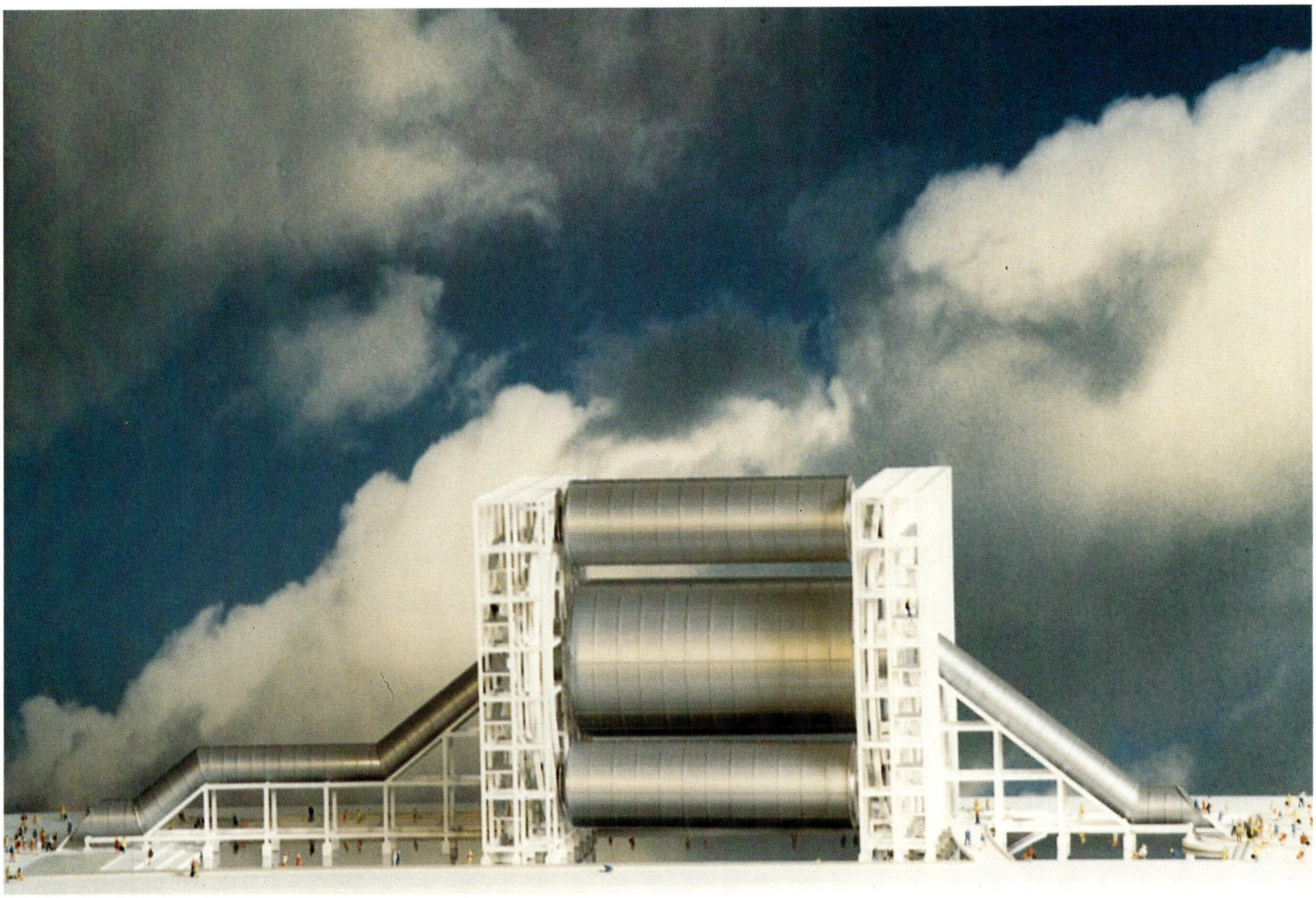

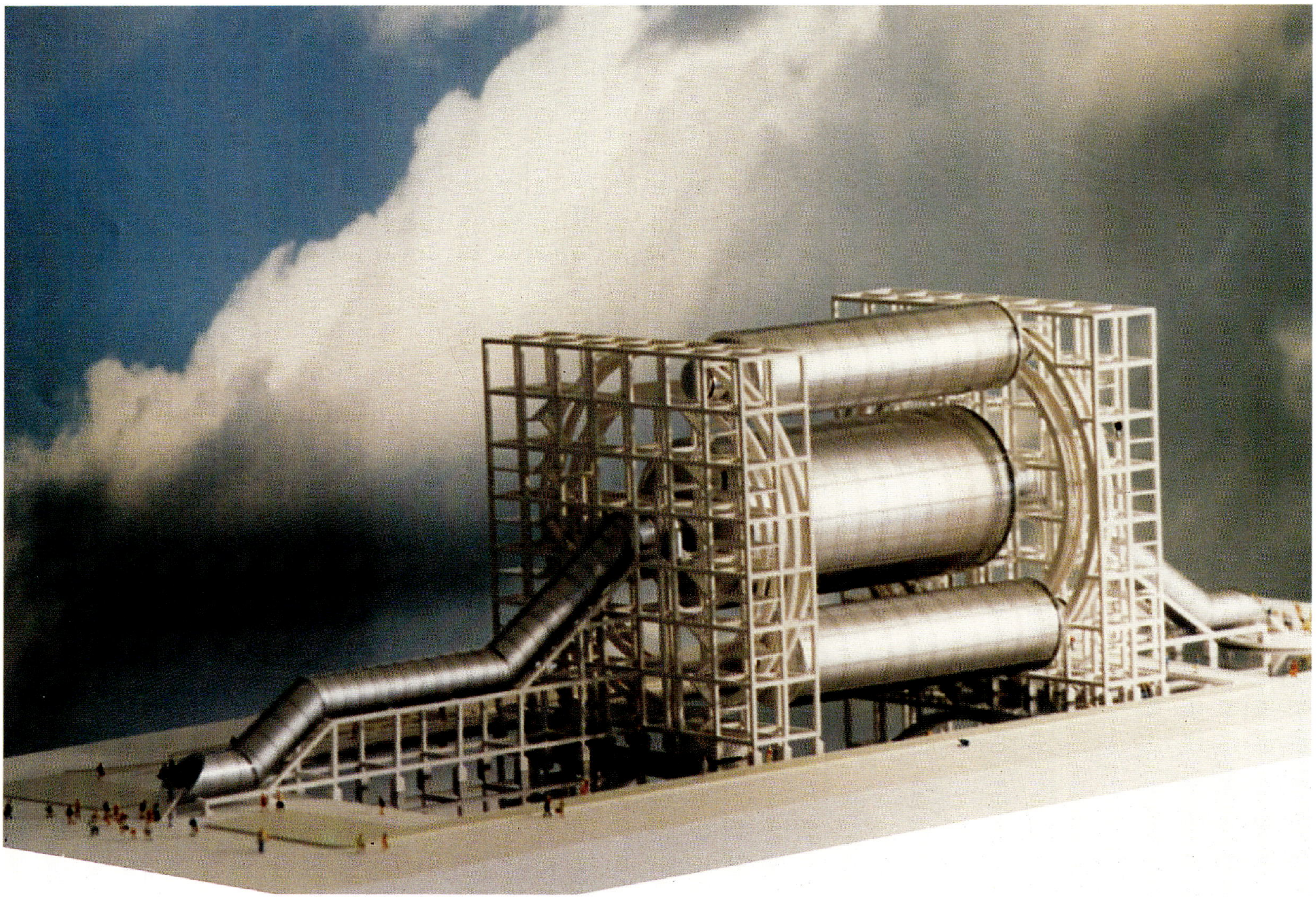

EXPO 2000
German Expo Pavilion
Deutscher Expo Pavillon

EXPO 2000 in Hanover is being held under the motto "Humankind-Nature-Technology" and is concerned less to display a picture of technical achievements than to provide insights into the future. The aim is to strike a balance between the three determinant and mutually interactive themes humankind, nature and technology. To see this as one dynamic entity entails being a visionary in many respects.

Such was the context for the design of the German pavilion. The architecture here was to be meaningful yet visionary, equally suitable for presentational and representational purposes.

The exterior appearance reminds one of a broader Ferris wheel or a revolving laboratory drum, but also of a child's toy. From all areas, indeed, associations also invariably flow into visionary ideas.

Yet specific associations are in fact lacking in this design. It's just that thoughts are constantly sparked off by a drum through which one may proceed into another, fresh world.

The whole complex is in three parts, linked up on each side by a transparent pedestrian tube. The central part consists of a large tube positioned horizontally and three narrower ones surrounding this. The tubular framework is supported by two steel lattice frames.

The central tube houses a hall on various themes, and the surrounding ones offer space for supplementary or more detailed displays. The tubes are about 40 metres long, conceived as extended pavilions, while the three rotating exhibition halls offer the experience of a height difference which is also almost 40 metres. The surrounding tubes are largely transparent and provide wonderful views across the exhibition grounds.

Mushroom-shaped entrance areas are planned for both sides of the static load-bearing steel structure. These put visitors in the mood and function as both the exits and ends of the transparent tubes to the exhibition halls.
Visitors can only enter the EXPO pavilion from one side and transit this in one given direction. Scrimmages caused by visitor flows in opposing directions are therefore avoided.

A pavilion of this kind offers an opportunity of showing that it is not technology per se which is a problem for the future, but the question of the resources, the goal and the viewpoint to be chosen in applying technology to regenerating nature and humankind.

Die EXPO 2000 in Hannover steht unter dem Motto „Mensch-Natur-Technik" und ist bestrebt, weniger ein Bild technischer Errungenschaften zu zeichnen, als vielmehr Ausblicke in die Zukunft zu geben. Es geht dabei um eine Ausbalancierung der drei prägenden und sich gegenseitig beeinflussenden Elemente Mensch, Natur und Technik. Dies als eine dynamische Einheit zu sehen, hat noch vielfach visionären Charakter.

Aus diesem Kontext heraus ist der Entwurf für einen Deutschen Pavillon entstanden. Es sollte eine signifikante und zugleich visionäre Architektur werden, die gleichwohl für Präsentations- und auch Repräsentationszwecke brauchbar ist.

Der äußere Eindruck kann an ein verbreitetes Riesenrad erinnern oder an eine sich drehende Labortrommel, aber auch an ein Kinderspielzeug. Aus allen Bereichen fließen immer ja auch Assoziationen in visionäre Vorstellungen ein.

Eindeutige Assoziationen gibt es bei diesem Entwurf allerdings nicht. Es blitzen nur immer wieder Gedanken an eine Trommel auf, durch die hindurch man zu einer anderen, neuen Welt gehen könnte.

Der gesamte Komplex ist dreiteilig und auf jeder Seite durch jeweils eine durchsichtige Lauf-Röhre verbunden. Der Mittelteil besteht aus einer horizontal positionierten großen Röhre und drei schmaleren, sie horizontal umkreisenden Röhren. Getragen wird das Röhrenwerk von zwei Gitter-Stahlgerüsten.

Die zentrale Röhre beherbergt eine Themenhalle, die kreisenden Röhren bieten Raum für ergänzende und vertiefende Darstellungen. Die Röhren sind als etwa 40 m lange, gestreckte Pavillons gedacht, wobei die rotierenden drei Ausstellungshallen einen Höhenunterschied von fast ebenfalls 40 m erleben lassen. Die kreisenden Röhren sind weitgehend transparent und gewähren großartige Überblicke über das Ausstellungsgelände.

Zu beiden Seiten der tragenden und statischen Stahlkonstruktion sind pilz-förmige Eingangsbereiche geplant. Sie stimmen ein und sind zugleich Ausgangs- und Endpunkte der durchsichtigen Zugangsröhren zu den Ausstellungshallen. Der Besucher kann den EXPO Pavillon nur von einer Seite betreten; die Laufrichtung ist vorgegeben. Turbulenzen durch gegenläufige Besucherströme sind damit vermieden.

Ein solcher Pavillon bietet die Möglichkeit, aufzuzeigen, daß nicht die Technik als solches ein Problem der Zukunft ist, sondern die Frage, mit welchem Aufwand, mit welchem Ziel und mit welchem Bewußtsein Technik zur Regeneration von Natur und Mensch eingesetzt wird.

Right: site plan, below: model of the Expo 2000 project and concept section.
Rechts: Lageplan, unten: das Modell des Projekts für die Expo 2000 und ein Systemschnitt.

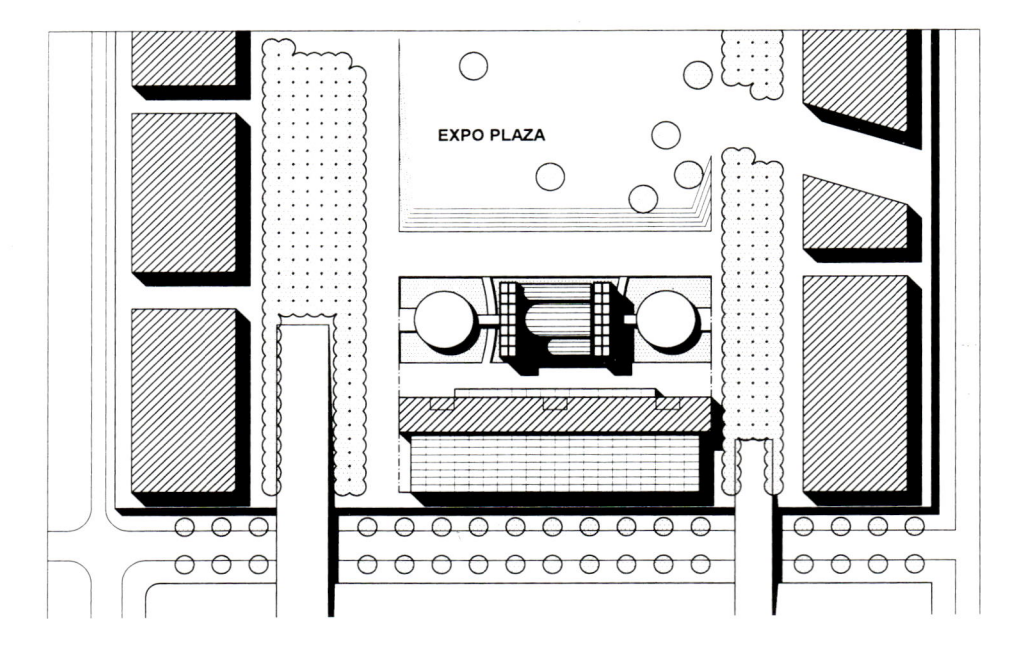

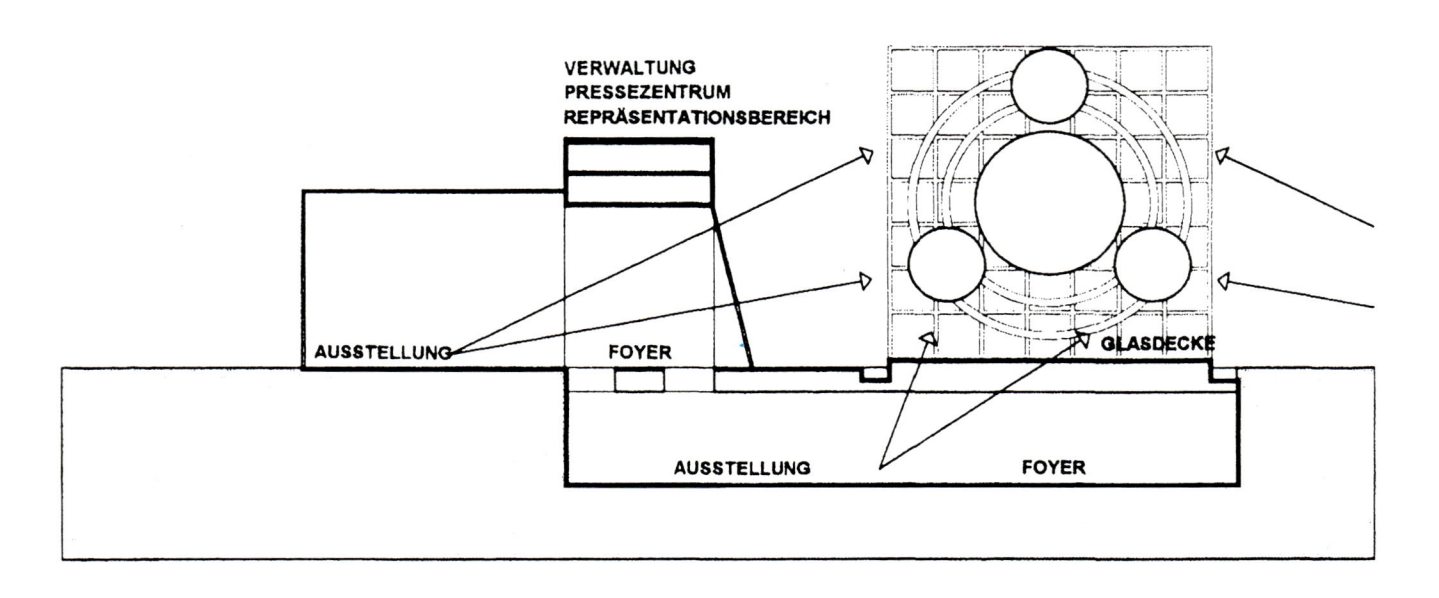

EXPO PLAZA

VERWALTUNG
PRESSEZENTRUM
REPRÄSENTATIONSBEREICH

AUSSTELLUNG   FOYER   GLASDECKE

AUSSTELLUNG   FOYER

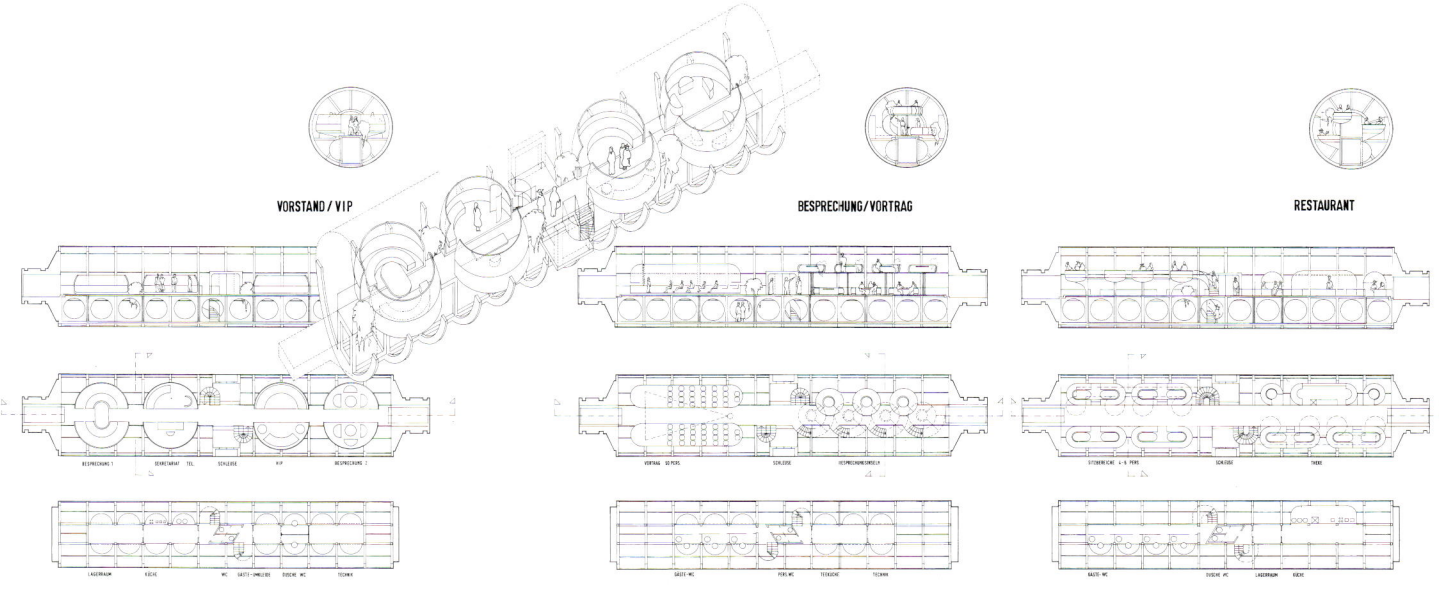

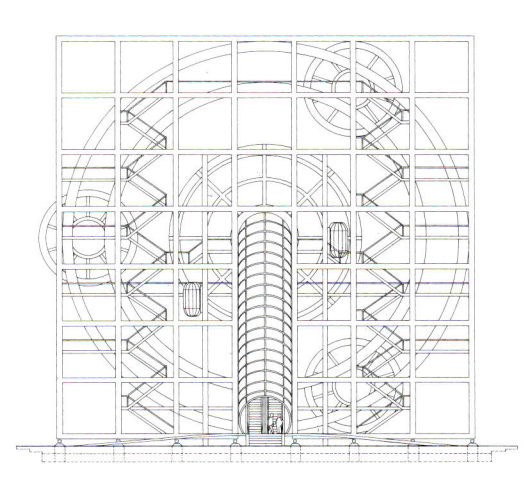

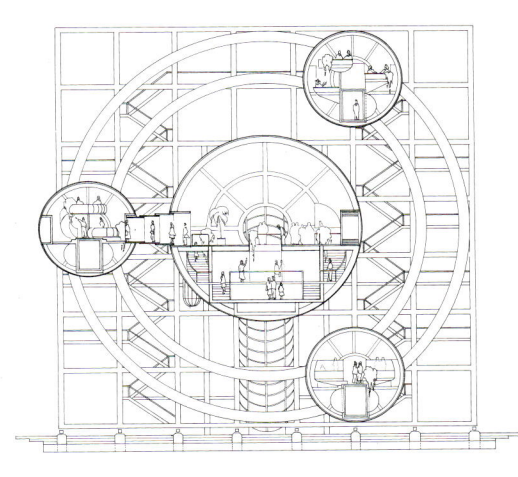

Top of page: longitudinal sections, axonometry and plans of the various building levels.
Above: south elevation and cross section.
Left: side view of the model.

Oben: Längsschnitte, Isometrie und Grundrisse der verschiedenen Ebenen des Gebäudes.
Oben: Südansicht und Querschnitt.
Links: Seitenansicht des Modells.

65

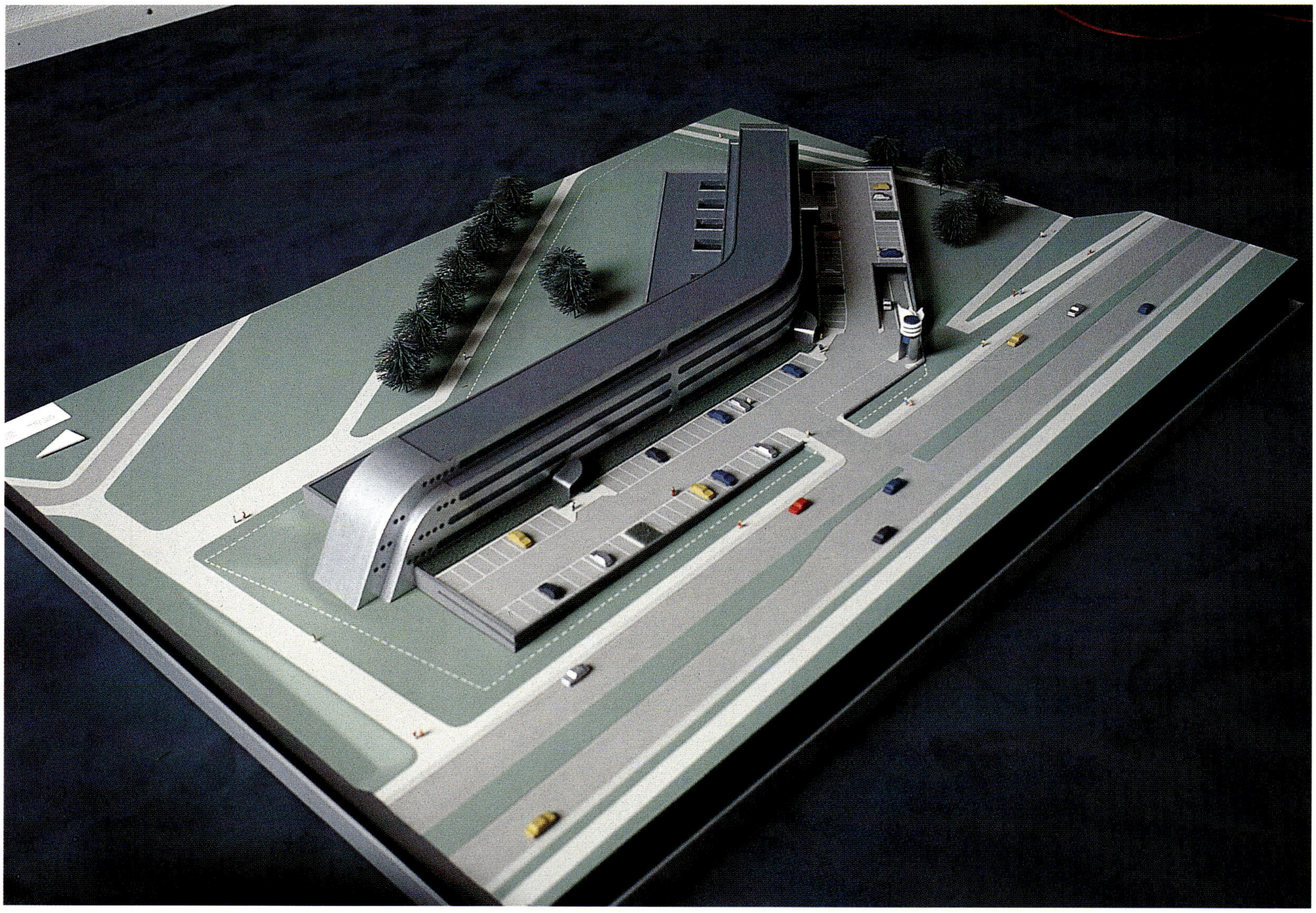

KW 2
Office Building for German Rail
Bürogebäude der DB AG

    Like an ICE express train, the office building for Deutsche Bahn AG (DB) slithers elegantly between road and railroad. 180 metres long, this is not exactly a small building, but no more than about half the length of a high-speed train.

    This complex of buildings has been planned to house the headquarters for DB's technical operations in Northern Germany. Lying along the Hanover-Berlin high-speed route inaugurated in September 1998, the look of the building underscores the desired image of German Rail. Elegance, innovation, smoothness and for all that, sturdy reliability also, are all signified by the architectural forms employed here.

    A gentle bend in the centre of the complex - consisting of a curve embodying an angle of 140° - plus rounded ends add a note of elegance to the compactness of the block. The curves also modify the appearance of the entire length of the building.

    Three storeys are topped by an additional recessed storey which thanks to a narrowing more felt than seen underscores the flow of the lines. Altogether, however, the building has six levels. The complex rests on a lower ground floor forming a plateau, below which two more underground levels house parking spaces and archive and basement areas.

    The block functions as noise insulation for the residential buildings behind it. Access is to the building is from the street side, i.e. Karl-Wiechert-Allee. A space in front provides a gap, "room for a view" and parking facilities for visitors.
The flowing elegance of the architectural lines can only be fully appreciated from a certain distance.

*   Wie ein ICE schlängelt sich das Bürogebäude der Deutschen Bahn elegant zwischen Straße und Schiene dahin. Mit etwa 180 Metern ist das Gebäude zwar nicht klein, aber doch nur etwa halb so lang wie die Hochgeschwindigkeitszüge der Bahn.*

*   Der Gebäudekomplex ist als technische Betriebszentrale des Bereichs Norddeutschland der Deutschen Bahn AG geplant. Entlang der im September 1998 eingeweihten Hochgeschwindigkeitstraße von Hannover nach Berlin unterstreicht das Erscheinungsbild der Betriebszentrale das Selbstverständnis der Bahn. Eleganz, Geschmeidigkeit, Innovation und bei alle dem dennoch robuste Zuverlässigkeit signalisieren die architektonischen Formen.*

*   Eine sanfte Biegung etwa in der Mitte des Gebäudekomplexes (durch ein Abknicken im stumpfen Winkel von 140°) und abgerundete Enden geben der Kompaktheit des Baukörpers die elegante Note. Die Schwünge verkürzen auch fürs Auge die Gesamtlänge des Gebäudes.*

*   Drei Geschosse werden von einem zusätzlichen Staffelgeschoß gekrönt, das durch seine mehr spürbare als sichtbare Verringerung in der Breite den Linienschwung unterstreicht. Insgesamt aber hat das Gebäude sechs Ebenen. Der Baukomplex liegt auf einem plateaubildenden Untergeschoß, das unter sich noch zwei Tiefgeschosse mit Parkplätzen und Archiv- und Kellerzonen aufweist.*

*   Der Baukörper wirkt auch als Schallschutz gegenüber der hinter ihm liegenden Wohnbebauung. Erschlossen wird das Gebäude von der Straßenseite (Karl-Wiechert-Allee) her. Ein Vorplatz bietet Abstand, „Sichtraum" und Parkmöglichkeiten für Besucher. Denn erst aus einer gewissen Entfernung wird die Eleganz der architektonischen Linienführung erkennbar.*

Site plan.
Below: the model seen from the west and south-west.
Lageplan.
Unten: das Modell von der West- und Südwestseite.

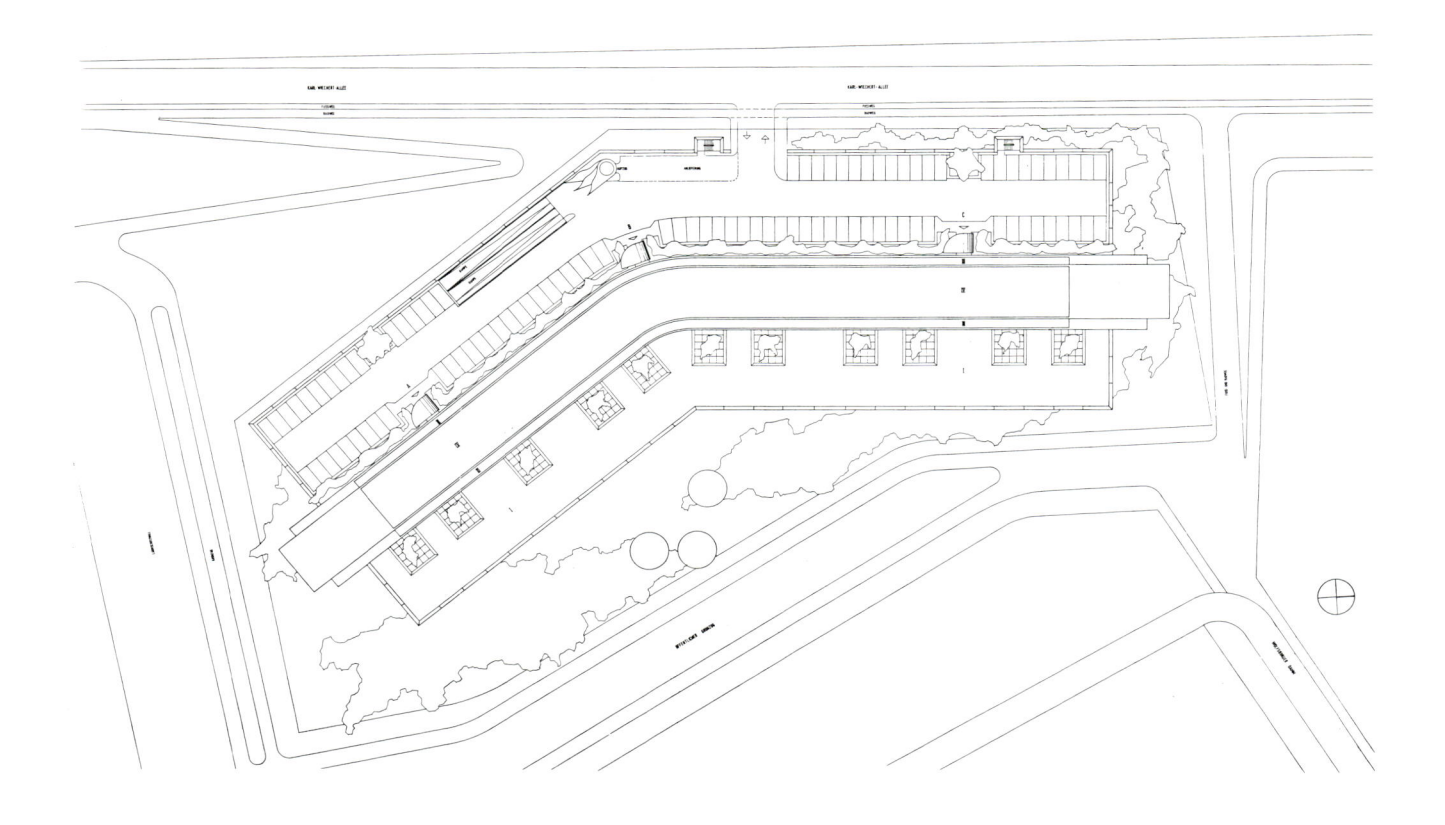

Partial elevations. Below: the model seen from the south and east.
Teilansichten. Unten: das Modell von der Süd-und Ostseite.

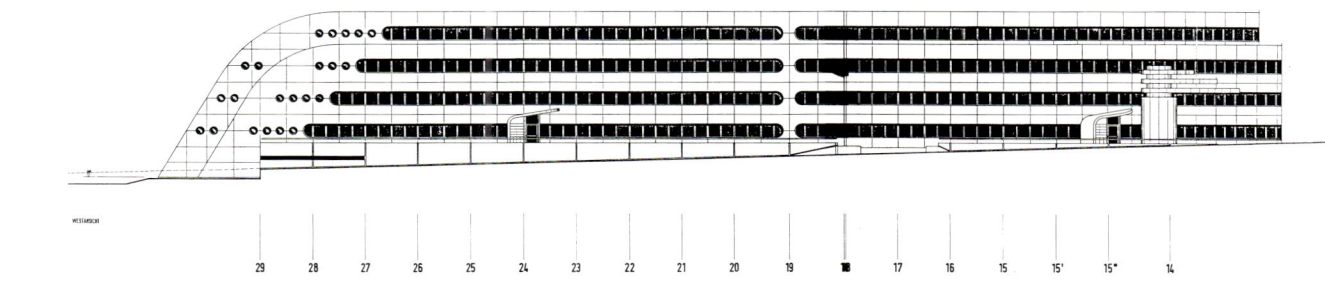

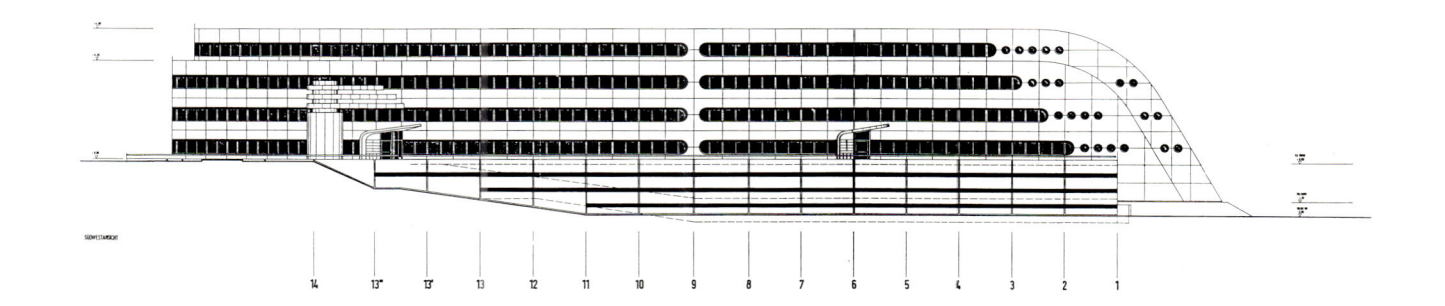

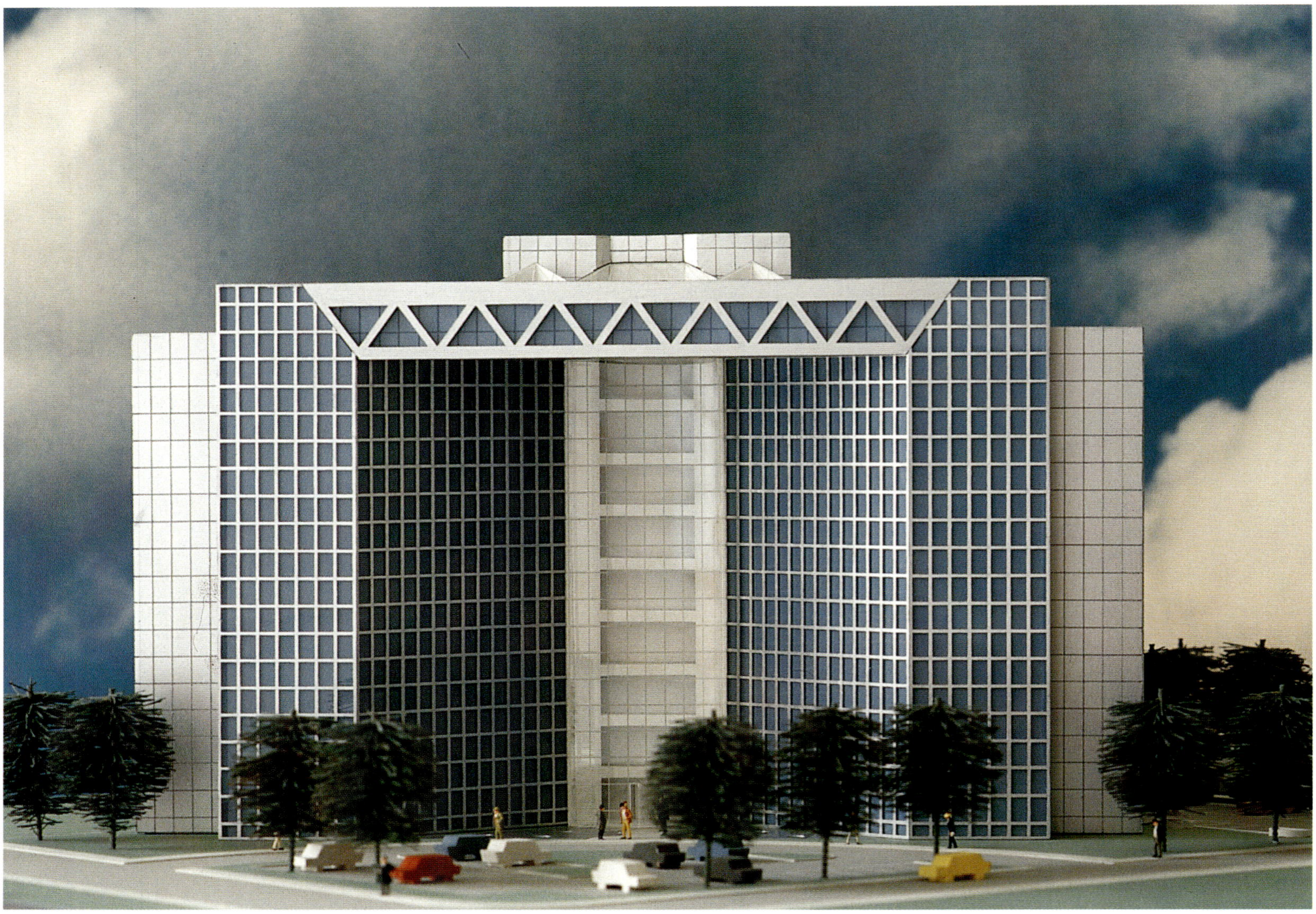

PITTLER
Headquarters
Hauptverwaltung

This ten-storey office building appears imposing, indeed extravagant, from the front, yet modest and compact when seen from behind or from the sides.

Two interlocking L-shapes form the ground plan of the building. The side open to the front has been used as the front entrance and completed by a glass facade the full height of the building. This transparent glass wall naturally also functions as an invitation to approach closer and enter.

The block has been positioned on the plot so as to leave adequate representational space along the street but also a sufficient gap to the nearest neighbours "at the back".

The building serves as the head office for Pittler, the Frankfurt-based engineering group. Its architecture provides a striking point of identity in what is most emphatically a location dominated by industrial and trading concerns. This terse structure also suggests something akin to a corporate identity. The building furnishes an unmistakable outward image.

The front of the building and its two sides have screen-type facades, but with very different emphases. The two side frontages forming the back, so to speak, of the open and welcoming "base" of the equilateral triangle, make a sequential, massive and constructive impression. The front side makes an airy and light impression and relieves the building of any ponderousness.

The lift units are on the middle axis of the triangle of buildings. They link both wings like some hinge. A steel structure carries the projecting roof and in providing a direct view of functional and aesthetic aspects is reminiscent of an architrave.

The architecture provides a play on solidity, expanse and volume in ever-changing aspects.

Repräsentativ und extravagant wirkt das zehngeschossige Bürogebäude von der Vorderfront, schlicht und geballt beim Blick von hinten und von den Seiten.

Zwei ineinander geschachtelte L-Formen bilden die Grundform des Gebäudes. Die nach vorne offene Seite wird zur Eingangsfront mit einer haushohen Glasfassade abgeschlossen. Aber natürlich ist die durchsichtige Glas-Wand zugleich auch die Einladung, näher- und einzutreten.

Der Baukörper ist so in das Grundstück hinein gesetzt, daß genügend repräsentativer Raum von der Straße her bleibt, aber ebenso auch im 'Rücken' genügend Abstand zu den nächsten Nachbarn.

Das Gebäude dient als Hauptverwaltung des Maschinenbaukonzerns Pittler in Frankfurt. Die architektonische Gestaltung setzt einen markanten Identifikationspunkt innerhalb eines stark industriell und gewerblich ausgerichteten Standortes. Darüber hinaus wirkt die Prägnanz der Konstruktion im Sinne einer Corporate Identity. Das Gebäude schafft ein unverwechselbares Erscheinungsbild.

Die Gebäudefront und die beiden Seiten haben rasterförmig geprägte Fassaden, doch mit sehr unterschiedlichen Gewichtungen. Die beiden Seitenfronten, die gewissermaßen die Rückseite der offenen und lichten „Basis" des gleichschenkligen Dreiecks bilden, wirken seriell, massiv und konstruktiv. Die Vorderfront macht einen luftigen und leichten Eindruck und nimmt dem Gebäude jegliche Schwere.

In der Mittelachse des Gebäudedreiecks befinden sich Liftanlagen. Sie verbinden wie ein Scharnier beide Flügel. Eine Stahlkonstruktion trägt das vorgezogene Dach und erinnert in der direkten Ansicht in Funktion und Ästhetik an ein Architrav.

Die Architektur umspielt Körperlichkeit, Flächigkeit und Volumen in jeweils neuen Ansichten.

Aerial view of the model.
Left, from bottom up: plan of the ground floor, standard floors, the ninth floor and the roof level.

*Vogelperspektive des Modells.
Links, von oben nach unten: Grundriß des Erdgeschosses, der neun Standardgeschosse, des Obergeschosses und der Dachaufsicht.*

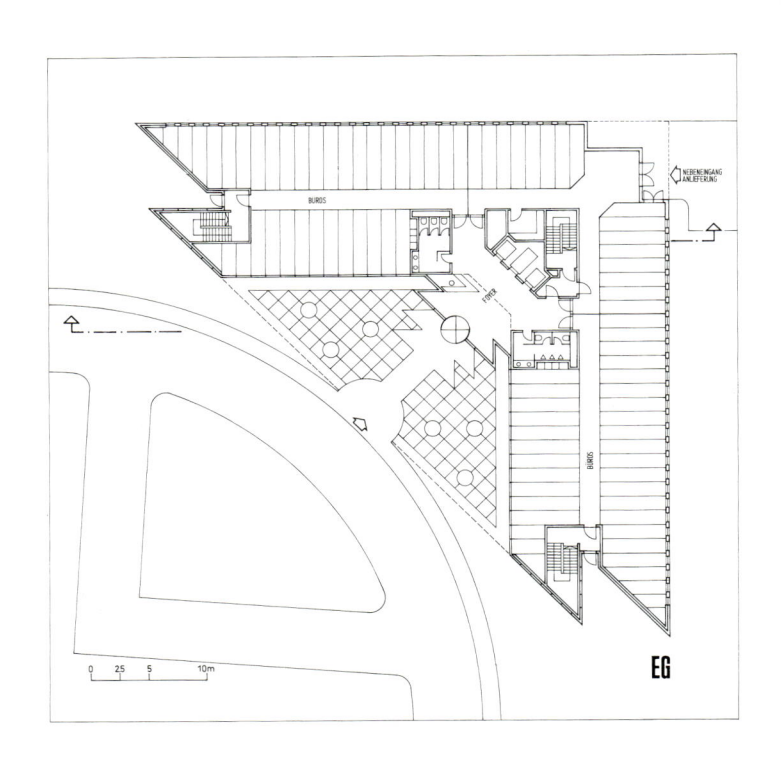

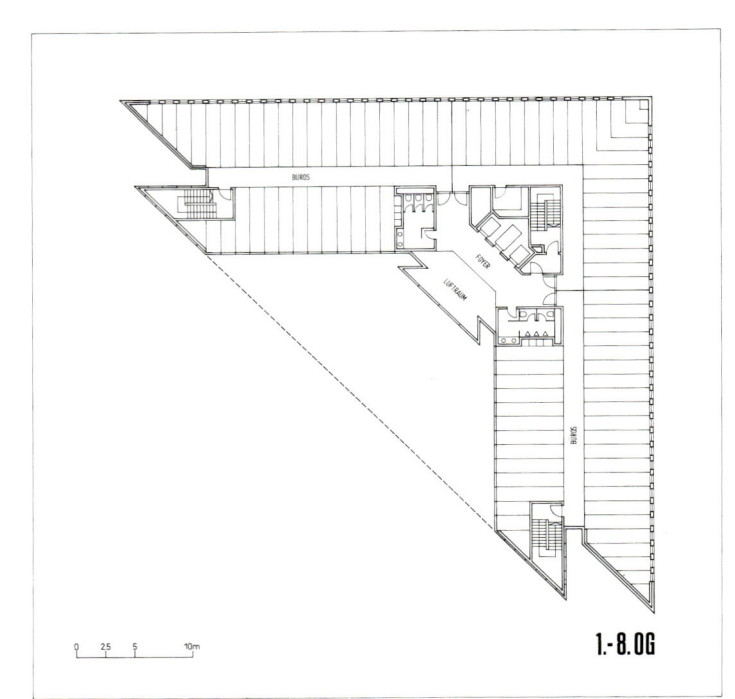

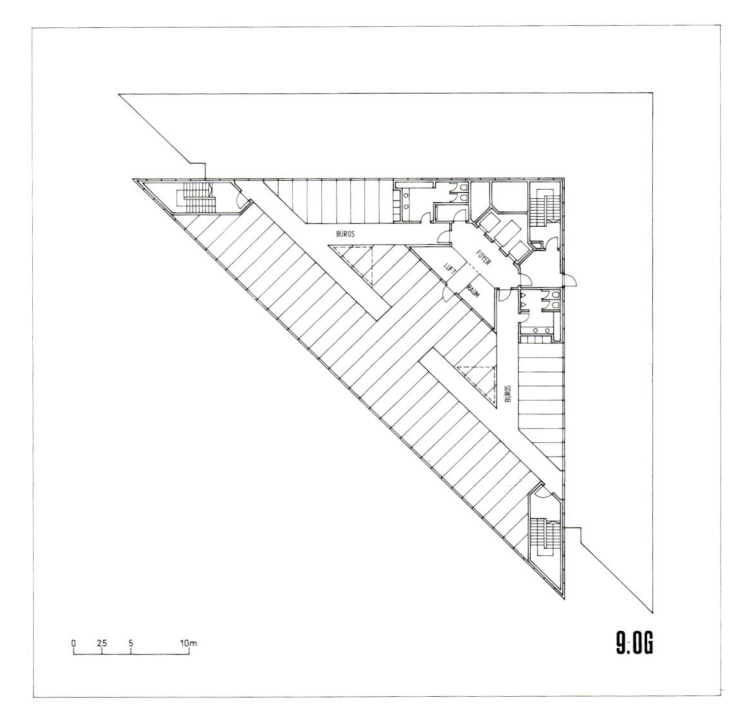

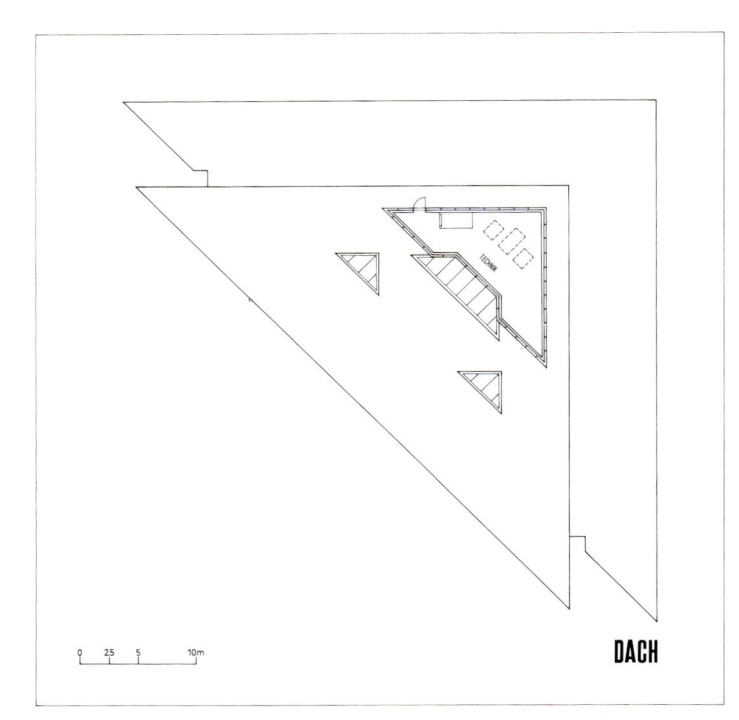

Main facade and below, north-east corner of the model.
Die Hauptfassade und unten: die Nord-Ost-Ecke des Gebäudes.

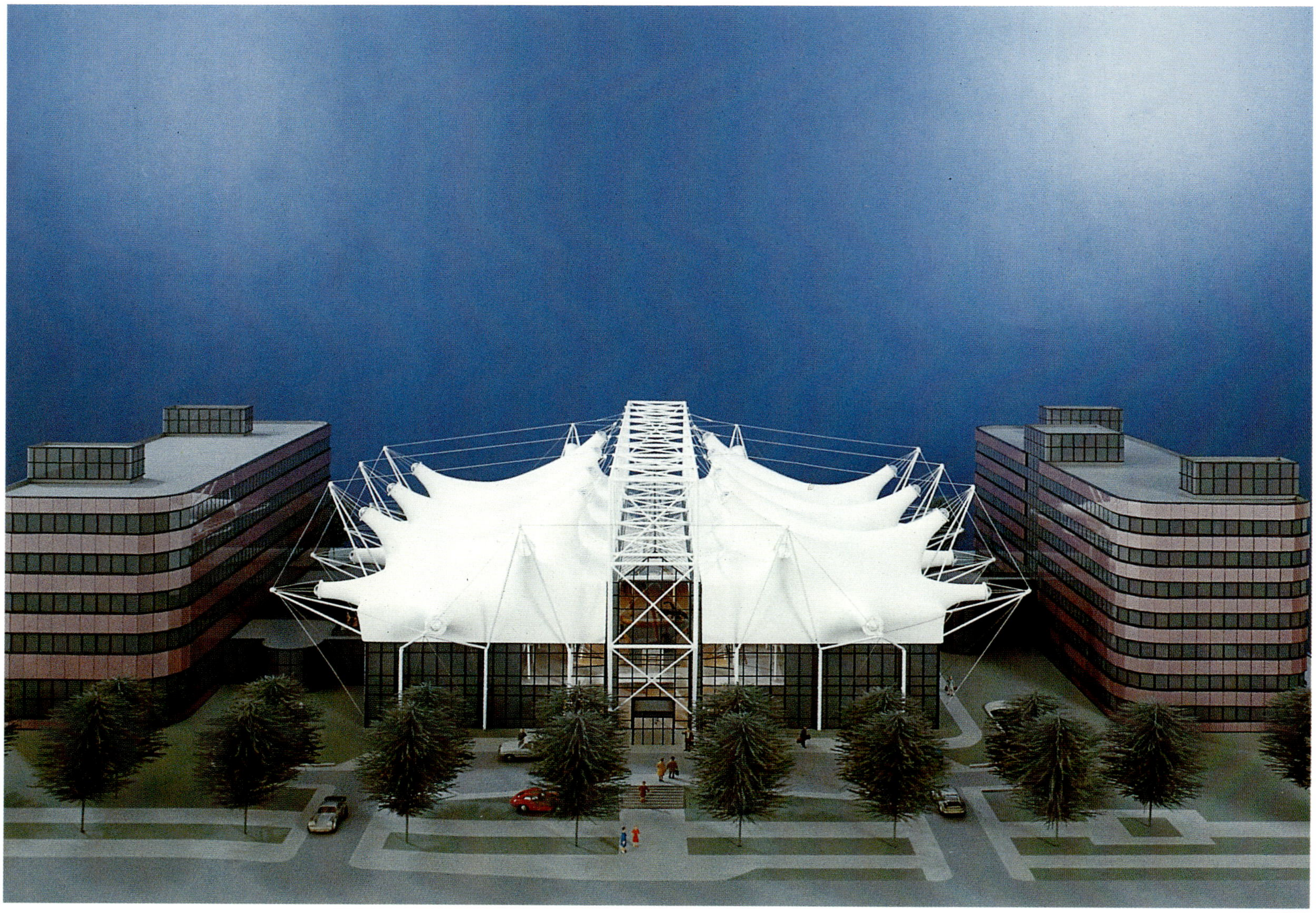

MPC
Medical Park Hotel and Office Centre
Medical Park Hotel-und Bürozentrum

Scientific centres such as the medical park and the biomedical industry are grouped around Hanover's medical university, but a communication centre has so far been lacking. The multi-lane Karl-Wiechert-Allee connects this lively and still growing scientific centre with motorways to the north, the fair and EXPO grounds to the south, and the city centre to the east. Yet at the same time the street also separates the expanding research and university centre from three differently structured residential areas.

Perpendicular to the street, a hotel and shopping centre will be inserted, joining up research, teaching, hospital and living areas. A complex of three buildings will link up the scientific areas in the north-south direction. A five-storey office building will mask a seven-storey hotel further back from the street. 140 suites of the US hotel company "Summerfield Suites" will reflect the representative tone of the complex as a whole.

Between the two buildings and linked with both is a hall building with a transparent tent roof. This permits a variety of usages and has been conceived as the central entrance to the office and hotel buildings. The rooms between the central hall and the buildings are for use as conference and convention rooms.

Thanks to the transparent tent roof, the glass roof below this and its glazed facade structure, the central hall will be light and extremely transparent.

Um die Medizinische Hochschule in Hannover gruppieren sich wissenschaftliche Zentren wie der Medical Park und Biomedizinische Industrie, aber es fehlt bislang ein kommunikatives Zentrum.

Die mehrspurige Karl-Wiechert-Allee verbindet dieses lebendige und immer noch aufstrebende wissenschaftliche Zentrum nach Norden hin mit den Autobahnen, nach Süden mit Messe- und EXPO-Gelände und nach Westen mit der Innenstadt. Die Straße trennt aber auch gleichzeitig das ausladende Forschungs- und Hochschulzentrum von drei unterschiedlich strukturierten Wohngebieten.

Senkrecht zur Straße wird sich in den Bereich zwischen Medizinischer Hochschule und Medical Park ein Hotel- und Geschäftscenter schieben, das die Bereiche Forschung, Lehre, Krankenbetreuung und Wohnen miteinander verknüpft. Ein dreiteiliger Baukomplex verbindet die wissenschaftlichen Bereiche in nord-südlicher Richtung. Die architektonische Lösung verbindet von der Straßenseite her durch einen langgestreckten Baukörper die bereits bestehenden Komplexe und bietet von Hochschule und Medical Park her durch seine Dreiteilung und die nord-südliche Ausrichtung Offenheit und Durchgang.

Eine Zeltdach bekrönte zentrale Halle wird von zwei kompakten Gebäuden flankiert. Zur Straße hin schirmt ein fünfgeschossiges Bürogebäude den weiter innen gelegenen siebengeschossigen Hotelbau ab. 140 Suiten der amerikanischen Hotelgesellschaft „Summerfield Suites" werden die repräsentative Note des Gesamtkomplexes widerspiegeln.

Zwischen beiden Gebäuden und mit beiden verbunden liegt ein Hallenbau mit einem lichtdurchlässigen Zeitdach. Er ermöglicht vielfältige Nutzungen und ist als zentraler Zugang zum Büro- und zum Hotelgebäude gedacht. Die Räume zwischen Hallenzentrum und Gebäuden werden für Tagungs- und Konferenzräume genutzt.

Die zentrale Halle ist durch das lichtdurchlässige Zeltdach, das darunter liegende Glasdach und seine gläserne Fassadenstruktur hell und geradezu transparent.

Detail of the model. Below, from bottom up: south, west and north elevations.
Opposite page: plan of the ground floor and aerial view of the model.
*Detailausschnitt des Modells.
Darunter, von unten: Süd-, West- und Nordansicht.
Auf der gegenüberliegenden Seite der Grundriß des Erdgeschosses und die Vogelperspektive des Modells.*

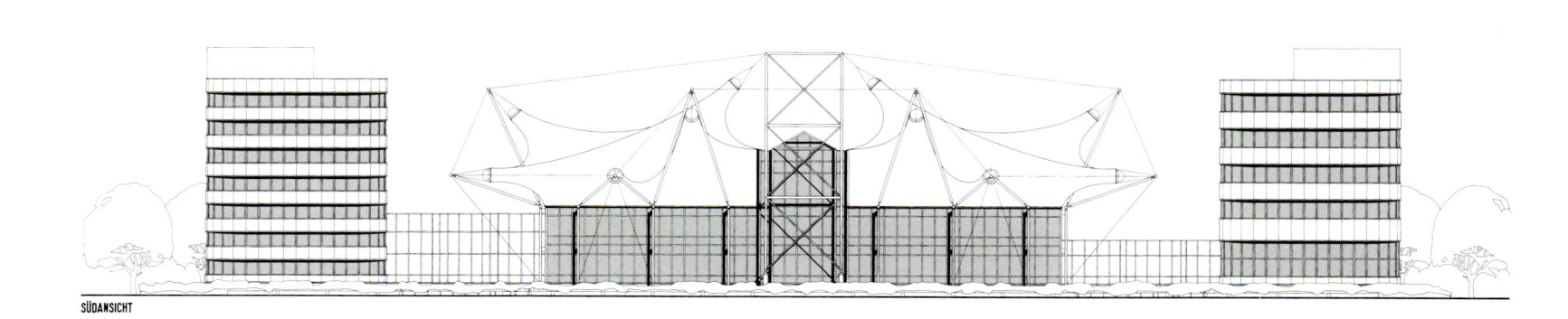

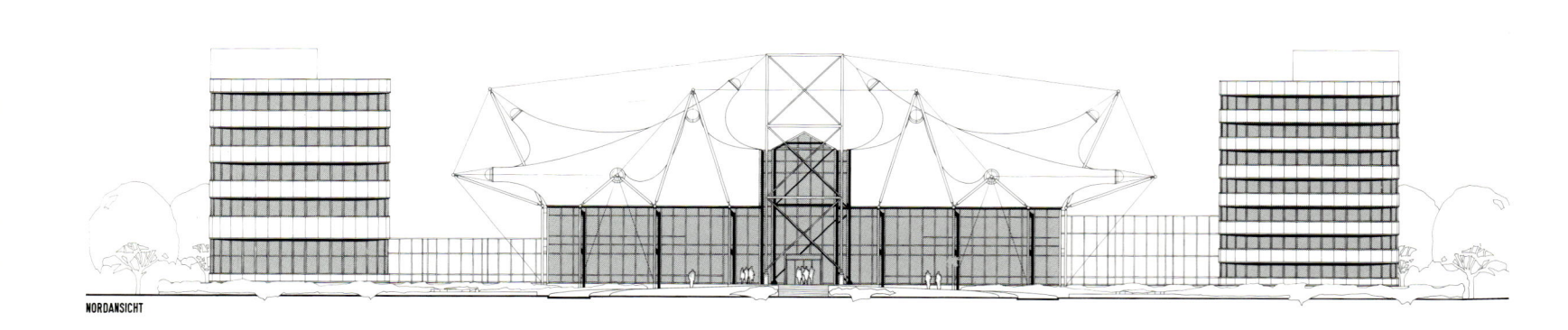

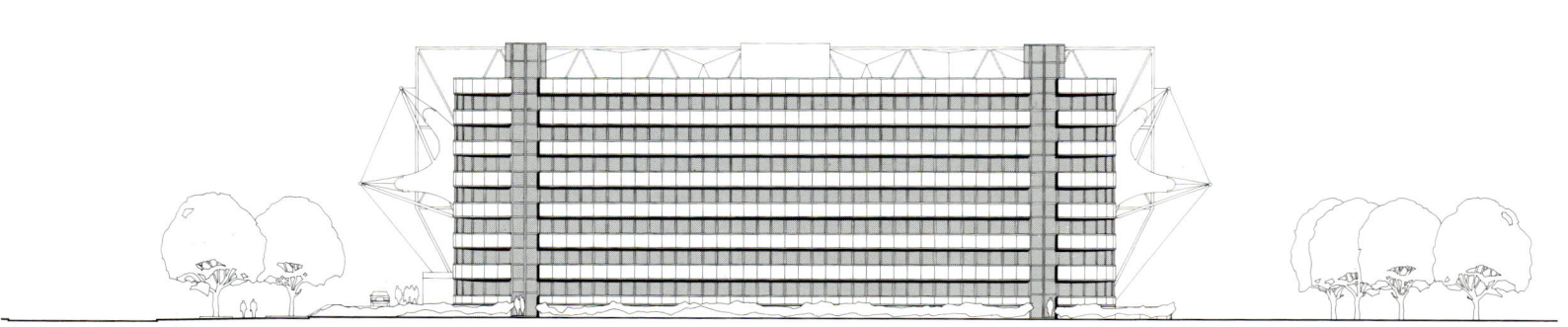

SÜDANSICHT

NORDANSICHT

WESTANSICHT

77

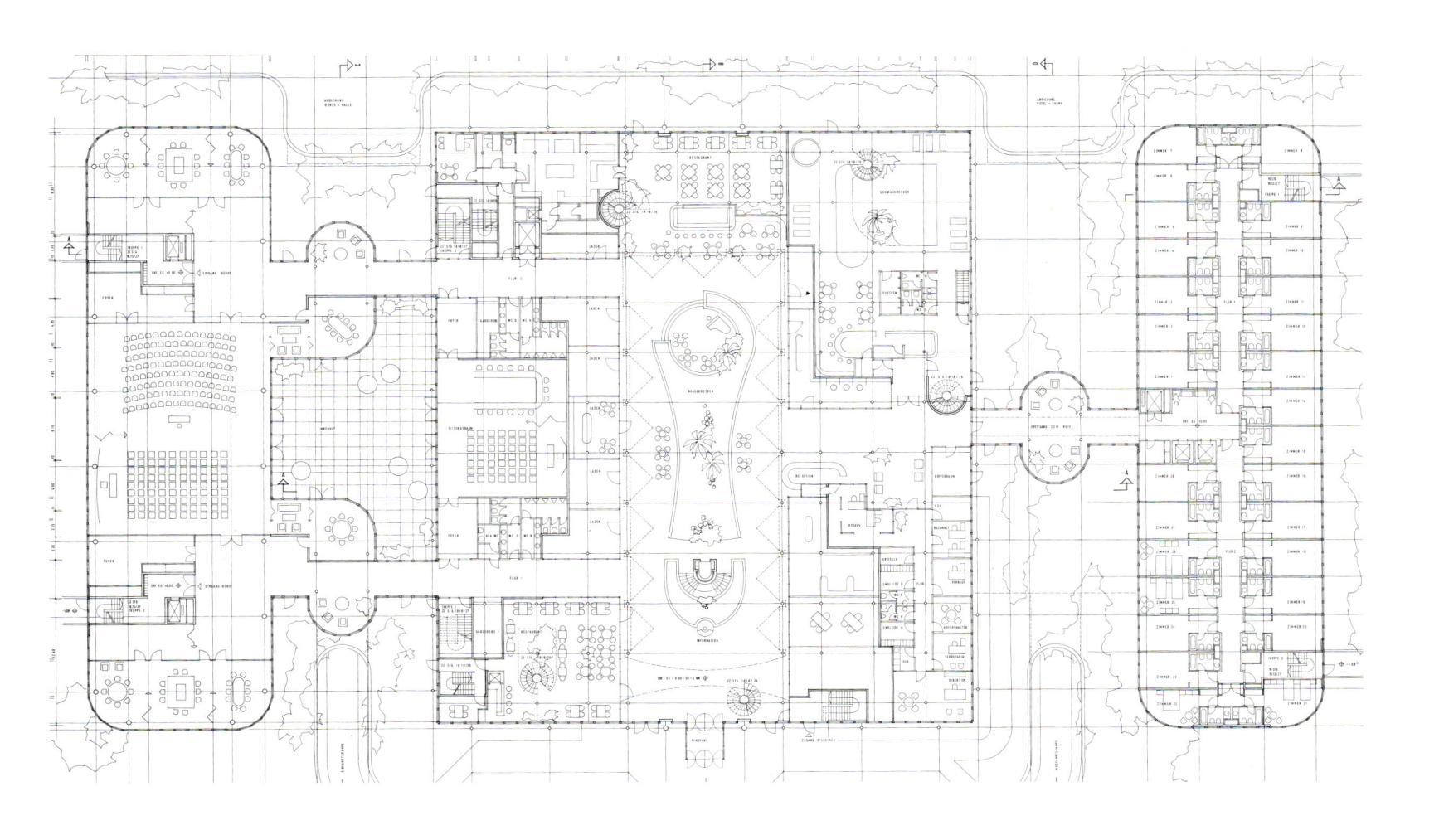

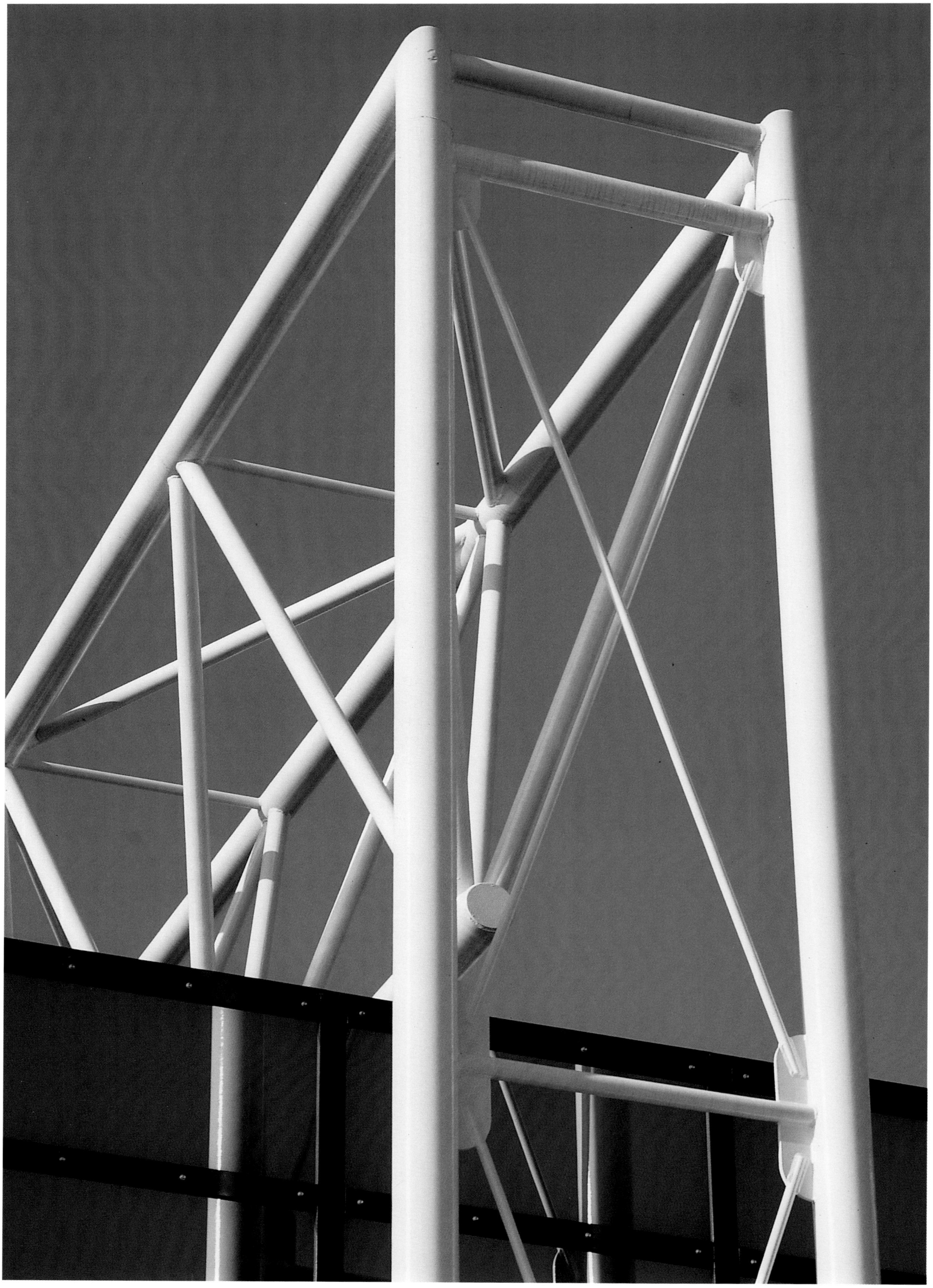

BOCO
Laundry
Wäscherei

The exterior shape of the building initially seems to consist of a truly brittle ashlar with a fully reflecting facade embodying a strong, uniform grid. The fluctuating reflections of the sky, the trees and the bushes of the surrounding green space bring life and vitality to the facade. The filigree elements of the supporting structure, holding the structure like iron rods, underline this appearance. The colouring of brilliant blue and gleaming white for the shell and the tubular construction demonstratively offset the architectural elements. The chimney in the foreground is an obtrusive irritation in an otherwise even layout.

Four striking lattice beams as triple girdle links with a height of 2.50 metres form the main supporting structure for the hall. These overstretch the 17.50-metre breadth of the hall with no supports.

The laundry building was conceived as a cubic shed construction without a basement. The hall is 8 metres high, 65 metres long and 45 metres wide. In the centre of the building is the single-storey washing hall. This is surrounded on three sides by two-storey utility rooms. The corresponding division of space is based on the flow of materials. With its own steel structure, this two-storey block is inserted into the interior of the main hall.

The colouring and design of the building are designed to conjure up associations with shimmering, clean blue water and white linen sails and to demonstrate that the company based here washes textiles expertly and with care.

In der äußeren Form zeigt sich der Bau zunächst als ein recht spröder Quader mit vollverspiegelter Fassade in kräftiger, gleichförmiger Rasterung. Die wechselnden Spiegelungen von Himmel, Bäumen und Büschen der umgebenden Grünanlagen verleihen der Fassade Leben und Lebendigkeit. Die filigranen Elemente des Tragwerks, die wie Bügel den Baukörper umgreifen, unterstreichen dieses Erscheinungsbild. Die Farbgebung von leuchtendem Blau und strahlendem Weiß für Gebäudehülle und Rohrkonstruktion setzen die architektonischen Teile demonstrativ voneinander ab. Der vorgesetzte Kamin ist eine markante Irritation in der sonst so bewußt gleichmäßigen Aufteilung.

Die Haupttragkonstruktion der Halle bilden vier markante außenliegende Stahlgitterträger als Dreigurtbinder mit einer Höhe von 2,50 m, die die Hallenbreite von 17,50 m stützungsfrei überspannen.

Das Wäschereigebäude wurde als nichtunterkellerter kubischer Hallenbau konzipiert. Der Hallenkörper ist 8 m hoch, 65 m lang und 45 m breit. Im Zentrum des Gebäudes liegt die eingeschossigen Waschhalle. An drei Seiten wird sie von zweigeschossigen Nutzungsräumen umgeben. Die entsprechende Raumverteilung orientiert sich am Materialfluß. Dieser zweigeschossige Baukörper ist mit einer eigenen Stahlkonstruktion versehen ins Innere der Halle gestellt worden.

Die Farbgebung und die Gestaltung des Gebäudes sollen Assoziationen zu blau schimmerndem, reinen Wasser und weißen Leinensegeln hervorrufen und verdeutlichen, daß hier ein Unternehmen tätig ist, daß das Waschen von Textilien ernsthaft und sorgfältig betreibt.

Bottom of page: ground floor plan. Below: top floor plan. Opposite page: general view of the complex and detail of the exposed steel framed glassfacades. The four beams span across a single 47,5 m bay, the same width as the building, which is also 65 m long and 8 m high.

Unten: Grundriß des Erdgeschosses. Darüber: der Grundriß des oberen Geschosses. Auf der Seite nebenan: die allgemeine Ansicht des Komplexes und Details der Glasfassaden mit der sichtbaren Stahlstruktur. Die vier freispannenden Stahlgitterträger überspannen die gesamte Hallenbreite mit einer Spannweite von 47,50 m. Die Anlage ist 65 m lang und 8 m hoch.

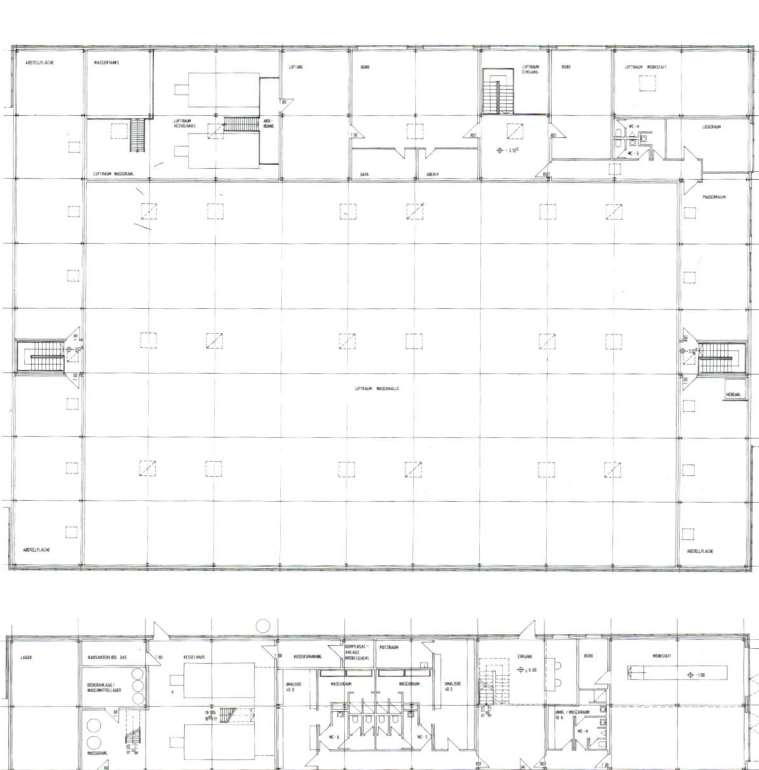

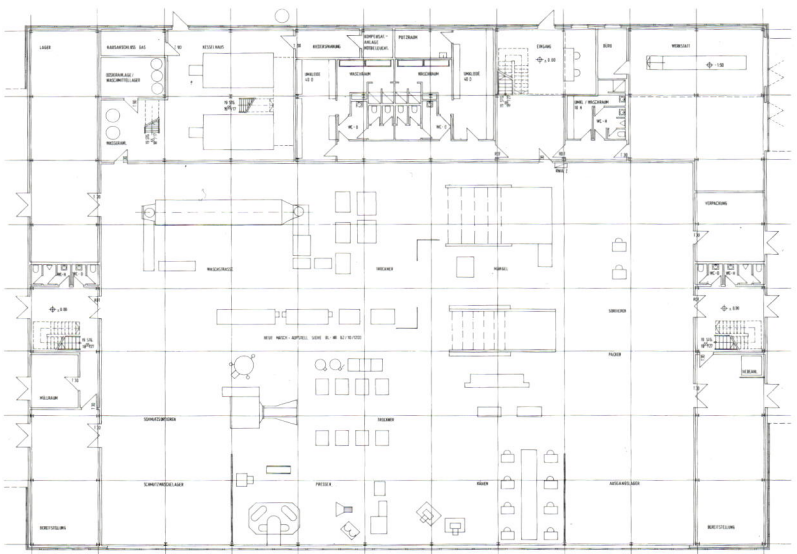

81

Cross section and opposite page: longitudinal section. Below: details of the steel structure and the glass facade.
Querschnitt und Seite nebenan: Längsschnitt. Darunter: Details der Stahlkonstruktion und der Glasfassade.

SCHNITT AA

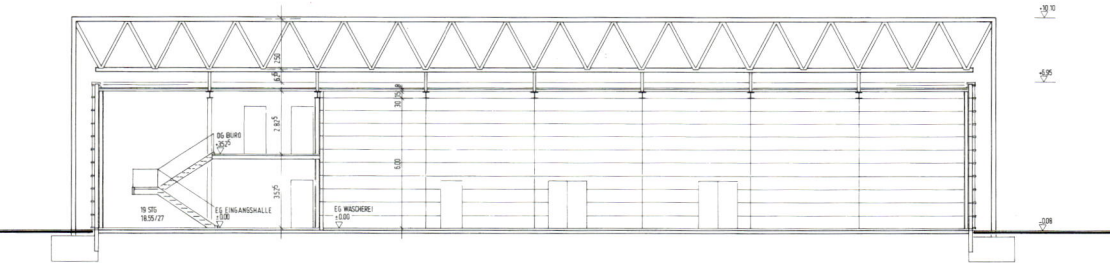

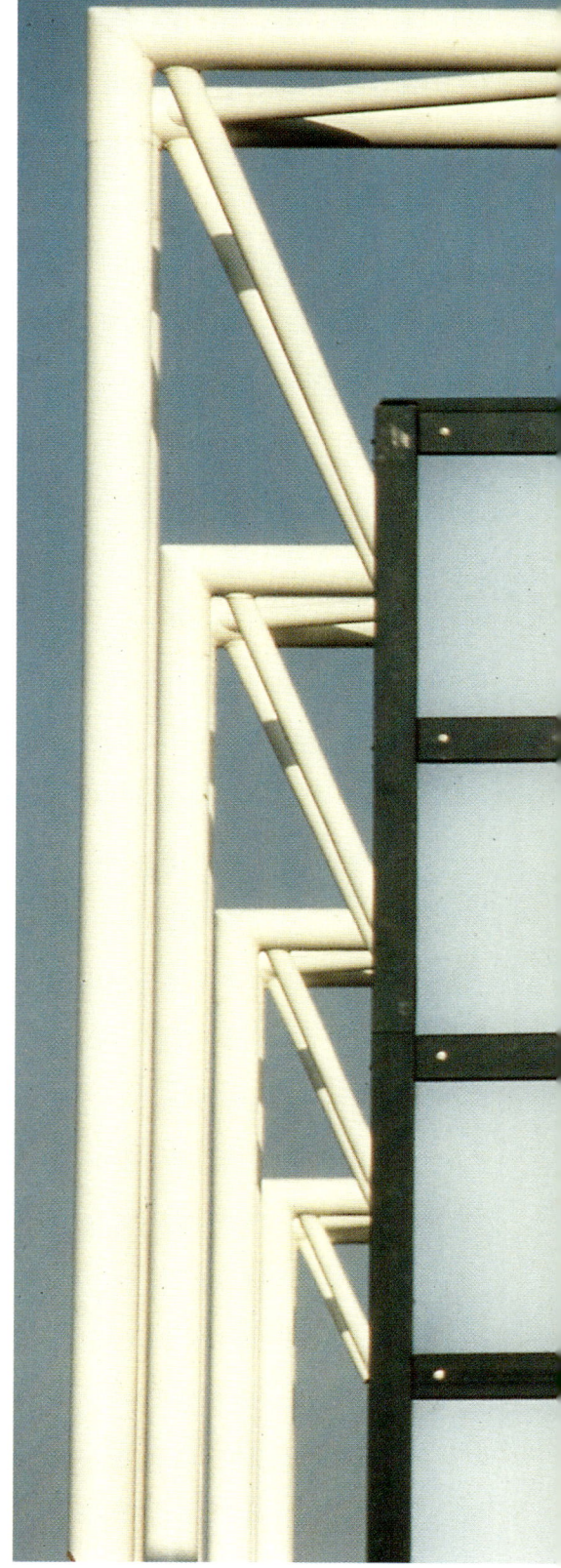

SCHNITT B B

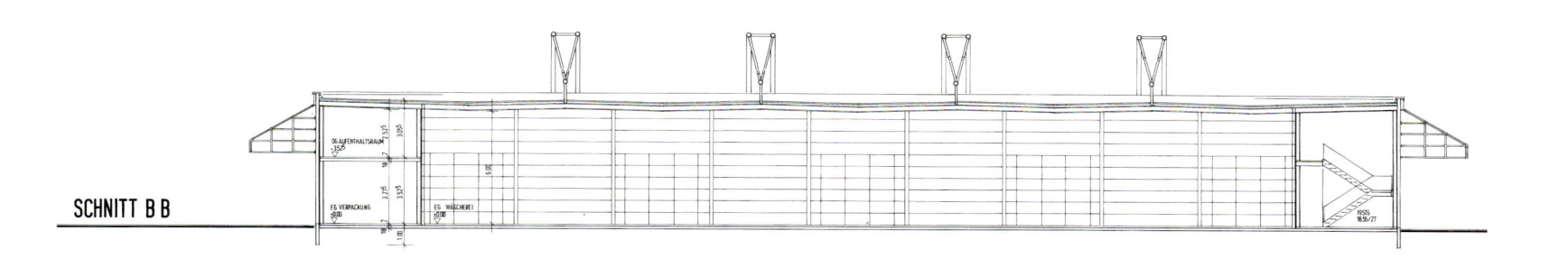

83

Detail of the bottom of the chimney where it is attached to the glass facade. Opposite page: detail of the suspended facade made of an aluminium-framing leg construction and clad with enamelled blue-coloured polished plate glass.
Detail des Schornsteinfußes mit der Verbindung an die Glasfassade.
Auf der Seite gegenüber: Details der vorgehängten Fassade, die als Aluminium-Pfosten-Riegel-Konstruktion erstellt ist und mit emaillierten blauen Spiegelgläsern in allen geschlossenen Bereichen ausgefacht ist.

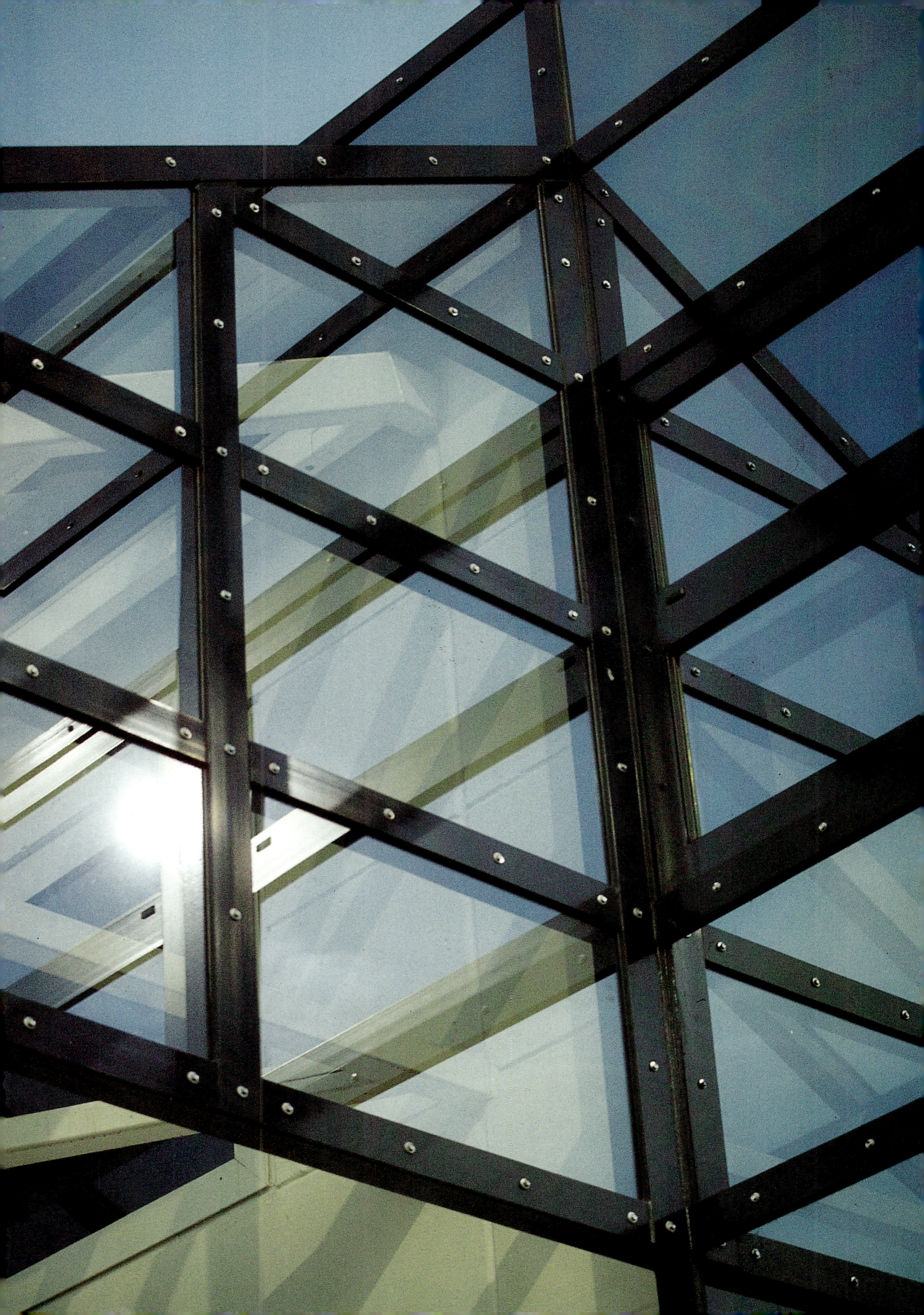

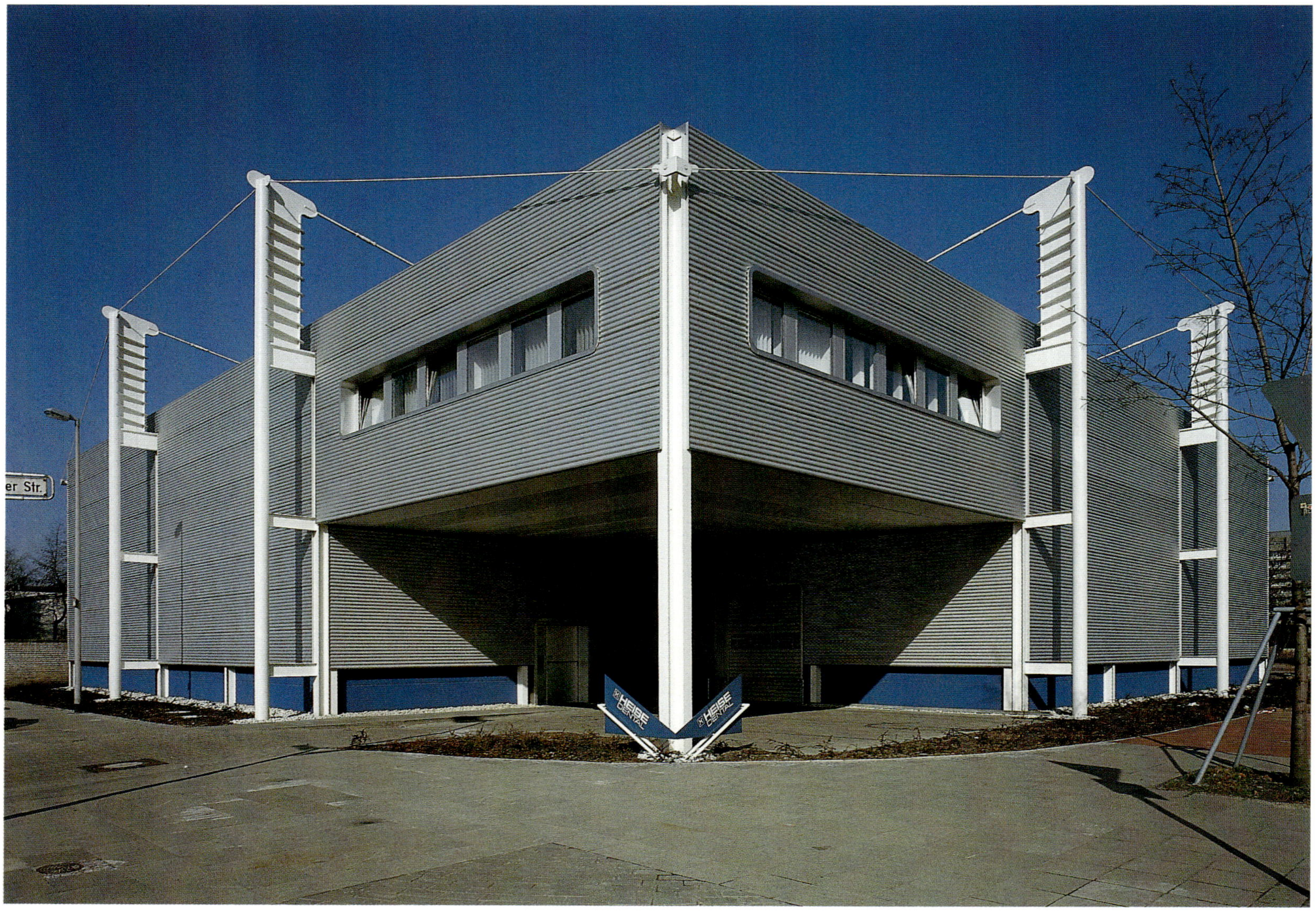
er Str.
HEISE DENTAL
HEISE DENTAL

DH 1
Dental Store
Dentallager

The aim was to provide a storage building for a firm trading in dental products from a lightly structured building - and an uninterrupted hall of 30 x 30 metres. Architectural planning had shown that despite the minimal building, the qualities and advantages of industrial steel construction could be exploited. The structure of the building consists of two tubular steel pylons on each of the four external sides of the building. These hold steel cables from which the roof of the hall is suspended.

Another factor in the technical subtlety of the scheme is that this building is separated from Norcon's office and administration block only by a road on which the dental trading company's head office is located. The two buildings are almost siblings, mutually protective and in dialogue.
It is immediately apparent that the architectural designs are offspring of the same family.

The storage hall seems compact and yet something of a jewel. The specification was for a single-storey hall with an interior height of about 7.50 metres and suitable for accommodating a two-tier shelving system. With the shelving system being fed semi-automatically, no supports were to interrupt the area of 30 square metres.

This was rendered possible by a steel structure with cable stays. Its basic square/cubic shape makes the building unspectacular in external appearance. Yet putting its structure outside banishes any memory of the monotony of normal storage buildings. Looking like fluttering flags with their diagonally reinforced welded panels, the tops of the supporting elements are especially striking.

The outer skin of the facade consists of naturally coloured, anodized corrugated aluminium which emphasizes the technical character of the building and the usage of its interior.

Eine kleine Bausubstanz und eine stützungsfreie Halle von 30 x 30 m sollten ein Lagergebäude für eine Firma ergeben, die mit Dentalprodukten handelt. Die architektonische Planung hat bewiesen, daß man trotz der kleinen Bausubstanz dafür die Vorteile und Qualitäten des industriellen Stahlbaus einsetzen kann. Die Gebäudestruktur besteht aus jeweils zwei Stahlrohrpylonen an den vier Außenseiten des Gebäudes. Sie halten Stahlseile, von denen das Hallendach abgehängt ist.

Zur technischen Delikatesse kommt noch hinzu, daß das Gebäude nur durch eine Straße vom Norcon Büro- und Verwaltungsgebäude getrennt ist, in dem sich die Verwaltung der Dentalhandelsfirma befindet. Die beiden Bauten haben ein fast geschwisterliches Verhältnis zueinander: beschützend und dialogisierend. Man sieht sofort, daß beide Architekturen Kinder der gleichen Familie sind.

Die Lagerhalle wirkt kompakt und dennoch wie ein Bijou. Gefordert war eine eingeschossige Halle mit einer Raumhöhe von etwa 7,50 m, die ein freistehendes zweistöckiges Regalsystem aufnehmen mußte. Da das Regalsystem halbautomatisch beschickt wird, durften keine Stützen die quadratische Grundfläche von 30 m teilen.

Eine Stahlkonstruktion mit Seilabspannungen ermöglichte das. Die äußere Gestalt des Gebäudes ist in seiner kubisch-quadratischen Grundform unspektakulär. Dennoch erscheint die Monotonie üblicher Lagerkontainer völlig vergessen angesichts dieser außenliegenden Konstruktion. Besonders markant sind die Stützenköpfe, die mit ihren querversteiften eingeschweißten Blechen wie flatternde Fahnen erscheinen.

Die Außenhaut der Fassade wird durch naturfarbenes, eloxiertes Well-Aluminium gebildet, das den technischen Charakter des Gebäudes und seiner inneren Nutzung betont.

General view. Plan of the ground floor and plan of the top floor of the warehouse distribution centre for dental products. The building was designed and built in less than six months.

Gesamtansicht. Grundriß des Erdgeschosses und des obersten Geschosses des Dentallagers. Die Anlage wurde in weniger als sechs Monaten geplant und gebaut.

OG

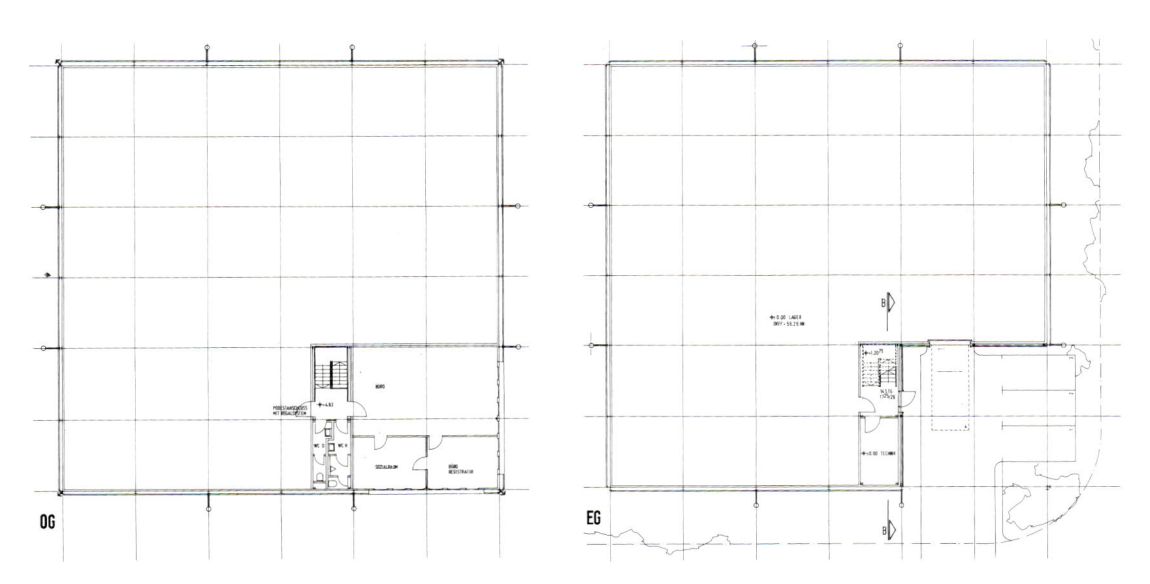

EG

89

Axonometry and details of the facade and structure made of two tubular steel pylons on each of the four sides, on which the purlins are suspended to the middle of the roof by pre-stressed ropes.

Isometrie und Details der Fassade und der Stahlstruktur. Die Gebäudestruktur besteht aus jeweils zwei Stahlpylonen an den vier Außenseiten des Gebäudes, an denen durch Spannseile zum Mittelquadrat der Halle die Dachpfetten abgehängt sind.

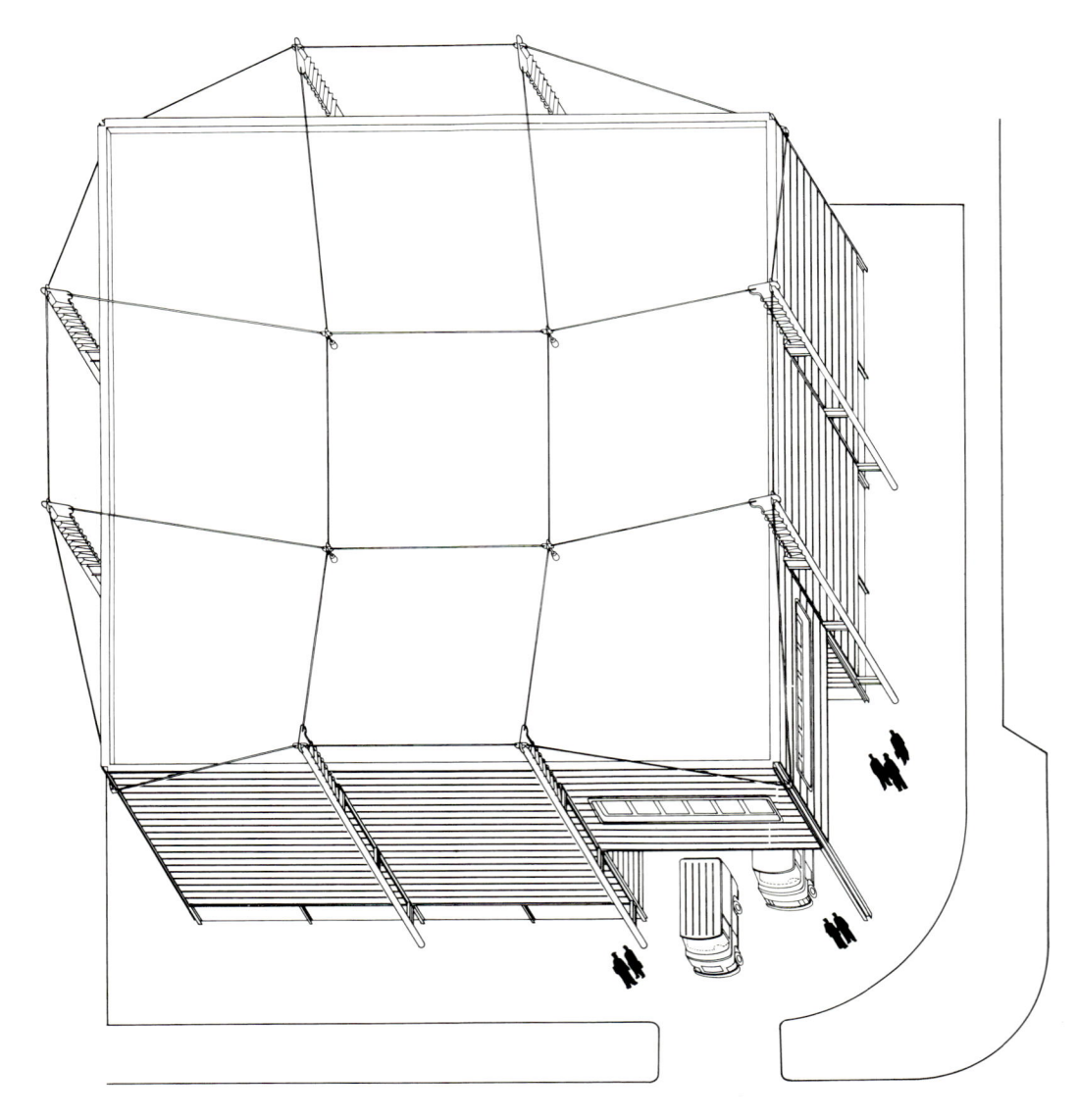

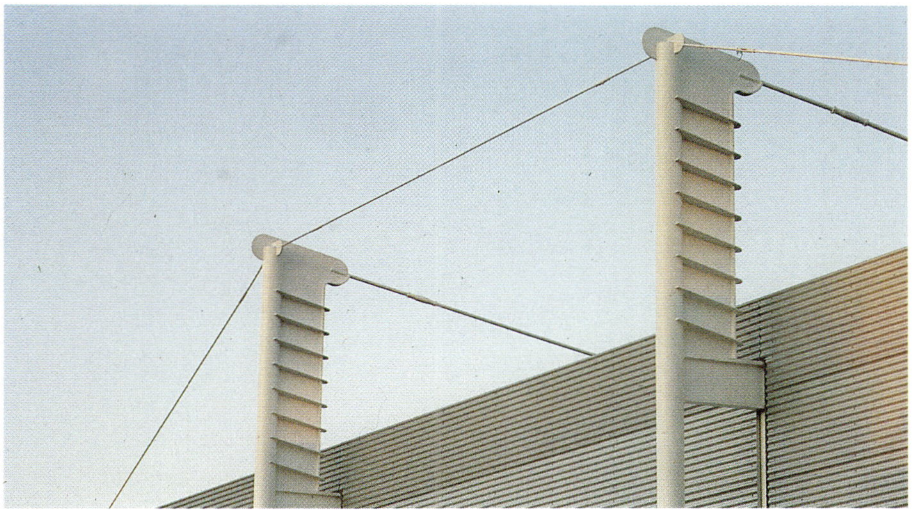

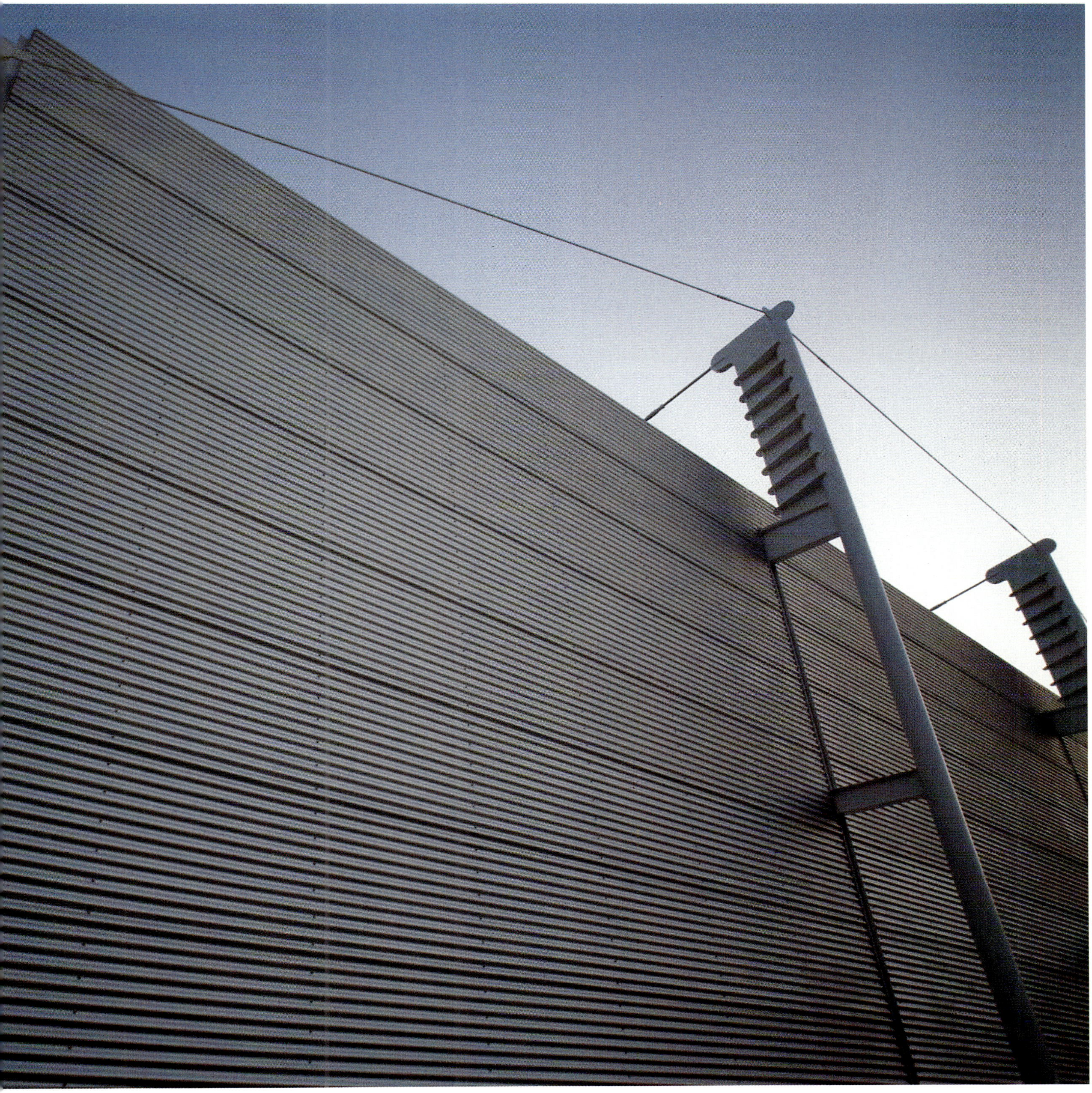

Details and axonometry of one of the tubular steel pylons.
Details und Isometrie eines Stahlpylons der Konstruktion.

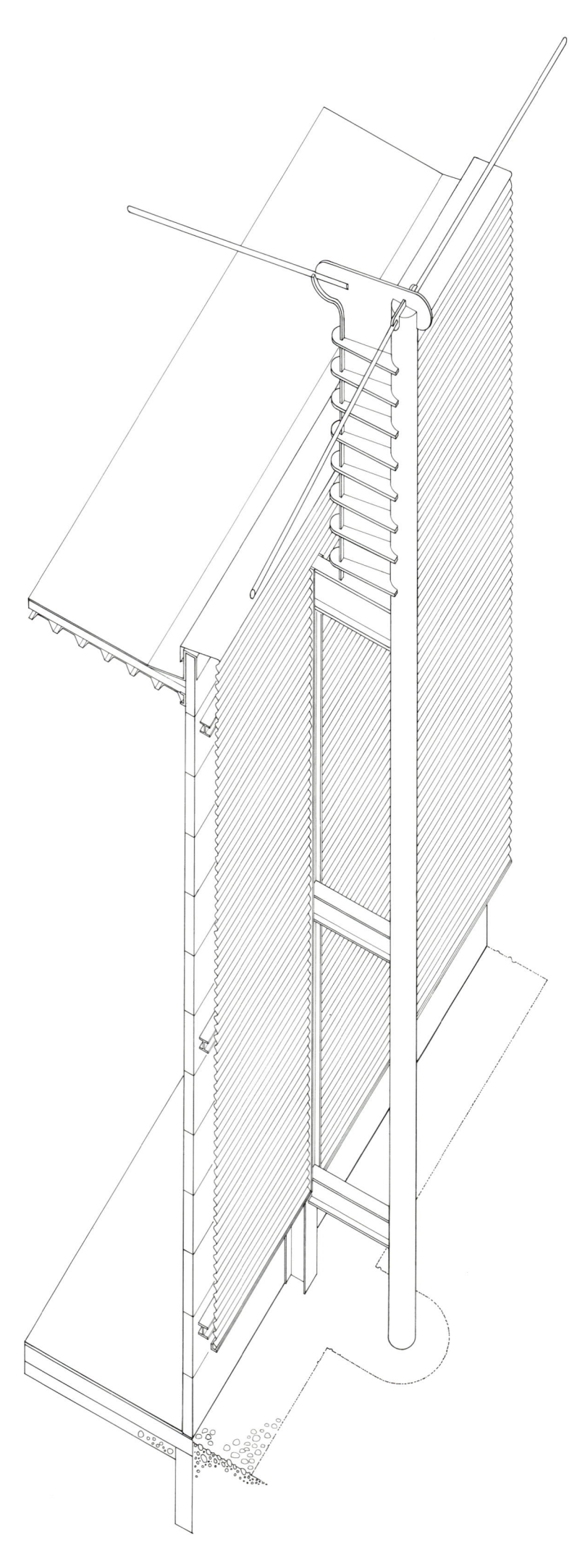

92

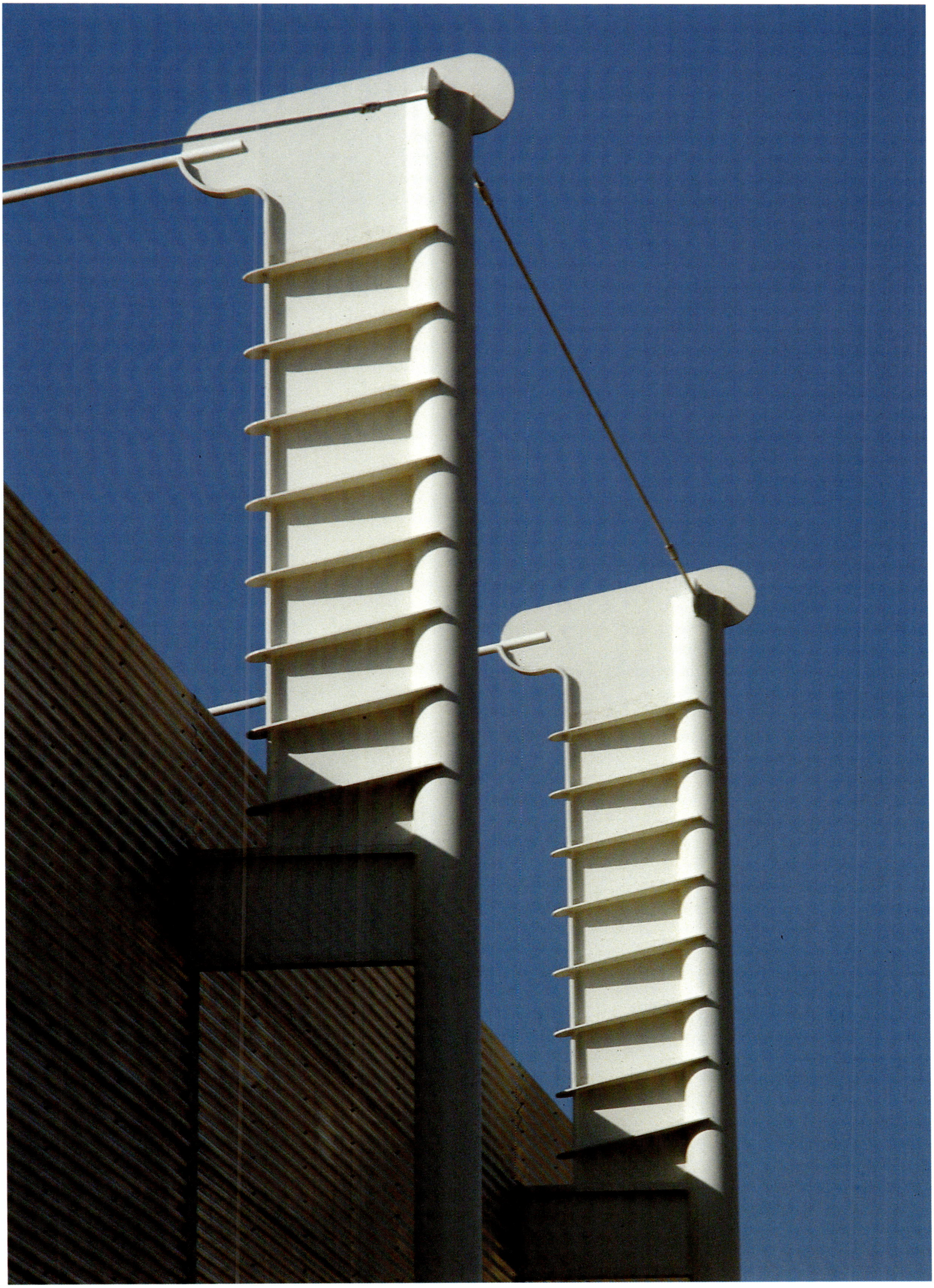

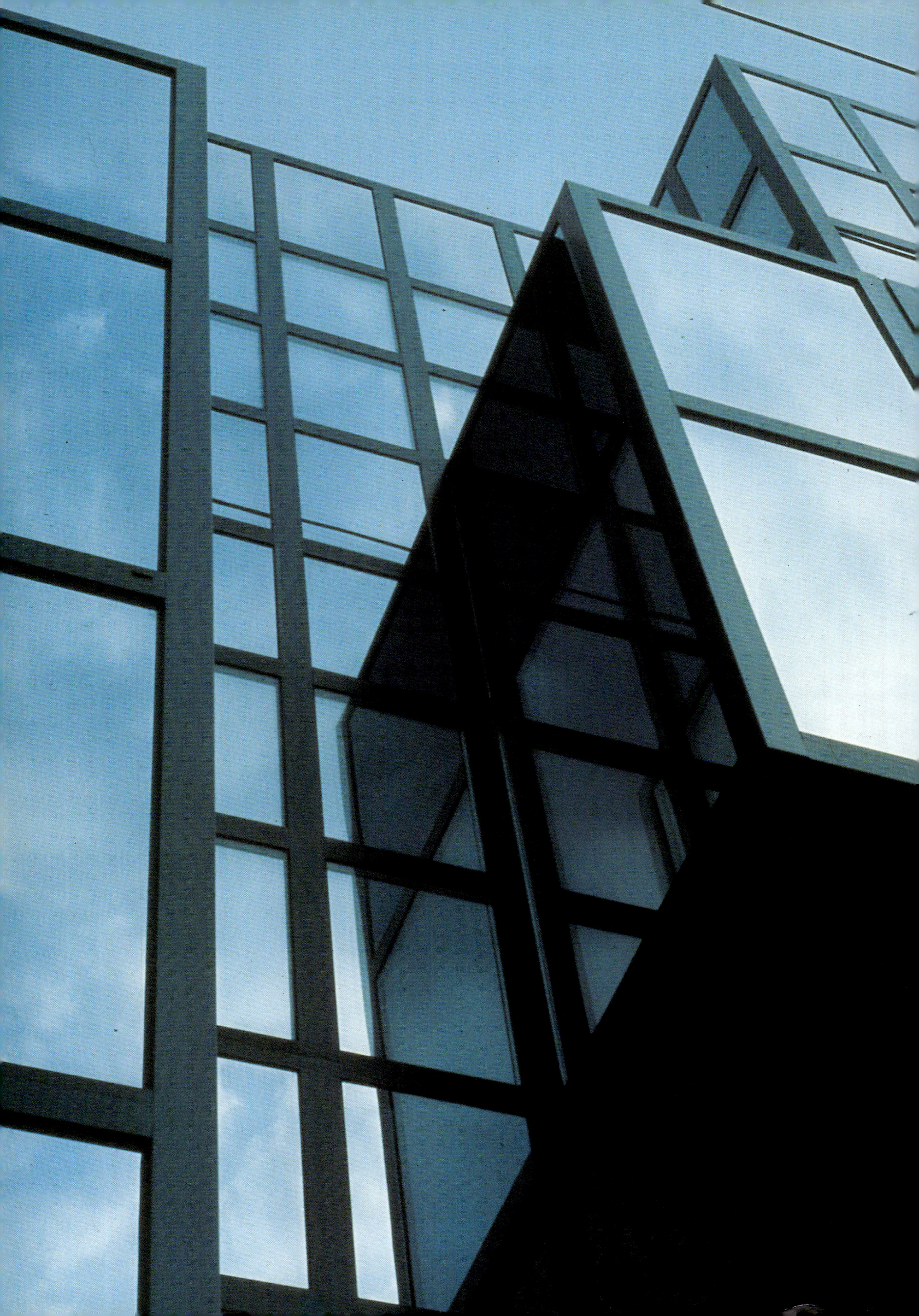

AF 16 B
Office Building
Bürohaus

A large, discreetly divided glass facade is the most striking feature of this office building. Yet it is also characterized by rejection of any firm ties with the ground. The plot has been left largely as it was and the block has been mounted on it. The cube only commences one and a half metres off the ground, supported and stabilized by an internal system of steel supports and an external wind-bracing system of all-steel ropes.

The plot lies in a former industrial zone in the northern part of the city of Hanover and borders a residential area and allotment gardens. The building is designed to provide a transition between the two without constituting any kind of visible boundary. The location was one ingredient in the design by the architects. A provisional character was therefore stressed rather than glossed over. A steel structure of interior roof beams and a facade in aluminium with silver-coloured reflecting glass elements naturally conjures up ideas of dismantling at any time. Nothing seems to have been affected permanently by the building.

The mobile character has been underlined by a stairway resembling a gangway looking as if it has simply been pushed in front of the building. The play with projecting and recessed building elements engenders aesthetic tensions within an intentionally passive volume and highlights the centre of the building.

Eine großflächige, ruhig gegliederte Glasfassade ist das Auffallendste an diesem Bürohaus. Das Charakteristische ist aber die Negierung einer festen Bodenhaftung. Das Grundstück wurde weitgehend so belassen, wie es war, und der Baukörper wurde aufgeständert. Erst eineinhalb Meter über dem Boden beginnt der Kubus, von einem inneren Stahlstützsystem und einem außenliegenden Windverband aus reinen Stahlseilen getragen und stabilisiert.

Das Grundstück liegt in einem alten Gewerbegebiet im Norden der Stadt Hannover mit angrenzender Wohn- und Kleingartenzone. Das Gebäude sollte zwischen diesen Bereichen vermitteln, ohne aber optisch eine Begrenzung festzulegen. Die Standortsituation floß in die architektonische Gestaltung mit ein. Deshalb wurde der Charakter eines Provisoriums unterstrichen und nicht übertüncht. Eine Stahlkonstruktion aus inneren Deckenträgern und einer Fassade in Aluminiumausführung mit silberfarbenen Spiegelglaselementen ermöglicht ganz selbstverständlich Gedanken an eine jederzeit mögliche Demontage. Nichts scheint durch das Gebäude nachhaltig beeinträchtigt zu sein.

Der Charakter des Mobilen wird durch die Gangway-ähnliche Treppe unterstrichen; sie wirkt so, als ob sie lediglich vor das Gebäude geschoben wäre. Das Spiel mit vorkragenden und zurückgesetzten Bauteilen erzeugt innerhalb des bewußt ruhig gehaltenen Volumens ästhetische Spannungen und hebt die Gebäudemitte hervor.

Plans of the first floor, second floor, and roof. Below: general view of the building. Top of opposite page: longitudinal and cross sections.

Grundriß des ersten und zweiten Obergeschosses des Gebäudes und der Dachaufsicht. Darunter die allgemeine Ansicht des Gebäudes. Oben auf der gegenüberliegenden Seite: Längs- und Querschnitt.

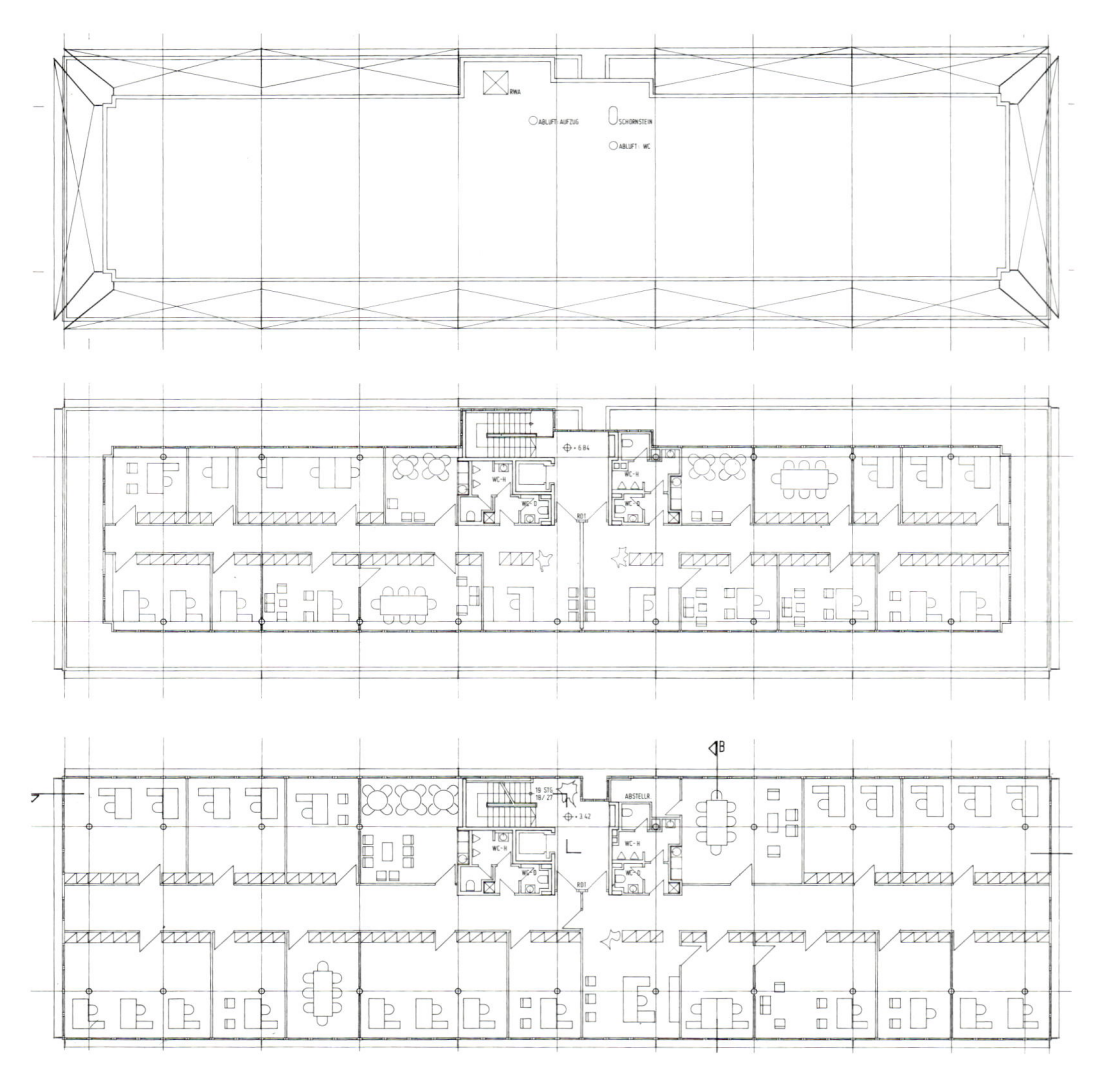

96

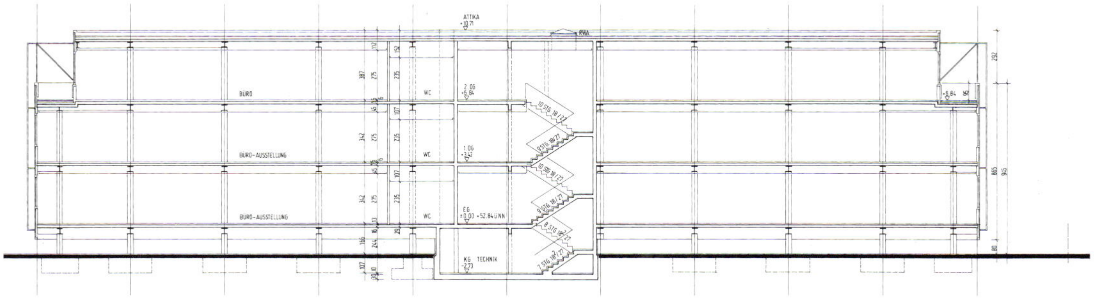

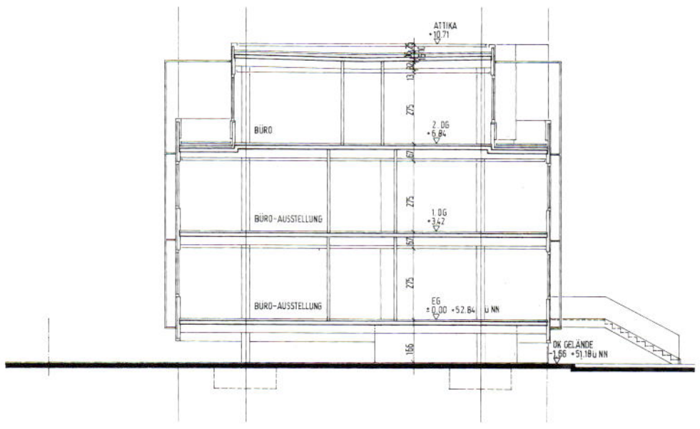

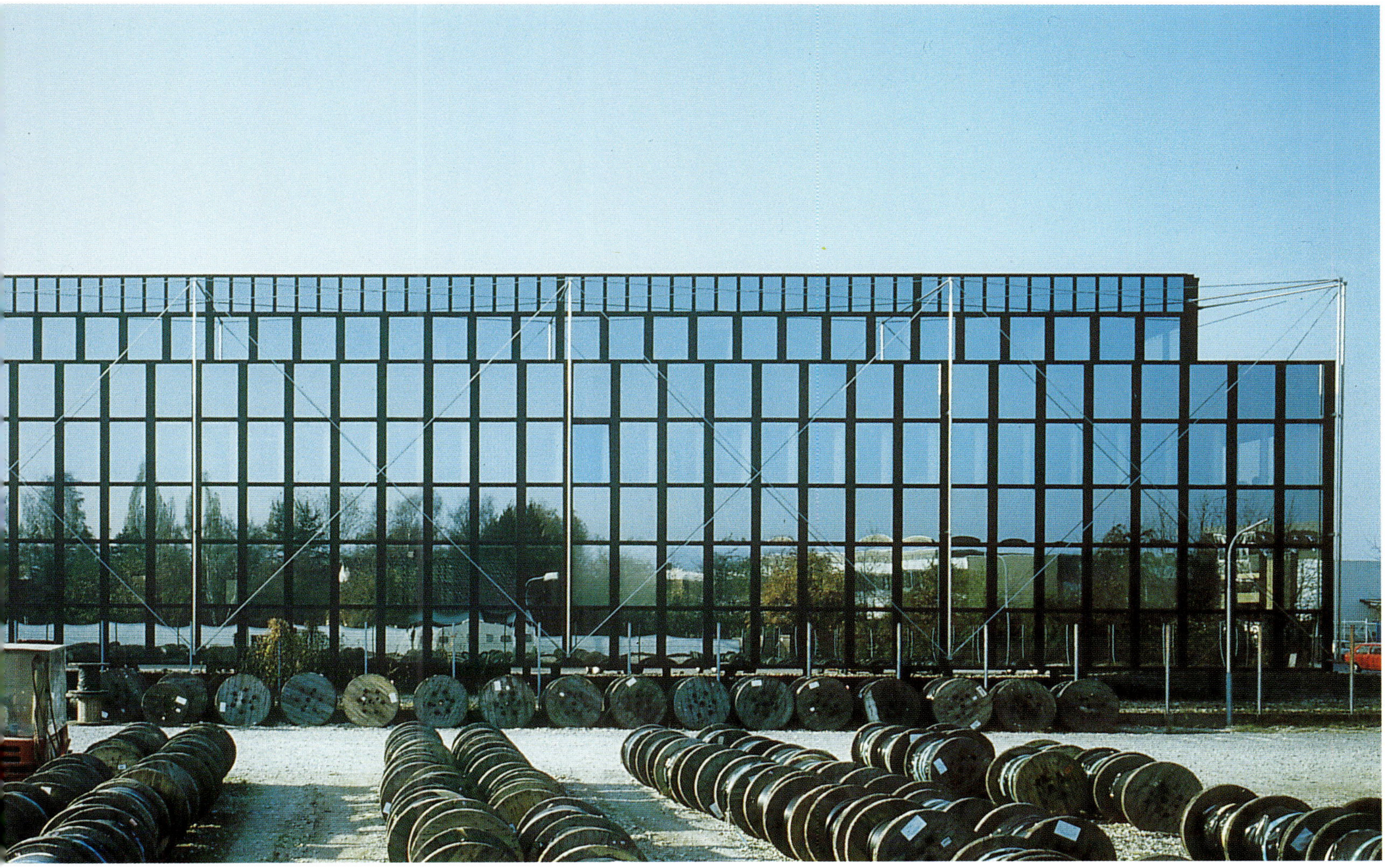

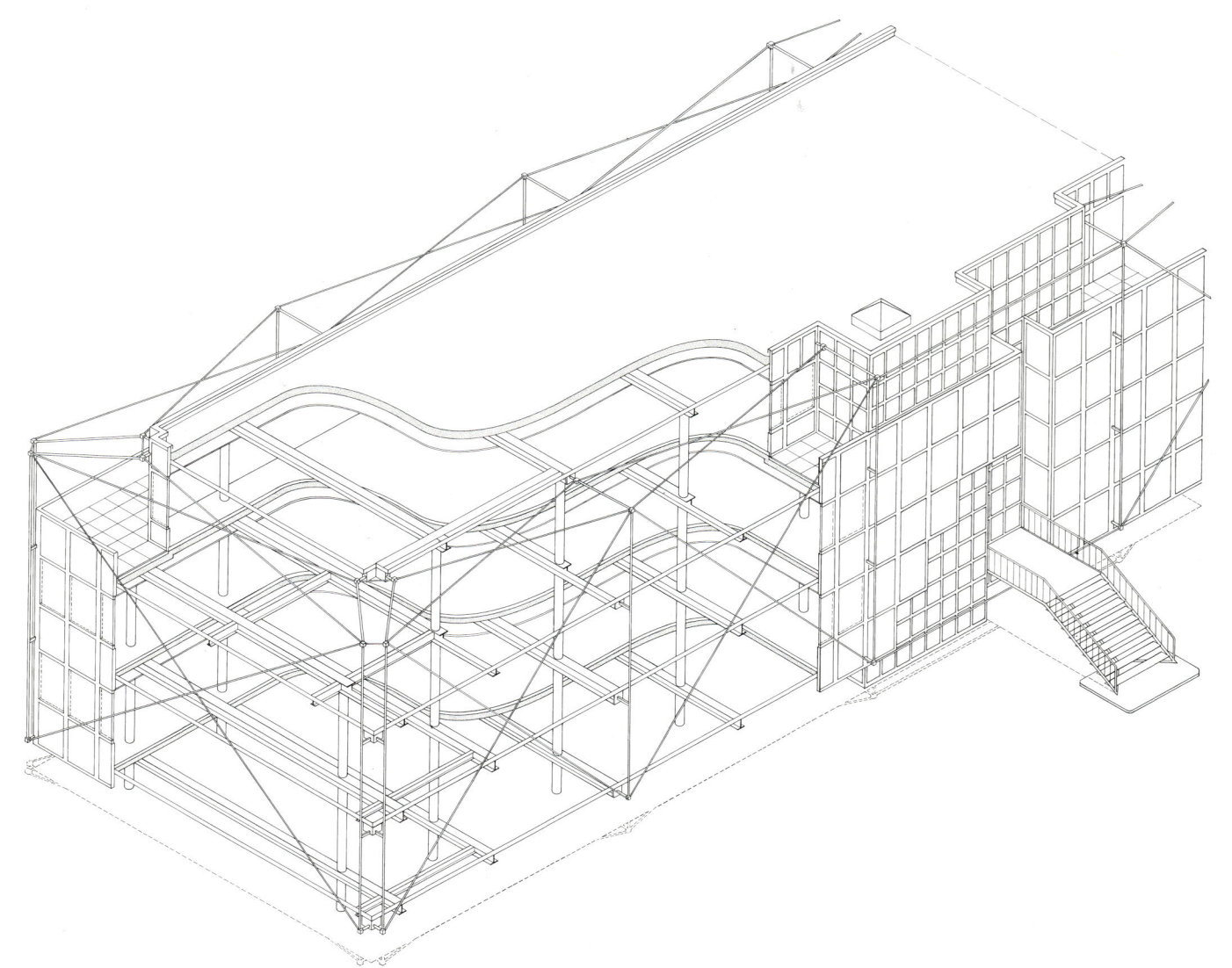

Above and opposite page: details of the entrance showing the stainless steel staircase. Left: axonometry.
Oben und auf der Seite gegenüber: Details des Eingangs mit der rostfreien Stahltreppe. Links: Isometrie.

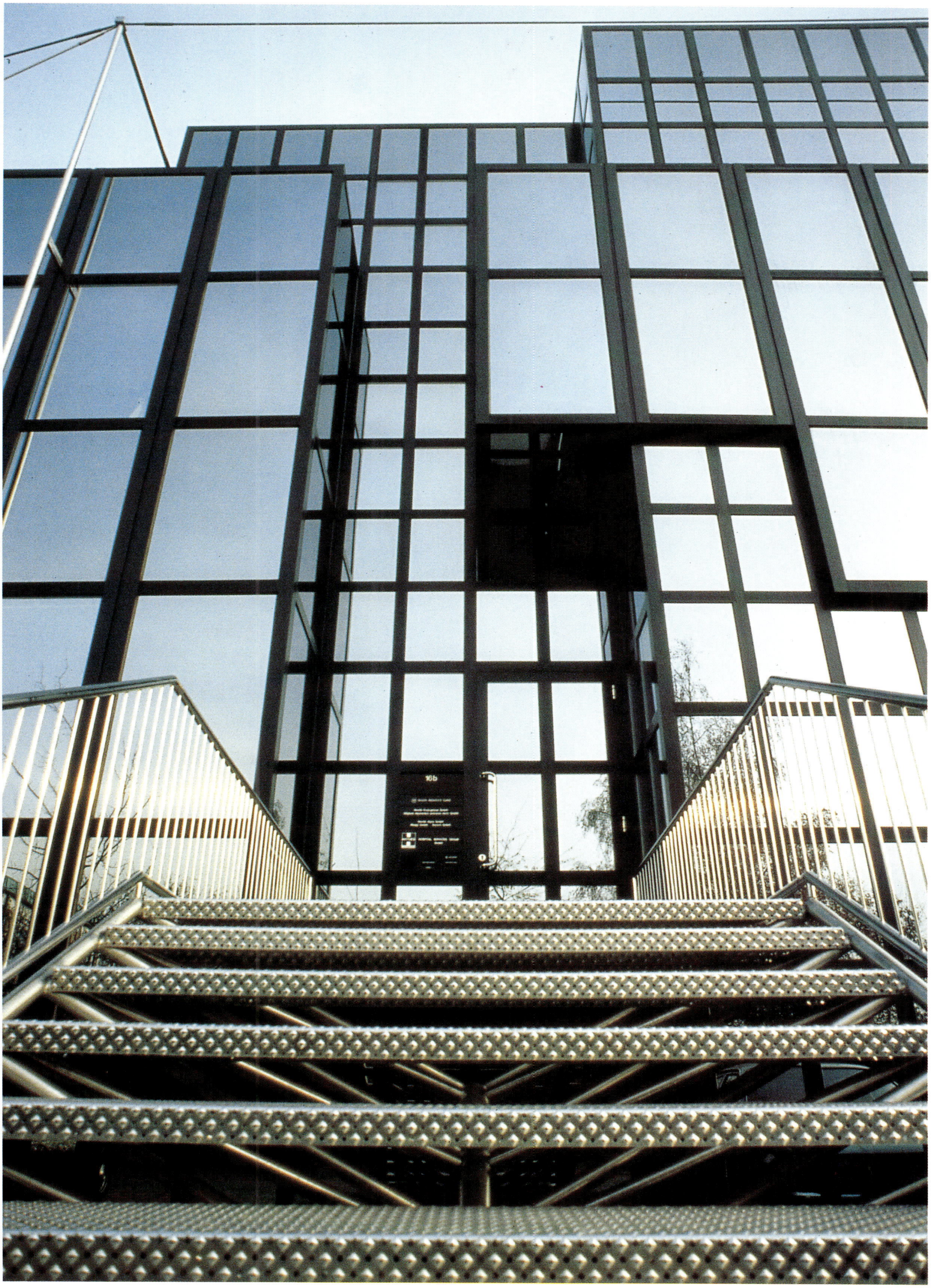

Detail of the base of the outside structural pylon.
Detail des Fußpunktes des äußeren Stahlpylons.

Details of the external wind-bracing-system made of stainless steel ropes.
Details der Stahlkabel des äußeren Windverbandes, der aus Edelstahl erstellt ist.

The entrance and below: detail of the side-facade. The silver-coloured plate glass facade is interrupted by stepped elements near the stair-well.

Der Eingang und unten ein Detail der Seitenfassade. Die lang durchlaufende Glasfassade wird mit Abtreppungen nur im Bereich der vertikalen Treppenhausschließung unterbrochen.

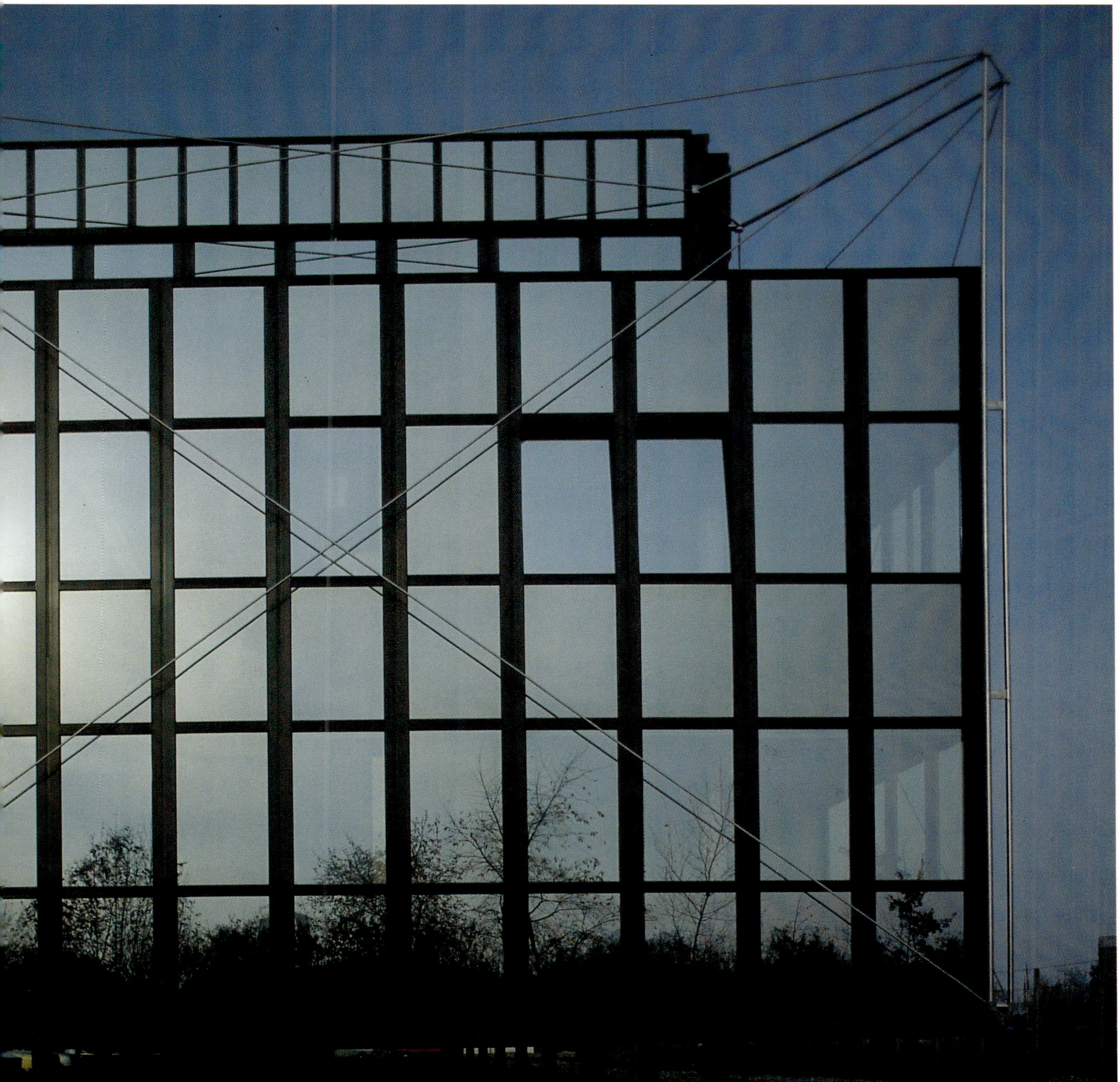

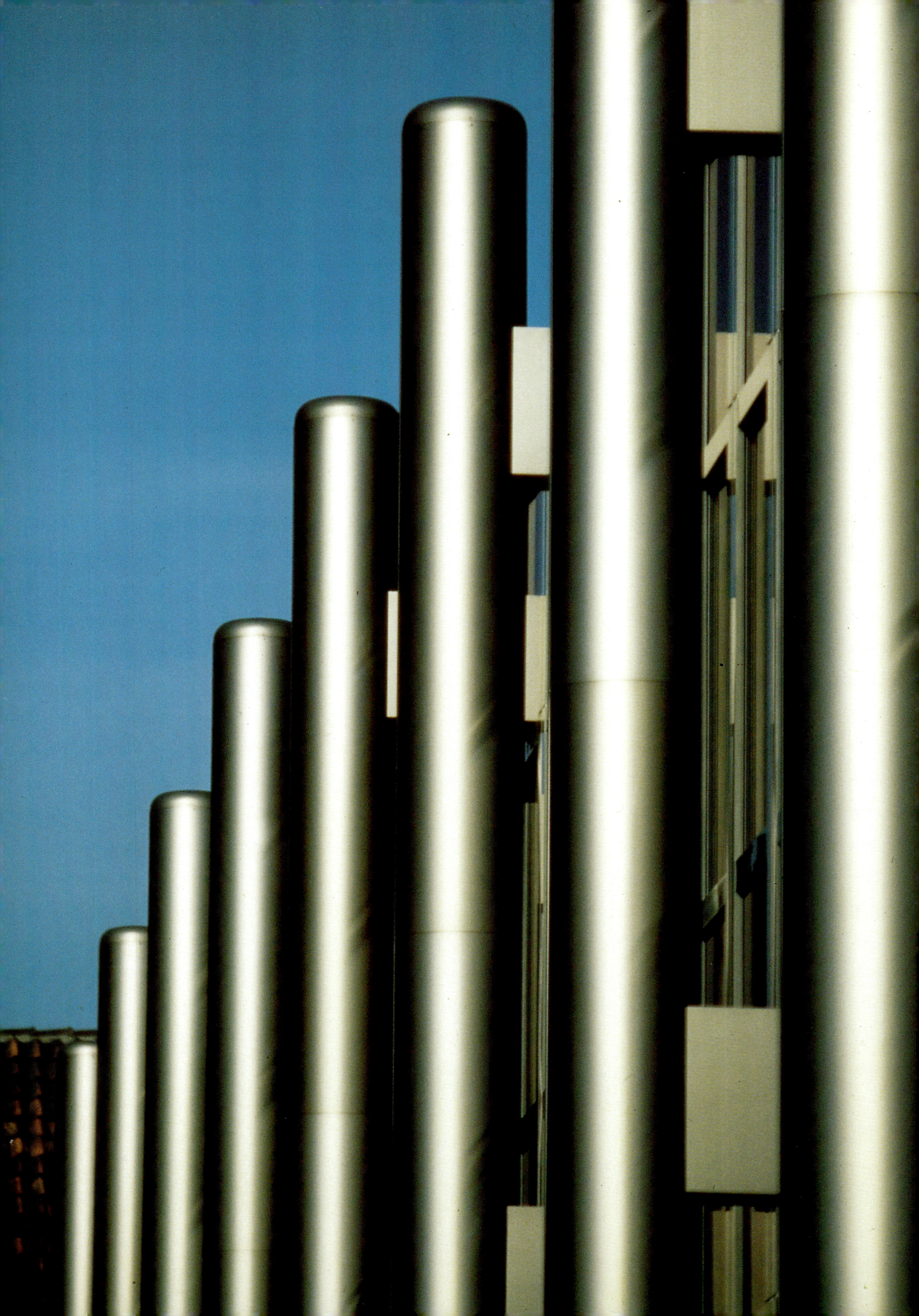

BSHG
Bosch- Siemens Service Centre
Bosch- Siemens- Kundendienstzentrum

The Hanover service and administration centre for the Bosch-Siemens Group was planned as a complex around the edge of a plot with a 15-storey high-rise as its main feature. This replaced an existing red-brick complex with smaller buildings dotted along the edge unsystematically. The plot lies about 100 metres from a heavily used road leading south and serving as access for the exhibition and EXPO grounds. It dominates a small industrial zone now containing no more than repair shops and practice rooms for musicians. To the west the plot borders an open space forming part of the southern bank of the River Leine.

The new complex of buildings provides a stimulus for the immediate vicinity. Over the next few years a completely new infrastructure will be created here and this will be influenced by the current architectural "landmarks". This service-and-administration centre sets a high standard for both usage and appearance.

The complex of buildings in front of the high-rise is of four storeys but without any visible horizontal division thanks to the curtain facade of anodized aluminium. Yet what is basically a massive block seems filigree and delicate. Aluminium elements and windows of polycolour reflecting glass provide a sequentially structured surface with a uniform colour characteristic which is vertically structured at intervals of six metres by supports running the height of the building.

A soaring lightness results and this is underscored by a raised ground floor. A scrubbed-concrete footing lifts the first layer from street level. The "round feet" around the round steel supports convey the impression that the entire building is anchored here.

Two recessed entrances almost the height of the building possess the aura of imposing portals, lending weight and gravity to the lightness of the architecture.

So far only the front section of building around the edge of the site has been realized.

Das Kundendienst- und Verwaltungszentrum für den Bosch-Siemens-Konzern in Hannover ist als Blockrandbebauung mit einem akzenturierenden 15-geschossigen Hochhaus geplant. Es ersetzt eine vorhandene rote Ziegelstein-Blockrandbebauung, an die kleinere Gebäude unsystematisch angestückelt sind.

Das Grundstück liegt etwa 100 m von einer stark frequentierten Straße entfernt, die nach Süden führt und als Zubringer für das Messe- und EXPO-Gelände genutzt wird. Es dominiert ein kleines Gewerbegebiet, das nur noch Reparaturbetriebe und Probenräume für Musiker umfaßt. Nach Westen hin grenzt das Grundstück an eine Grünzone des südlichen Maschbereichs der Leine.

Der neue Gebäudekomplex setzt für die nähere Umgebung einen Impuls gebenden Akzent. Im Laufe der kommenden Jahre wird hier eine völlig neue Infrastruktur entstehen, die entscheidend durch die derzeitigen architektonischen „Marken" beeinflußt wird. Das Kundendienst- und Verwaltungszentrum gibt einen hohen Standard für Nutzung und Erscheinungsbild vor.

Der dem Hochhaus vorgelagerte Gebäudekomplex ist viergeschossig, aber durch eine Vorhangfassade aus eloxiertem Aluminium ohne eine sichtbare horizontale Teilung. Dennoch wirkt der im Grunde massive Baukörper filigran und kleinteilig. Aluminiumelemente und Polycolorspiegelglas-Fenster ergeben eine seriell strukturierte Fläche mit einer einheitlich farblichen Charakteristik, die durch gebäudehohe Stützen im Abstand von sechs Metern vertikal strukturiert wird. Es entsteht eine aufstrebende Leichtigkeit, die durch ein erhöhtes Erdgeschoß unterstrichen wird. Ein Waschbeton-Sockel hebt die erste Ebene vom Straßenniveau ab. Die mächtigen „Rundfüße" an den Stahlrundstützen vermitteln den Eindruck, daß hier das gesamte Gebäude verankert ist.

Zwei zurückgesetzte, fast haushohe Eingänge vermitteln einen imposanten Portalcharakter, der der architektonischen Leichtigkeit Gewicht und Eindrücklichkeit verleiht.

Bisher ist nur der Frontalbereich der Blockrandbebauung realisiert worden.

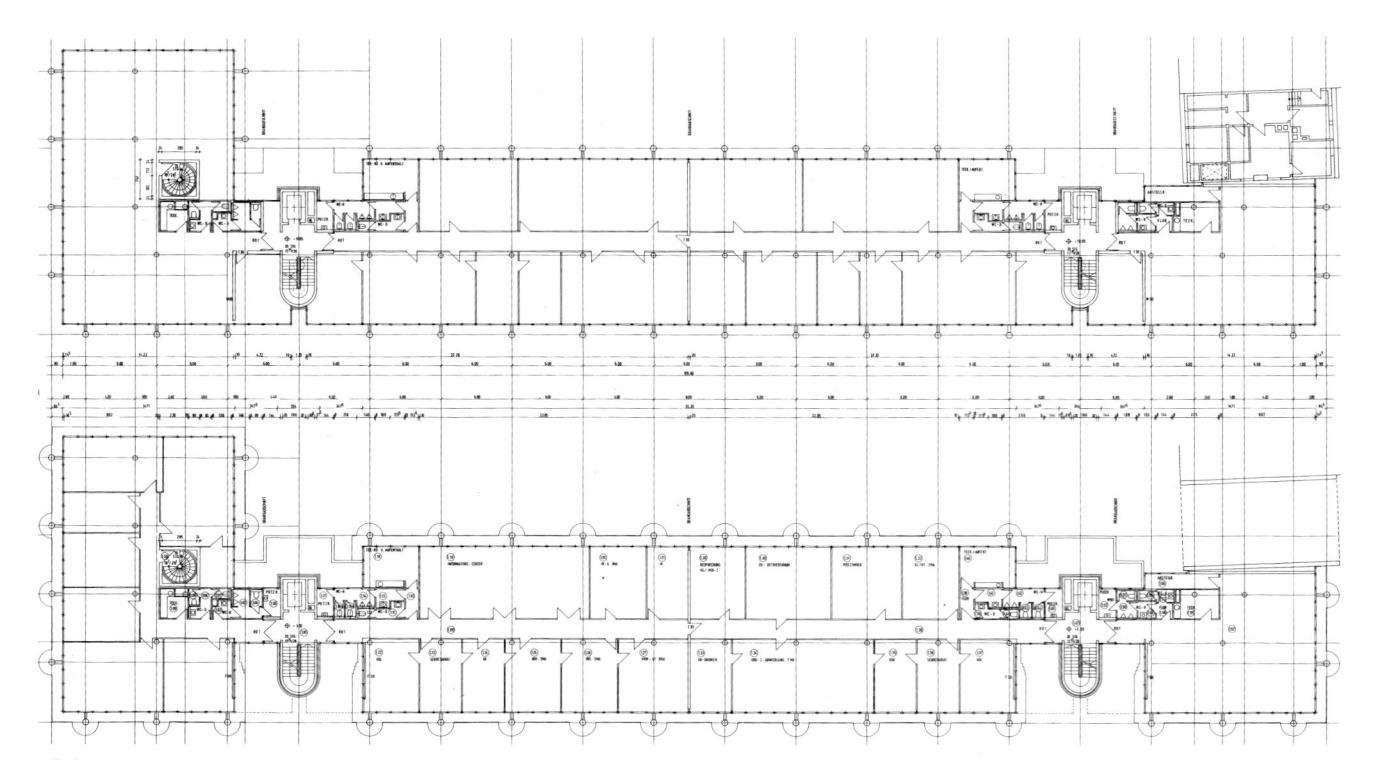

From bottom up: plans of the ground floor, basement, first floor and third floor. Opposite page: the heroic entrance and the bottom detail of the glass curtain facade made of a construction grid of either 1.20 m or 6.0 m.

Von unten nach oben: Grundriß des Erdgeschosses, Kellergeschosses, ersten und dritten Obergeschosses. Gegenüber: der monumentale Eingang und darunter: ein Detail der lang durchlaufenden Glasfassade. Das Grundkonzept für die Gestaltung der Fassade ist die Vorhangfassade im Konstruktionsraster von 1,20 bzw. 6,0 m.

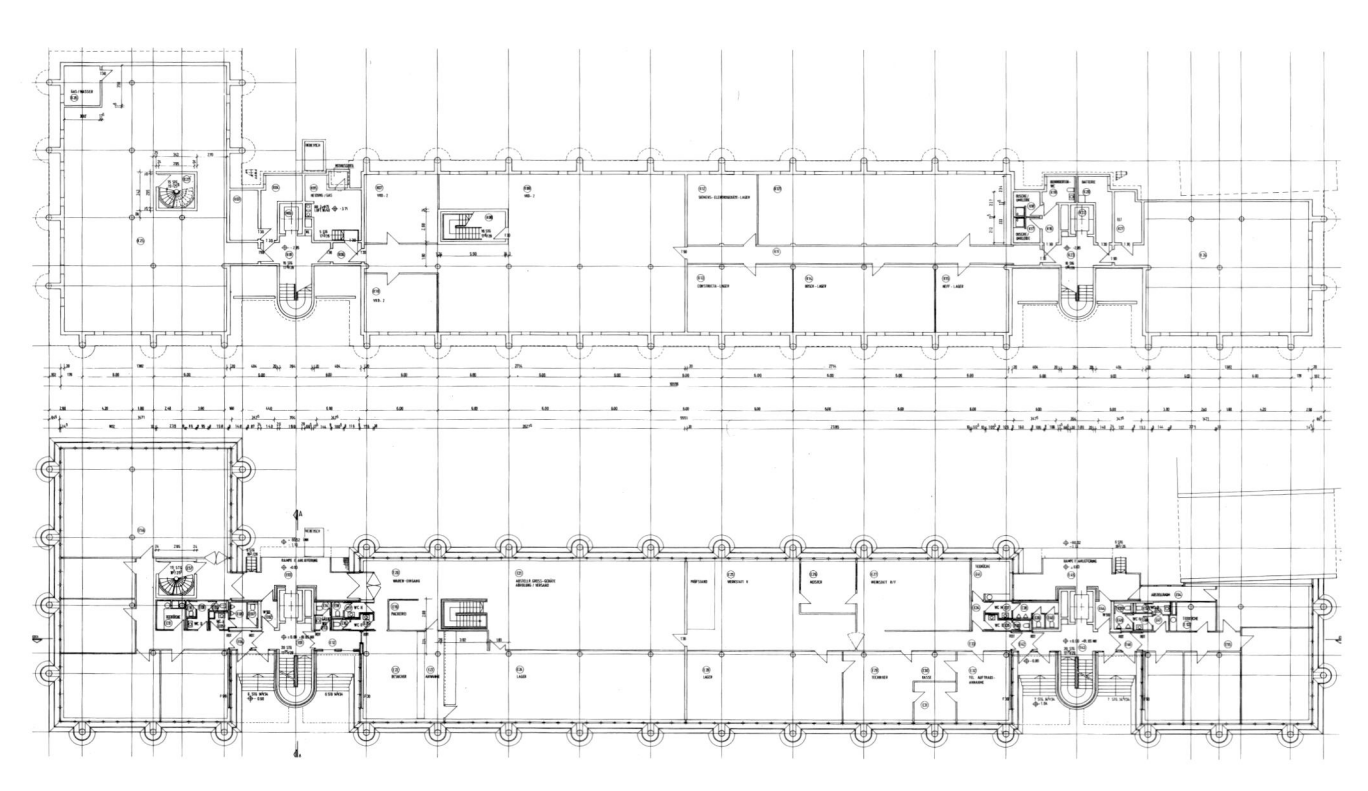

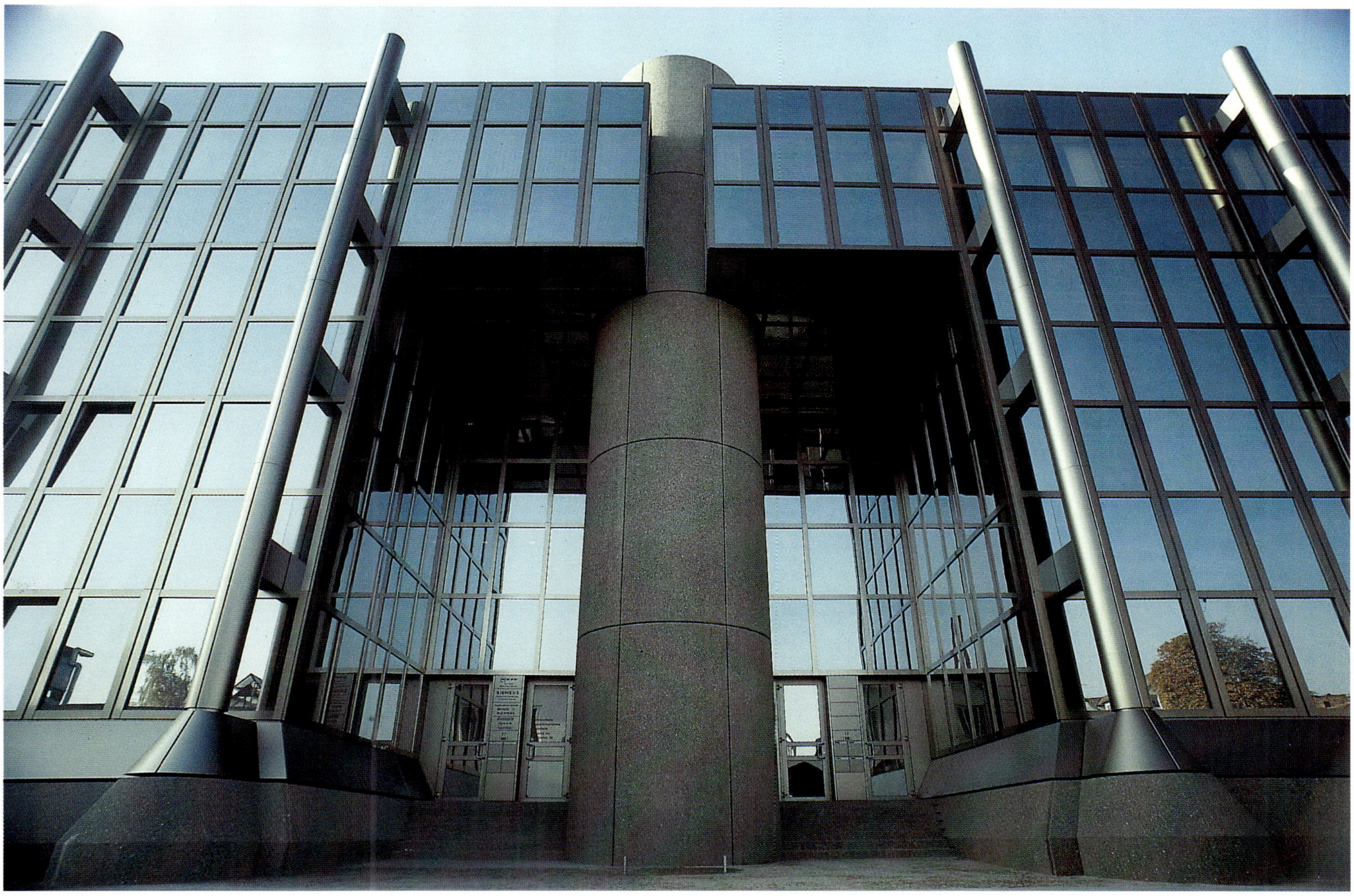

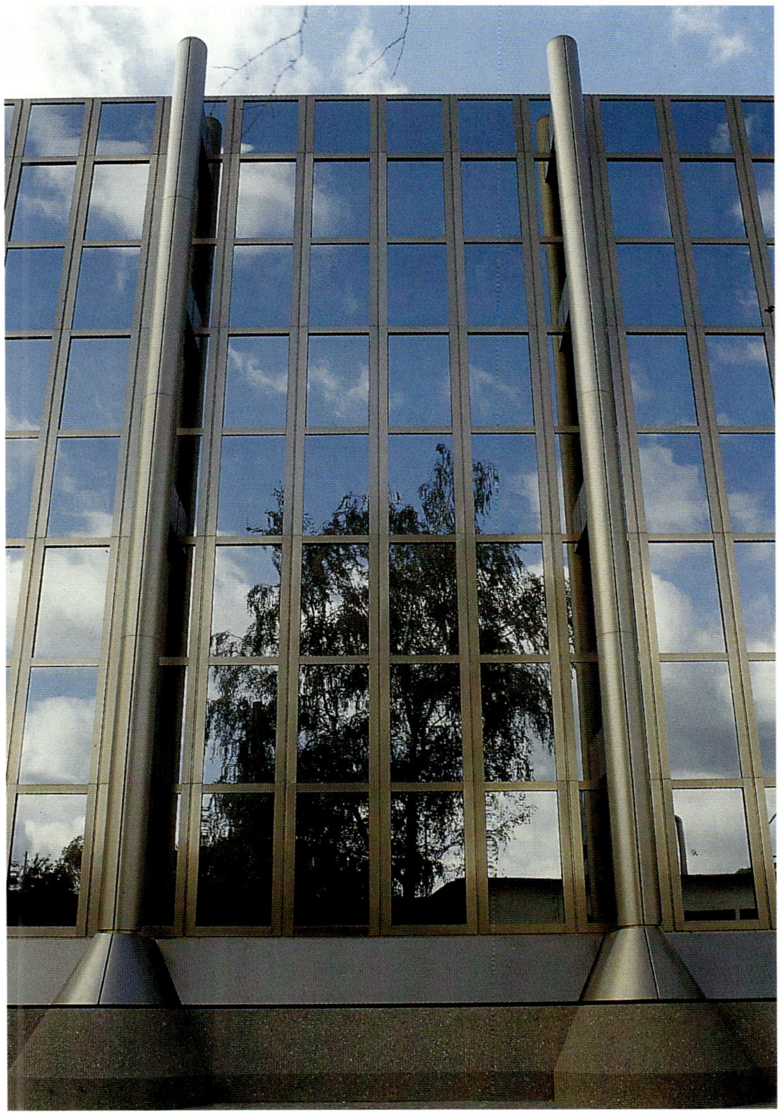

Axonometry and partial views of the facade vertically constructed around steel structural columns.
Isometrie und Details der Fassade mit außenstehenden Stahlrundstützen.

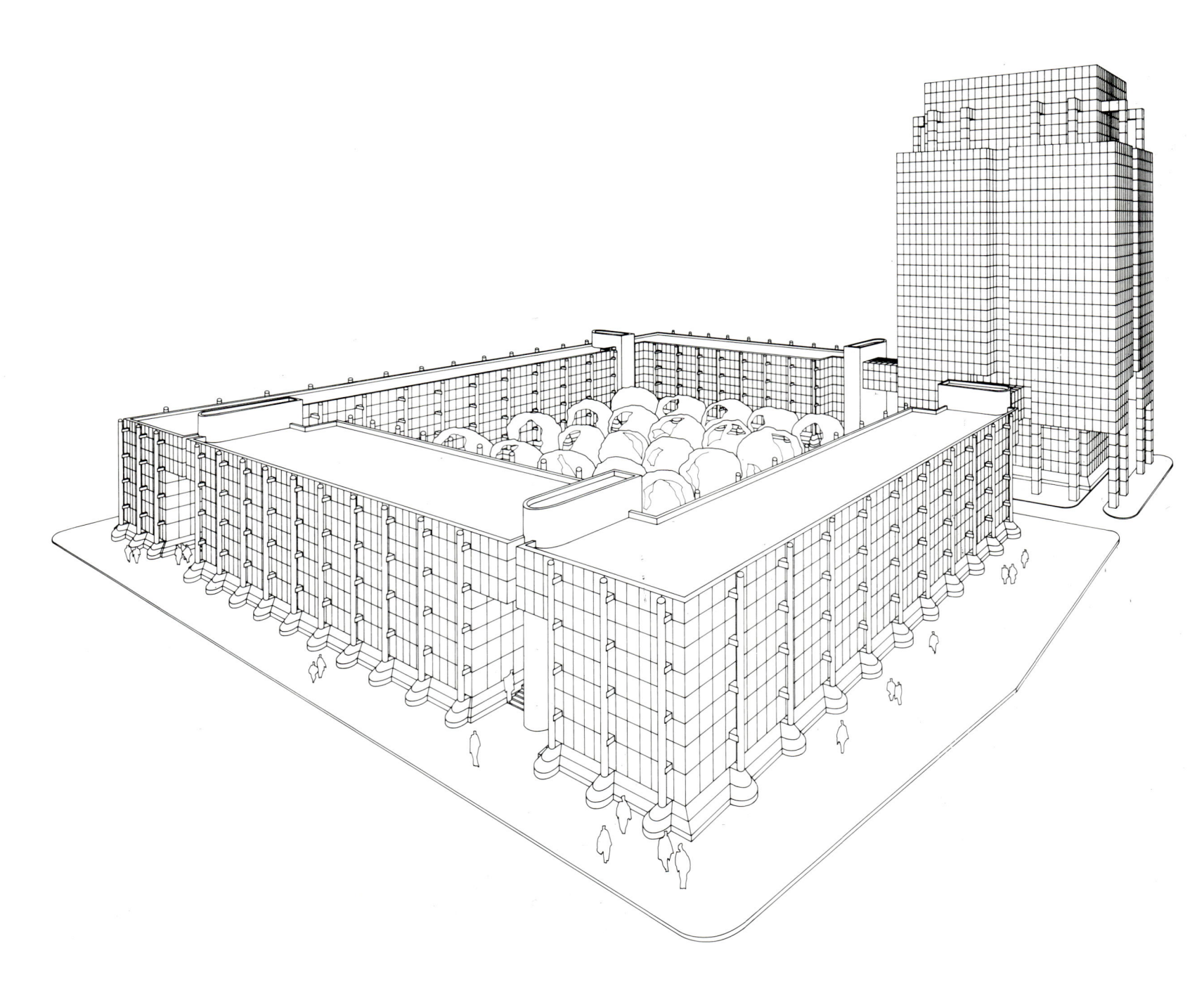

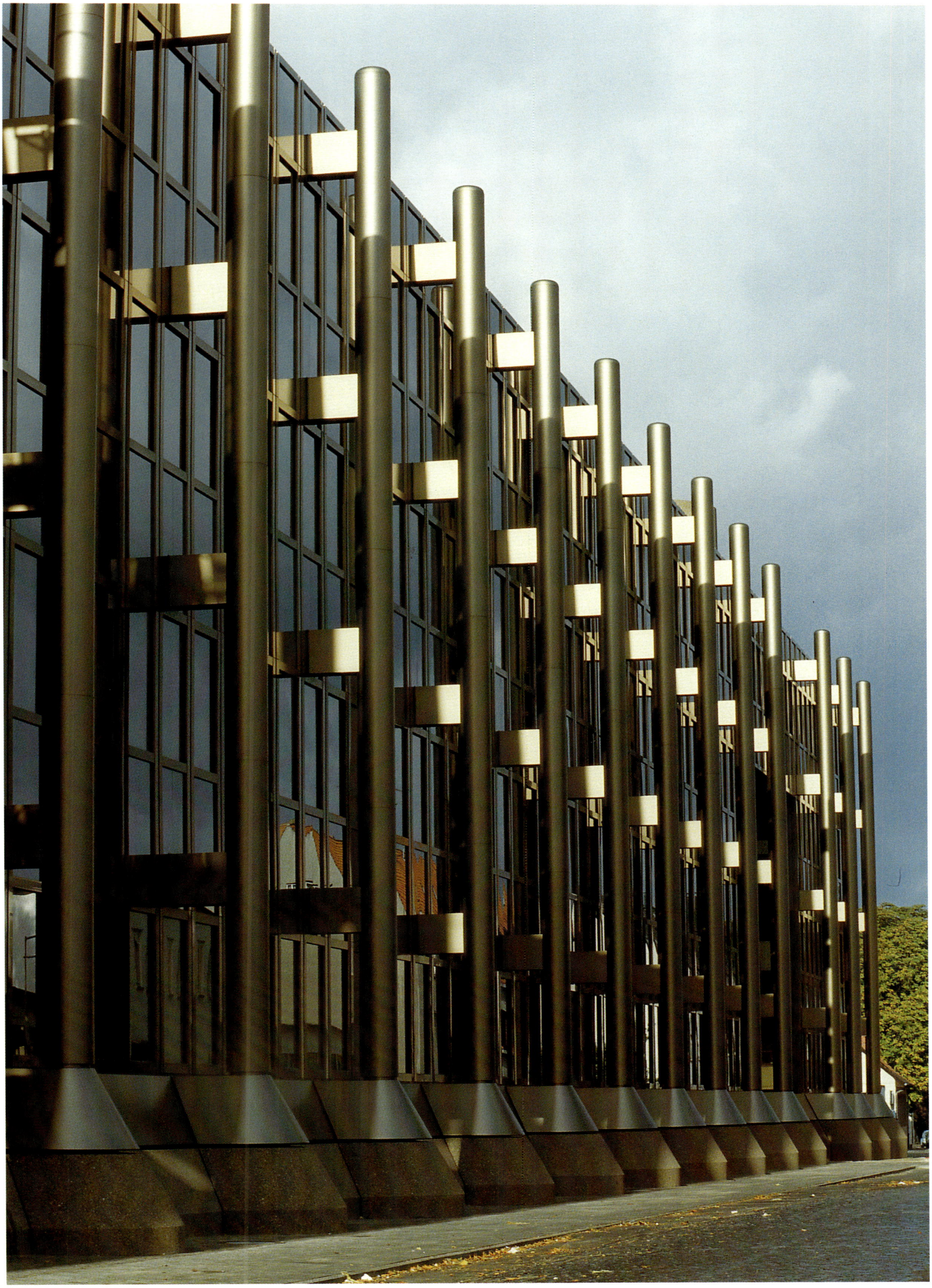

Details of the bottom of the steel columns clad with aluminium and arranged at a distance of 6 m from each other to enliven the facade.

Fußpunkte der Stahlrundstützen im Bereich der Glasfassade. Hier bilden die außenstehenden, im Abstand von 6 m, 4-geschossig verlaufenden alumimumverkleideten Stahlstützen eine rhythmische Gliederung des Gebäudes.

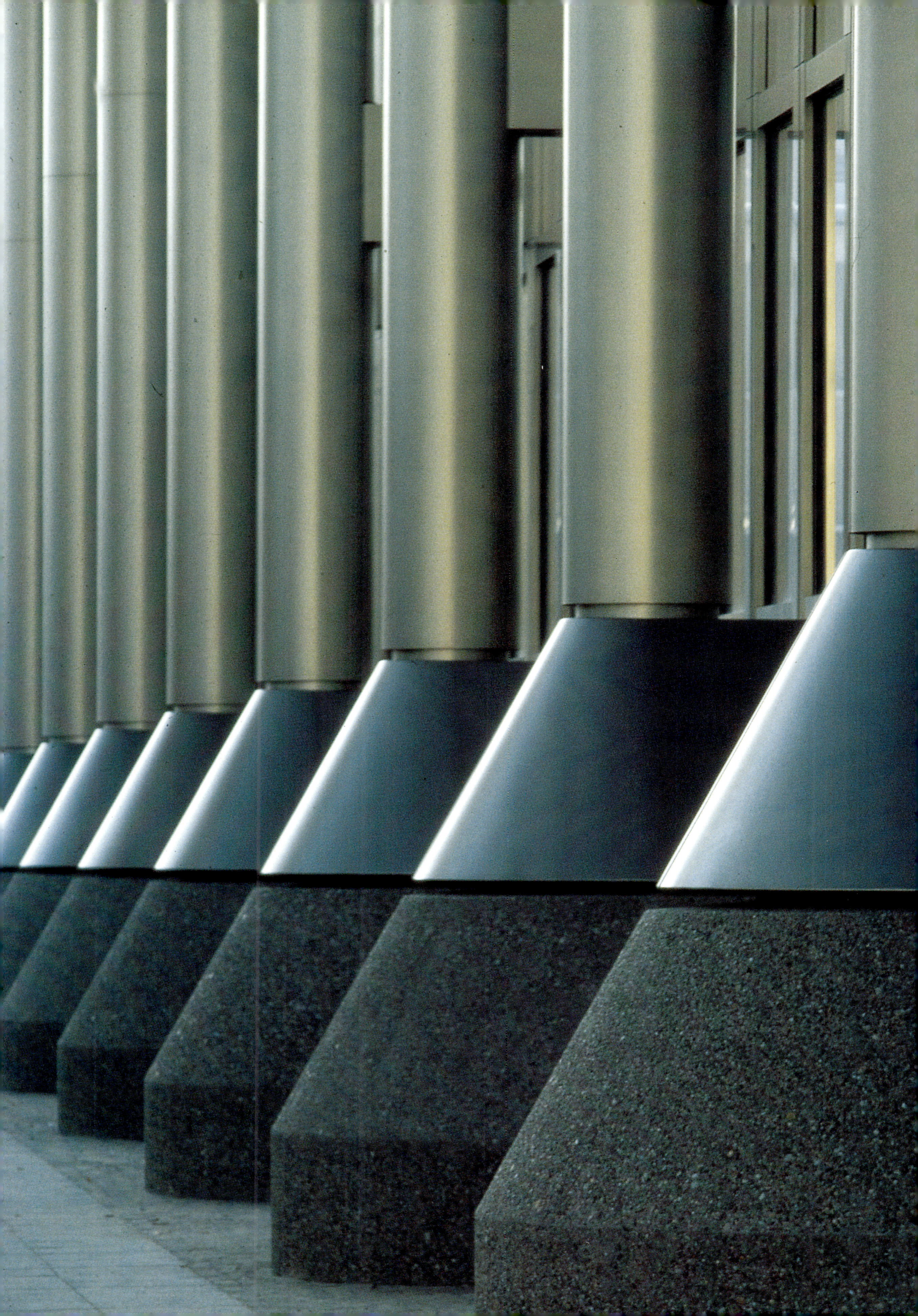

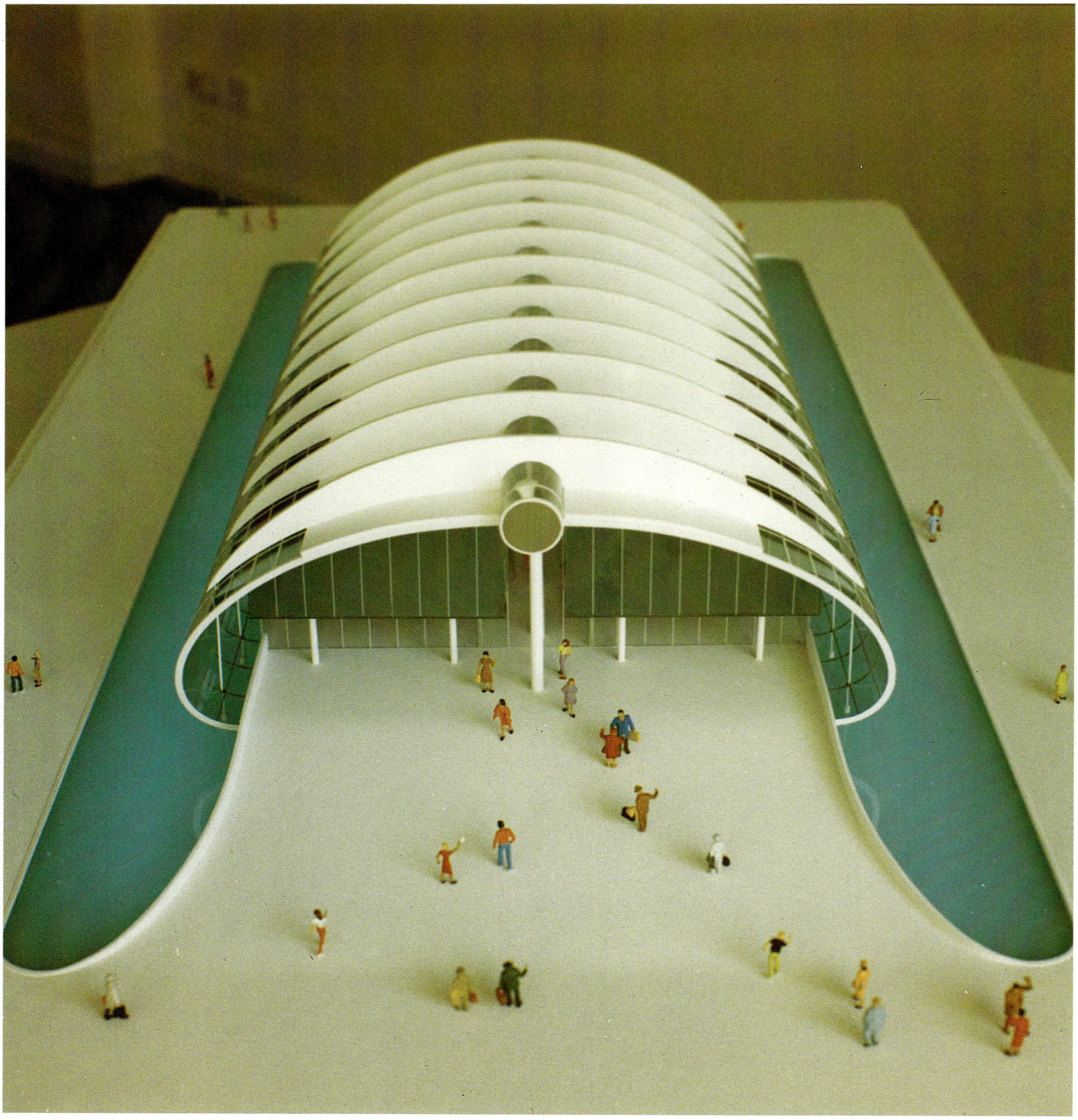

KRUPP EXPO
Exhibition Centre
Ausstellungspavillon

Shapes convey more than an insight into functions, they also reveal visions. And visions then not infrequently make an impact on functions. All this needs to be remembered in an exhibition pavilion designed to harness ideas and emotions to point to the future.

With the pavilion conceived for the Krupp group, the chosen "outer skin" alludes to vegetable shapes - without drawing on any specific association - and also to fantasy technology of the type used in sci-fi films. Innovations are here approached by way of emotional response. What is suggested by the "exterior" may be verified in the "interior".

A purpose-built block on two floors in customary rectangular shape has been inserted under a filigree steel/glass skin comprising an ellipsoid cylinder. Yet to some extent one sees only an upper section of the "reclining" cylinder, for the path to the pavilion climbs continuously and leads directly inside. There seems to be no more "ground" for the architectural form - and this applies both to the "earth" on which the pavilion stands and to the reason for its being as it is.

Technically the structure exudes dynamism and this "visual feeling" conveys conceptions of the future immediately realized in the images conveyed by technical structures.

Formen vermitteln mehr als die Einsicht in Funktionen, sie vermitteln auch Visionen. Und die Visionen wirken dann nicht selten zurück auf die Funktionen. Das muß mitbedacht werden, wenn man mit einem Ausstellungspavillon ideell und emotional in die Zukunft weisen will.

Bei dem für den Krupp-Konzern entwickelten Pavillon verweist die gewählte „Außenhaut" auf vegetabile Formen - ohne eine bestimmte Assoziation anzusprechen - und zugleich auf eine Phantasie-Technik, wie sie in Science-Fiction Filmen eingesetzt wird. Innovationen werden hier über ein emotionales Wahrnehmen angesprochen. Was das „Außen" suggeriert, kann im „Innen" verifiziert werden.

Ein zweigeschossiger Zweckbau in gewohnter Rechteckform steckt unter einer filigranen Stahl-Glas-Hülle, die einen ellipsoiden Zylinder bildet. Aber man sieht gewissermaßen nur einen oberen Teil des „liegenden" Zylinders, denn der Weg auf den Pavillon zu steigt stetig an und führt geradezu in ihn hinein. Es scheint keinen „Grund" mehr für die architektonische Form zu geben - und das meint sowohl den „Boden", auf dem der Pavillon steht, als auch die Begründung für ihr So-Sein.

Die technische Konstruktion drückt Dynamik aus und dieses „visuelle Gefühl" vermittelt Zukunftsvorstellungen, die sich gleich wieder in technischen Konstruktionen imaginiert umsetzen.

View of the entrance to the Expo centre. Bottom of page: ground floor plan. Left: plan of the basement and right: plan of the first floor.
Ansicht des Ausstellungspavillons. Darunter: Grundriß des Erdgeschosses. Darüber links: Grundriß des Teilkellergeschosses und rechts: das eingeschobene Obergeschoß.

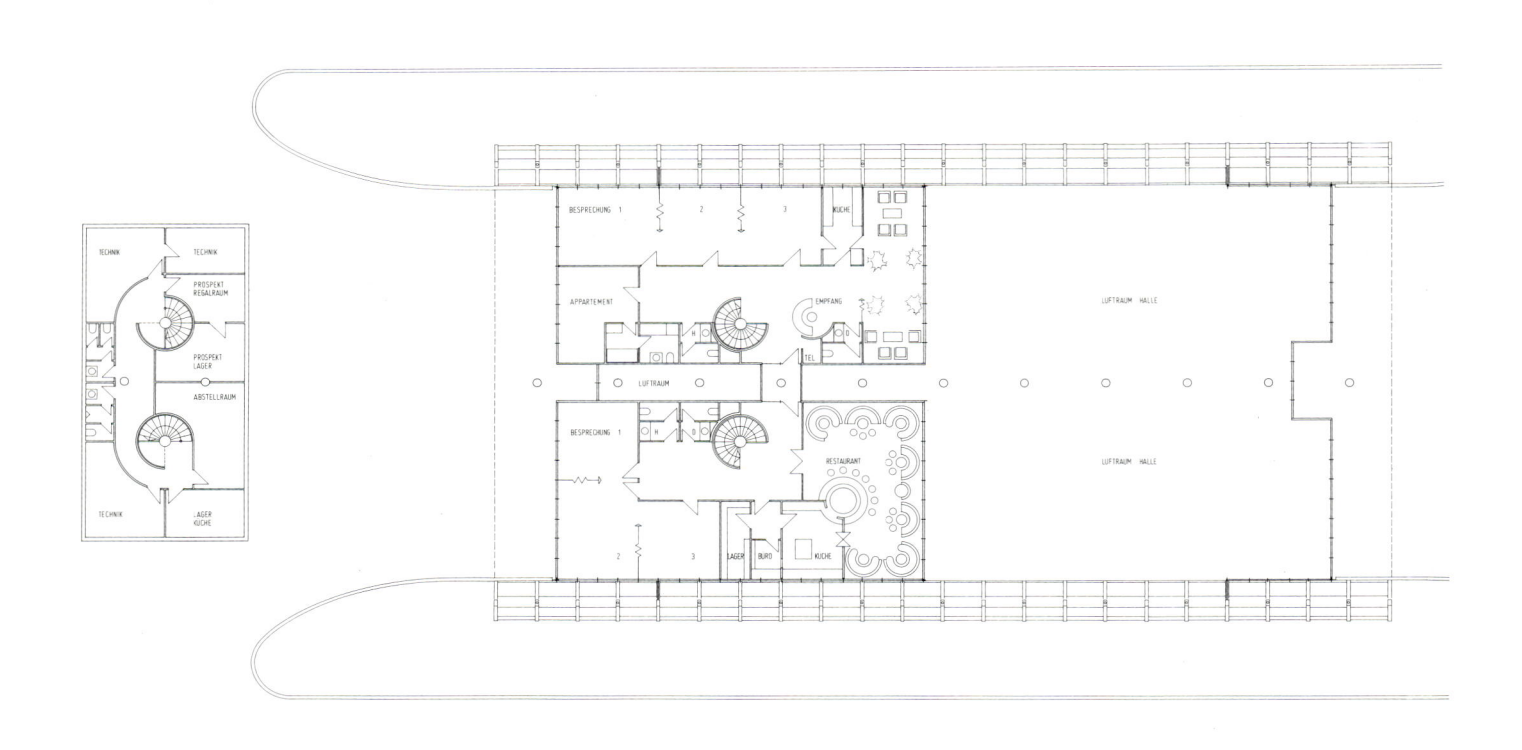

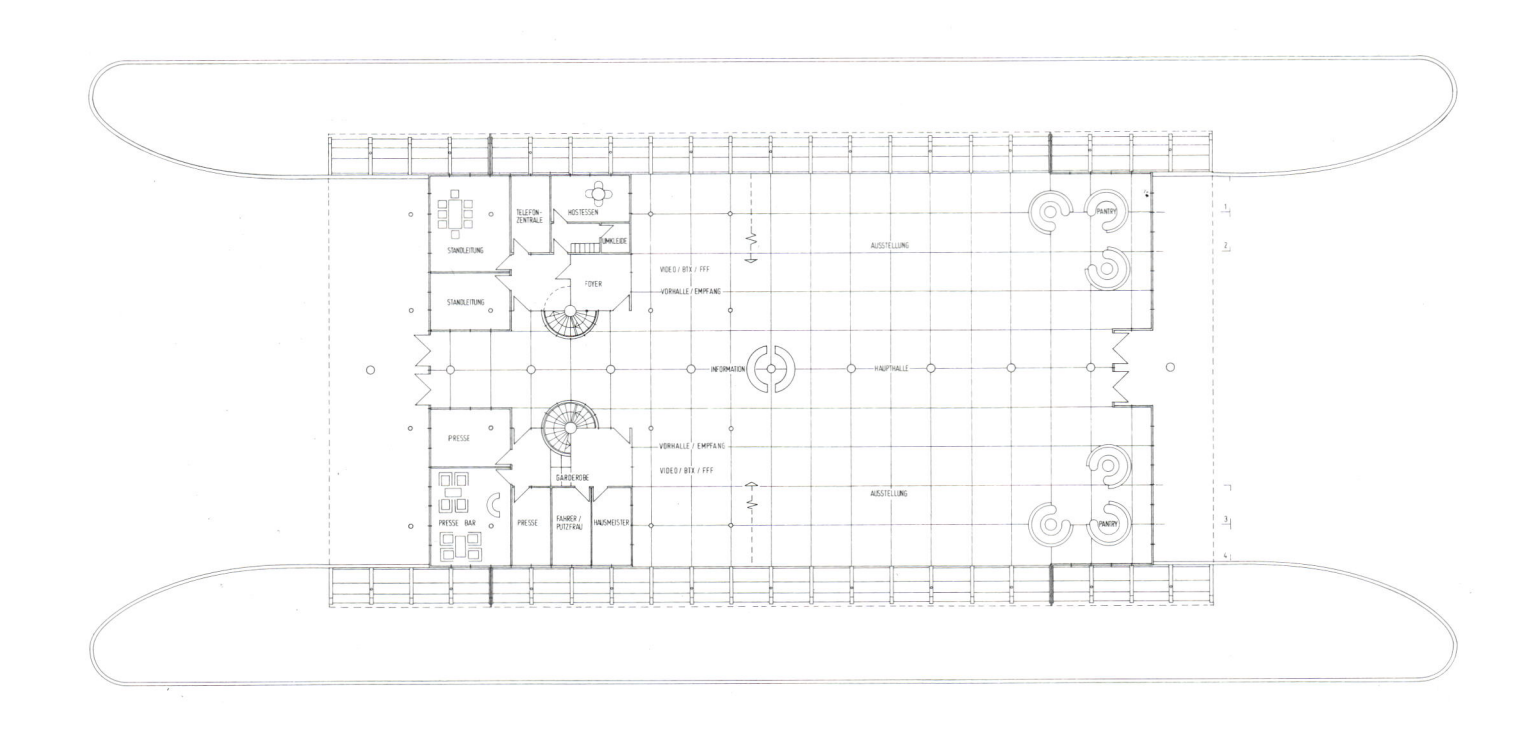

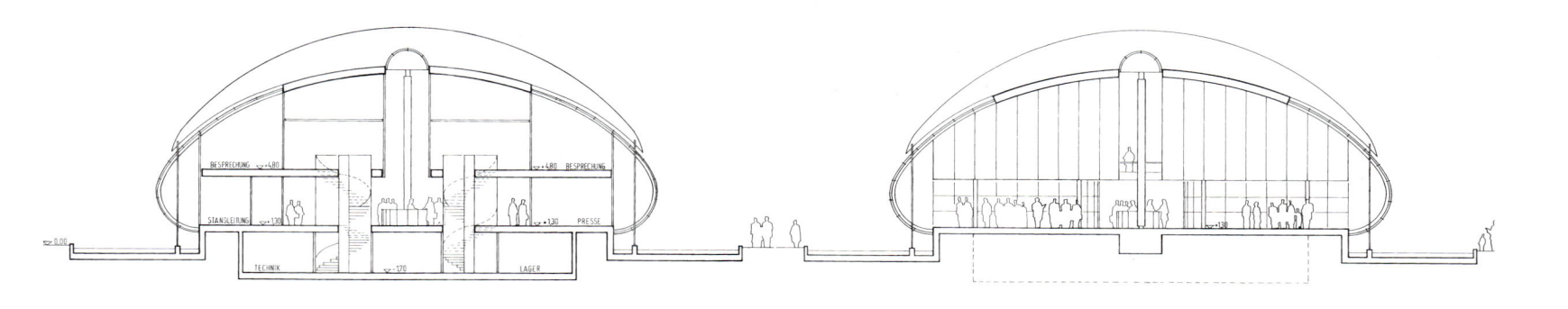

Top of page: cross sections.
Above: general view of the model.
*Querschnitte.
Darunter: Gesamtansicht des Modells.*

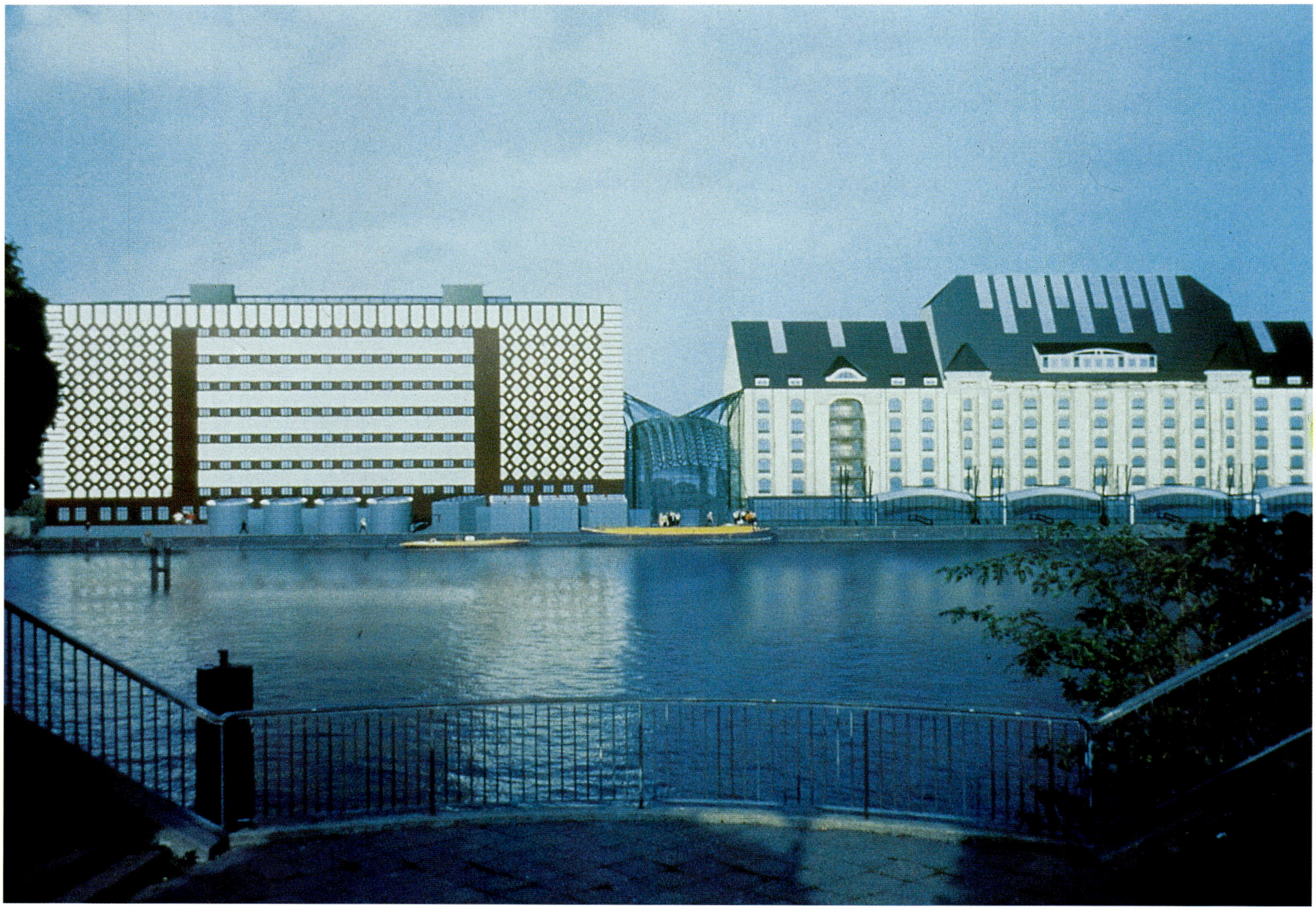

DSS
The Spree Warehouses
Die Spree Speicher

Two listed warehouses in the derelict Osthafen on the River Spree are to become a modern creative centre. Both requirements and solutions here are equally simple and complicated. The two isolated buildings used to serve as storehouses for grain and eggs. Although erected at an interval of a mere 15 years, in style they represent two entirely different epochs: the former grain store was built in neo-classical style in 1913, the coolstore for eggs built in 1928/29 features an original Bauhaus facade (white-yellow brick with patterns). This facade actually lay masked for years by typical GDR panel masonry and was regarded as decayed.

Offices premises, display areas, lofts and communication centres along with restaurants, bars and bistros are to be created in the two buildings. Planning for the two buildings provides for de-coring with internal atria surrounded by galleries. The idea is to allow daylight to flood these from the roof to the ground floor.

The seven-storey granary and the eight-store coolstore are to be linked by a steel-glass tract beneath a suspended roof.

Lofts and mezzanine offer a host of possibilities for different usages and layouts. The mezzanine, especially, is a big part of the attraction, permitting undisturbed work on the (inner) second floor at the same time as the general public are coming and going at the "basic" level.

These two historic buildings are both listed. The coolstore in Bauhaus style understandably has no windows. Fire protection regulations, so it has emerged, preclude a de-coring of this and it will accordingly be impossible to light it from the roof. Thus was born the idea of "virtual historic building protection". The old facade is to be replaced by a double glass facade with the original brick pattern silk-screen printed on this. Whether the Historic Buildings Agency can accept this is still unresolved, but the idea has triggered a spirited debate.

Aus zwei denkmalgeschützten Lagerhäusern am verwaisten Osthafen der Spree soll ein modernes Kreativ-Zentrum werden. Vorgaben und Lösungen sind gleichermaßen einfach wie kompliziert. Die beiden solitären Gebäude dienten ehemals der Lagerung von Getreide und Eiern. Obwohl nur fünfzehn Jahre nacheinander errichtet, entstammen sie zwei grundverschiedenen Stilepochen: der ehemalige Getreidespeicher wurde 1913 im neoklassizistischen Stil gebaut und das 1928/29 errichtete Eierkühlhaus weist eine originale Bauhaus-Fassade (weiß-gelber Klinker mit Musterung) auf. Diese Fassade allerdings lag lange Jahre hinter einer typischen DDR-Platten-Verblendung und gilt als marode.

In beiden Gebäuden sollen Büroräume, Ausstellungsflächen, Lofts und Kommunikationszentren mit Restaurants, Bars und Bistros geschaffen werden. Die Planung sieht für beide Gebäude eine Entkernung vor mit inneren Atrien in galerieartiger Ausstattung. Vom Dach her soll Tageslicht bis ins Erdgeschoß fließen können.

Der siebengeschossige Getreidespeicher und das achtgeschossige Kühlhaus werden mit einem Stahl-Glas-Trakt verbunden, der von einem hängenden Dach abgeschlossen wird.

Lofts und Mezzanine bieten vielfältige Nutzungs- und Gestaltungsmöglichkeiten. Gerade die Mezzanine machen einen Teil der Attraktion aus, denn sie gewähren im (inneren) zweiten Stock ein ungestörtes Arbeiten, wenn auf der „Basis"-Ebene Publikumsverkehr herrscht.

Beide historischen Gebäude stehen unter Denkmalschutz.

Das Kühlhaus im Bauhaus-Stil hat (verständlicherweise) keine Fenster. Es kann, so stellte sich heraus, aus Brandschutzgründen nicht entkernt und somit auch nicht vom Dach her belichtet werden. Daraus entwickelte sich die Idee eines „virtuellen Denkmalschutzes". Die historische Fassade soll einer doppelten Glasfassade weichen, auf die das ursprüngliche Klinkermuster per Siebdruck aufgedruckt wird. Ob der Denkmalschutz sich damit anfreunden kann, ist noch nicht entschieden, aber die Idee hat eine intensive Diskussion ausgelöst.

General view of the project area. Below: detail of the 1920's building and opposite page: of the warehouse built at the turn of the century, joined together by a full-height glass gallery.
Bottom: plan of the ground floor of the complex.
Gesamtansicht des Projekts. Darunter: Detail des Speichergebäudes, das um die Jahrhundertwende gebaut wurde. Gegenüber: Teilansicht des Gebäudes aus den 20er Jahren. Der Zweck des Gesamtprojekts ist die Vereinigung der zwei bestehenden Denkmalsbauten über eine Glashalle zu einem Gesamtkomplex. Unten: Grundriß des Erdgeschosses der Gesamtanlage.

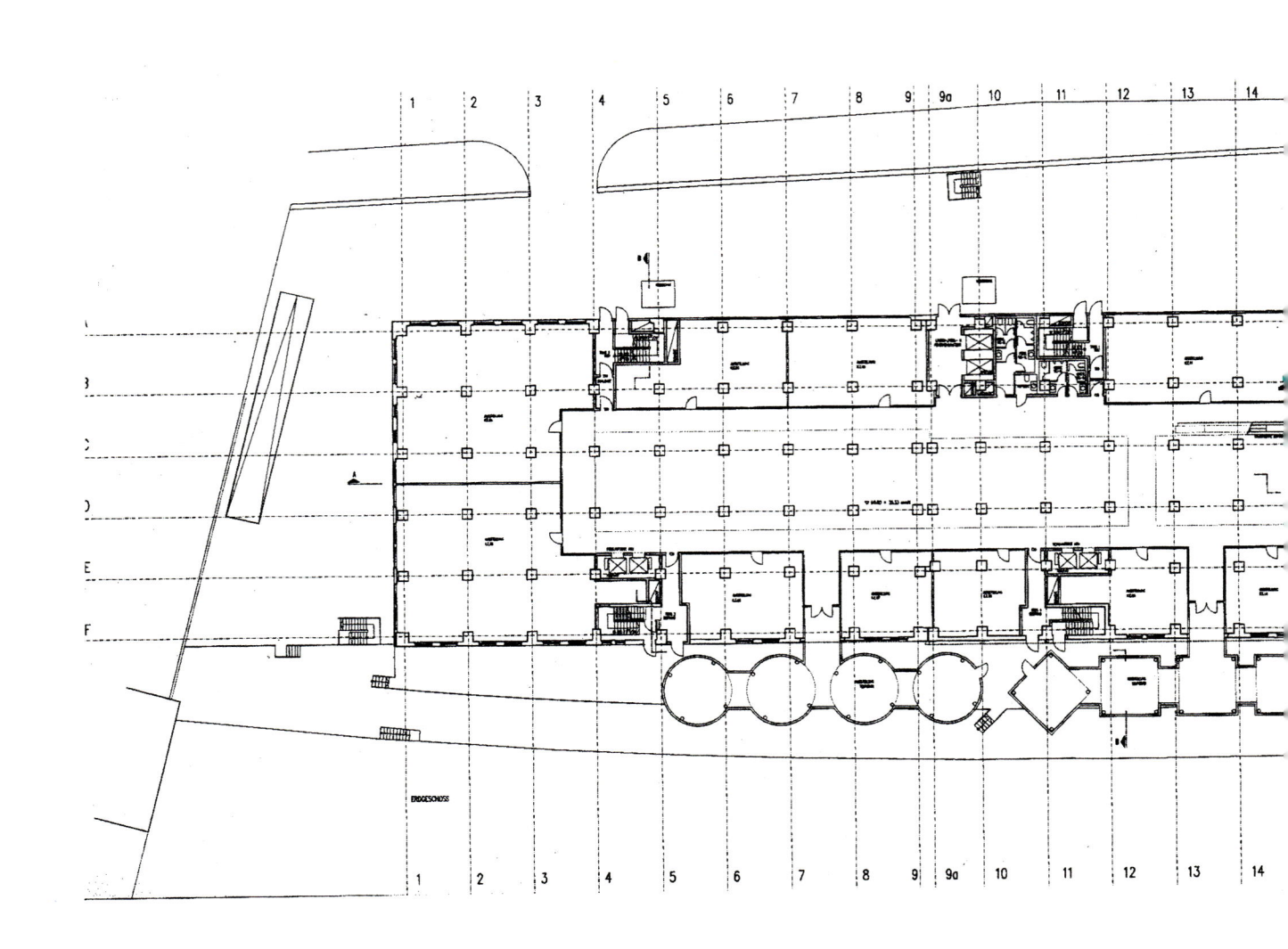

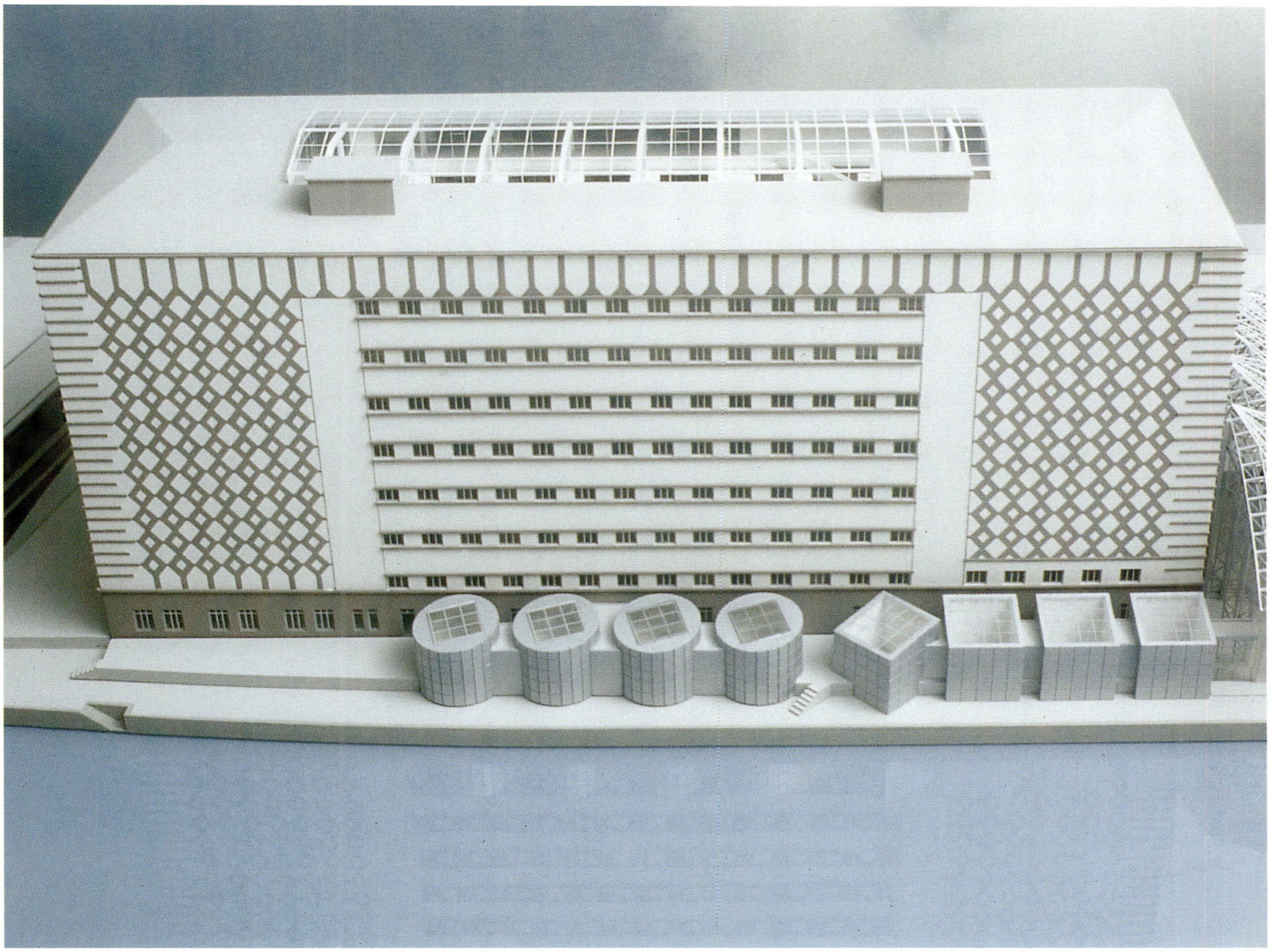

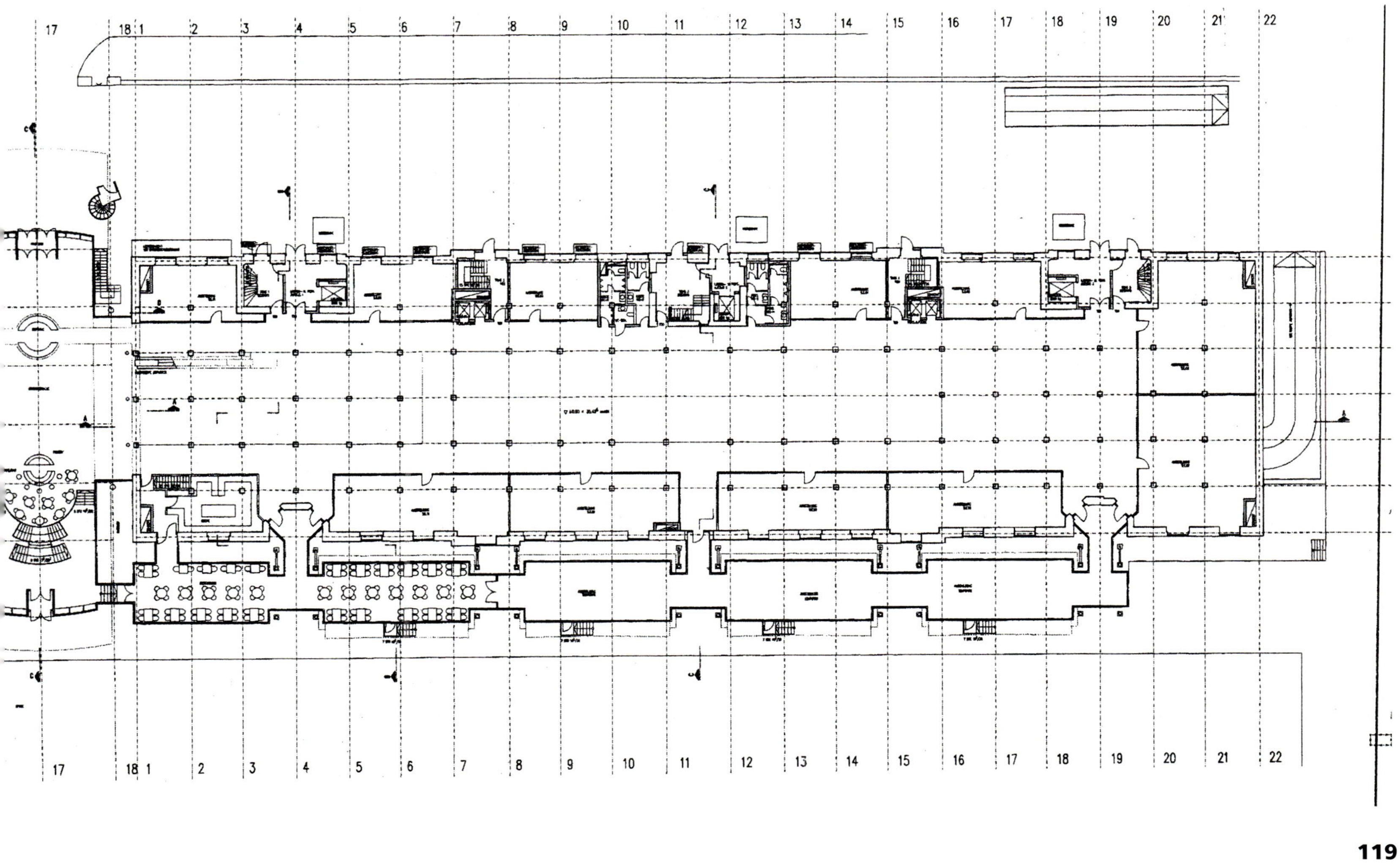
17 18 1 2 3 4 5 6 7 8 9 10 11 12 13 14 15 16 17 18 19 20 21 22

Rendering of the inside of the glass gallery designed to join together the two existing buildings. Right: cross sections of the complex.
Perspektivzeichnungen der inneren Glashalle, die die Rolle des Verbindungselements zwischen den bestehenden Bebauungen spielen wird. Rechts: Querschnitte des Komplexes.

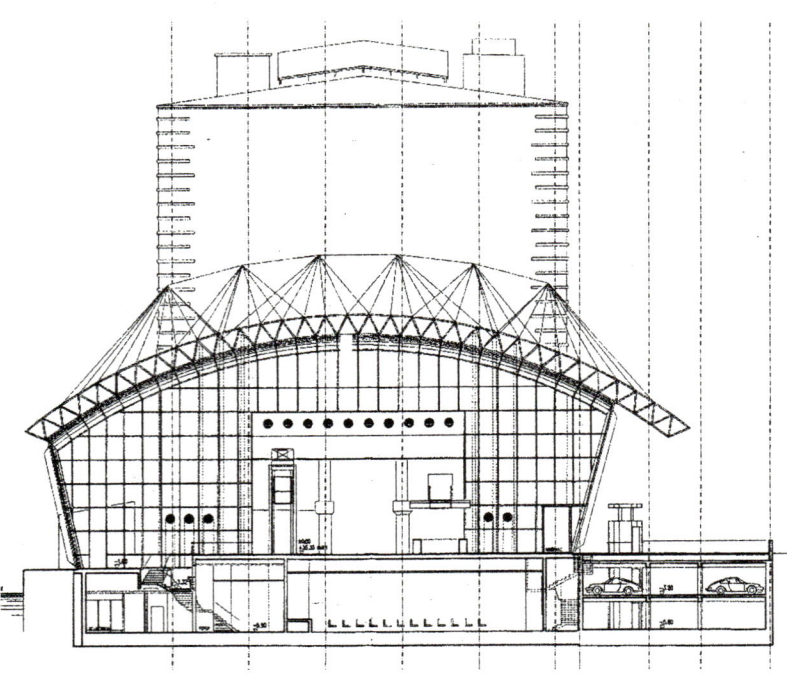

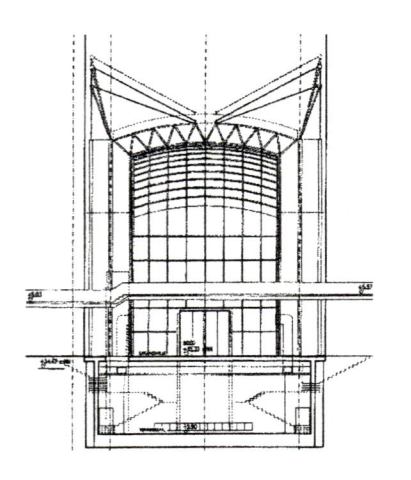

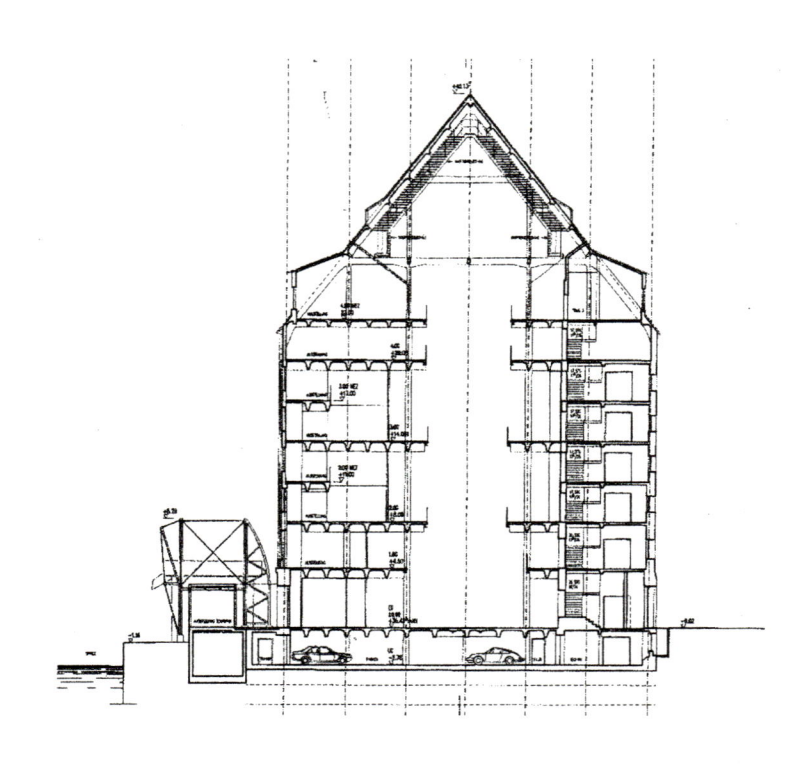

Rendering of the inner office space and below the inner atrium.
Perspektive der inneren Bürofläche und darunter das innere Atrium.

121

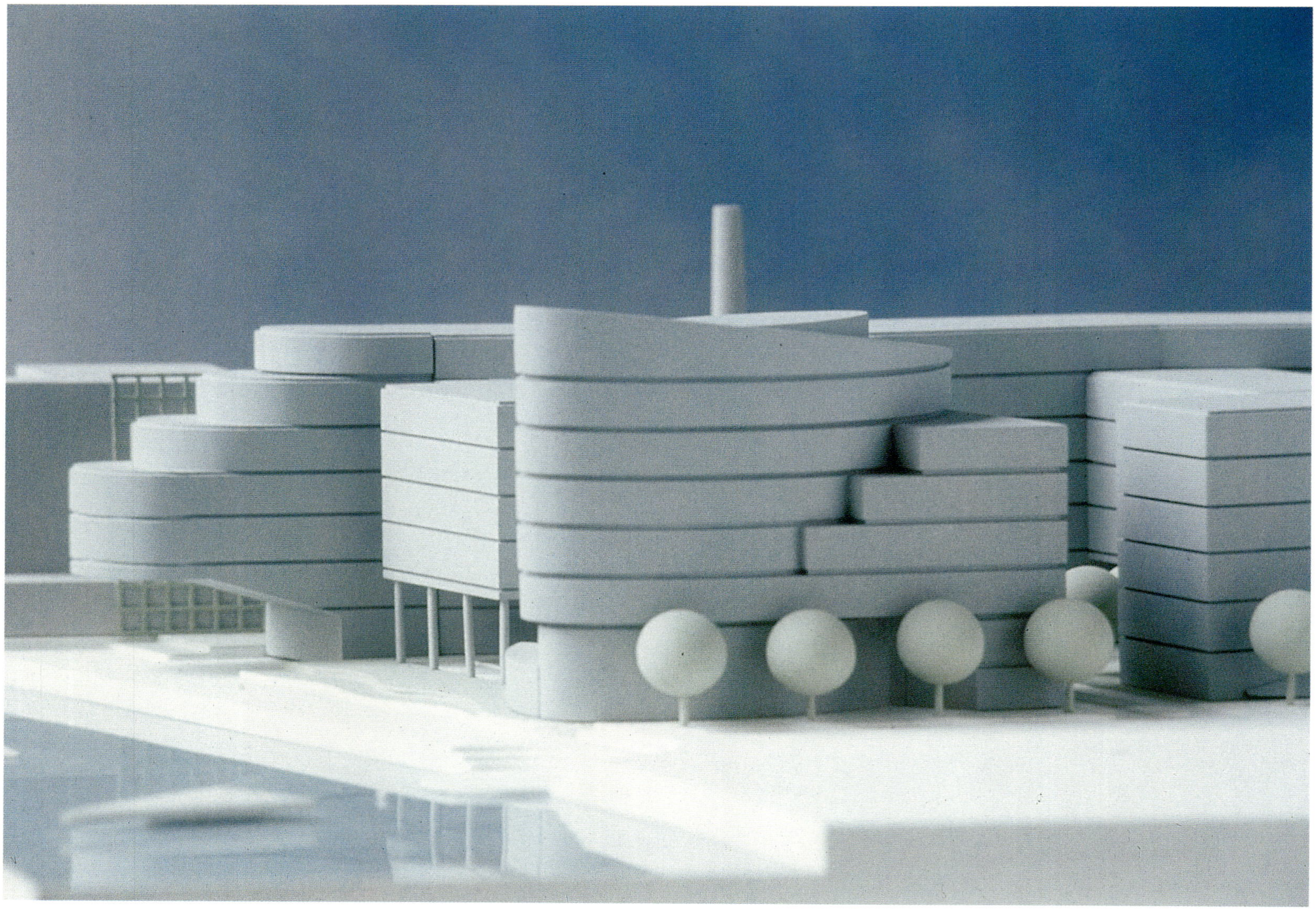

KTC
Technology Centre
Technologiezentrum

The idea behind the "Kreuzberger Technology Centre" was to inject some architectural vitality into the area lying between compact buildings of five and six storeys east of the Cuvrystrasse and the street itself.

The design provides for a very open block layout only still existing in schemes and opening up slightly towards the Spree. A series of three buildings slides along compact buildings from the turn of the century (mainly in commercial use). This row consists of three buildings on the Cuvrystrasse, which runs down to the Spree. Each of these has been given a distinct shape. The one facing the Spree has departed farthest from the basic rectangular pattern, being oval and positioned diagonally in the plot - albeit on a plateau which remains very rectangular.

When compared to the surrounding buildings, the plan provides for very dense usage.

One of its themes is "fragmented order". It may be abundantly clear that the separate blocks have developed from the original square blocks, yet the structure worked out here dissolves the previous clear relationships.

In its efforts towards divergence or convergence - and both approaches are possible - this architectural ensemble reflects social and political sensitivities in Berlin. Commercial usage (shops) is envisaged for the ground floor areas of the buildings running along the Spree, while a restaurant in the oval building is intended to provide a link with the riverside promenade.

Blocks built at the turn of the century in Berlin are generally accessible only from one side. In this case, generous access has been laid on for pedestrians. This ensemble of buildings can be reached on foot from both sides of the street and from the riverside promenade. For cars and trucks, an underground garage with separate entrances and exits is also planned.

Zwischen eine geschlossene fünf- und sechsgeschossige Bebauung östlich der Cuvrystraße und der Cuvrystraße selbst soll mit einem „Kreuzberger Technologiezentrum" architektonische Bewegung gesetzt werden.

Der Entwurf sieht eine nur noch in Schemen vorhandene sehr offene Blockbebauung vor, die sich zur Spree hin leicht öffnet. Entlang einer kompakten Bebauung aus der Jahrhundertwende (mit vornehmlich gewerblicher Nutzung) schlängelt sich ein dreiteiliges Gebäudeband. An der Cuvrystraße, die auf die Spree zuläuft, ist das Band in drei einzelne Gebäude gelöst. Jedes der Gebäude findet dabei zu einer eigenständigen Form.

Das spreeseitig orientierte Gebäude ist am weitesten aus dem rechteckigen Grundmuster ausgeschert: es ist oval und schräg in das Grundstück versetzt - allerdings auf einem noch rechteckig geschnittenen Plateau.

Gemessen an der umliegenden Bebauung sieht der Entwurf eine überaus hohe Nutzungsdichte vor. Der Entwurf thematisiert eine „gebrochene Ordnung". Man sieht zwar noch sehr deutlich, daß die einzelnen Baukörper sich aus ursprünglichen Quaderbauten entwickelt haben, aber die ausformulierte Struktur löst die klaren Konstellationen auf.

Im Auseinander- oder Zusammenstreben (beide Sichtweisen sind möglich) spiegelt der architektonische Komplex gesellschaftliche und politische Empfindungen in Berlin wider. In den Erdgeschoßzonen der auf die Spree zulaufenden Bauten sind gewerbliche Nutzungen (Ladenflächen) vorgesehen, im ovalen Gebäude soll ein Restaurant die Verbindung zur Uferpromenade entstehen.

Berliner Blockbebauungen der Jahrhundertwende sind meist nur von jeweils einer Seite zugänglich. Hier hat man eine großzügige Erschließung für Fußgänger eingeplant. Von beiden Straßenseiten und von der Uferpromenade ist das Gebäudeensemble zu Fuß zu betreten. Für PKWs und LKWs ist eine Tiefgarage mit getrennten Zu- und Abfahrten projektiert.

From bottom of page up: plans of the first and third floor.
Von unten nach oben: Grundriß des ersten und dritten Geschosses.

Aerial view of the model and site plan of the centre built along the Spree over an area of 10,066 square metres.
Luftbild des Modells und Lageplan des Gesamtkomplexes der in Nord-Süd-Richtung zum Spreeufer abfällt und 10.066 m2 umfaßt.

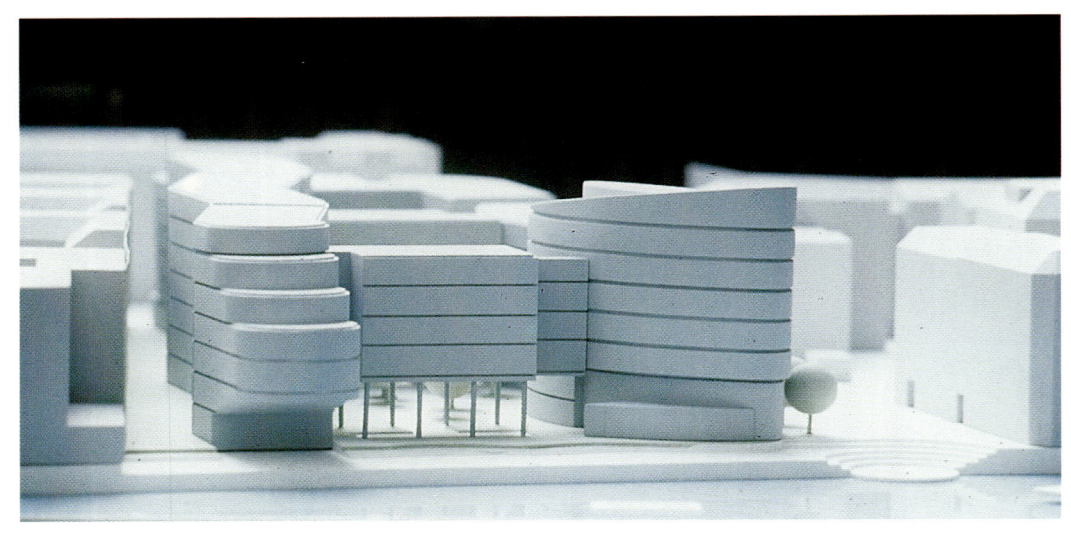

Views of the model. The technology centre is designed like a block of separate buildings instilling the area with a sense of spatial transparency and openness.

Ansicht des Modells. Das Technologiezentrum bildet im Grundriß die Figur eines langgestreckten, sich zur Spree hin U-förmig öffnenden und transparenten Baukörpers.

GUYRSTRASSE

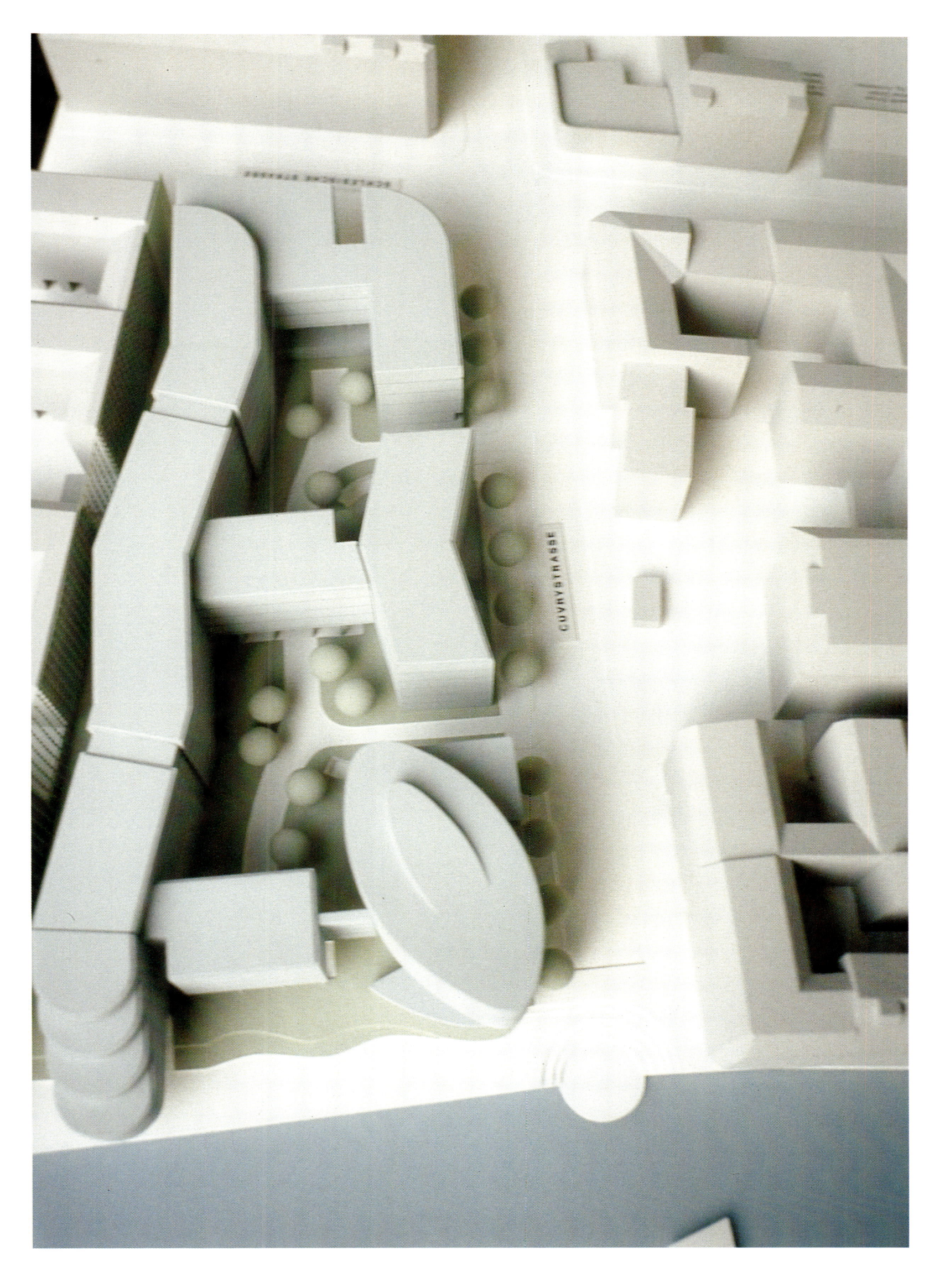

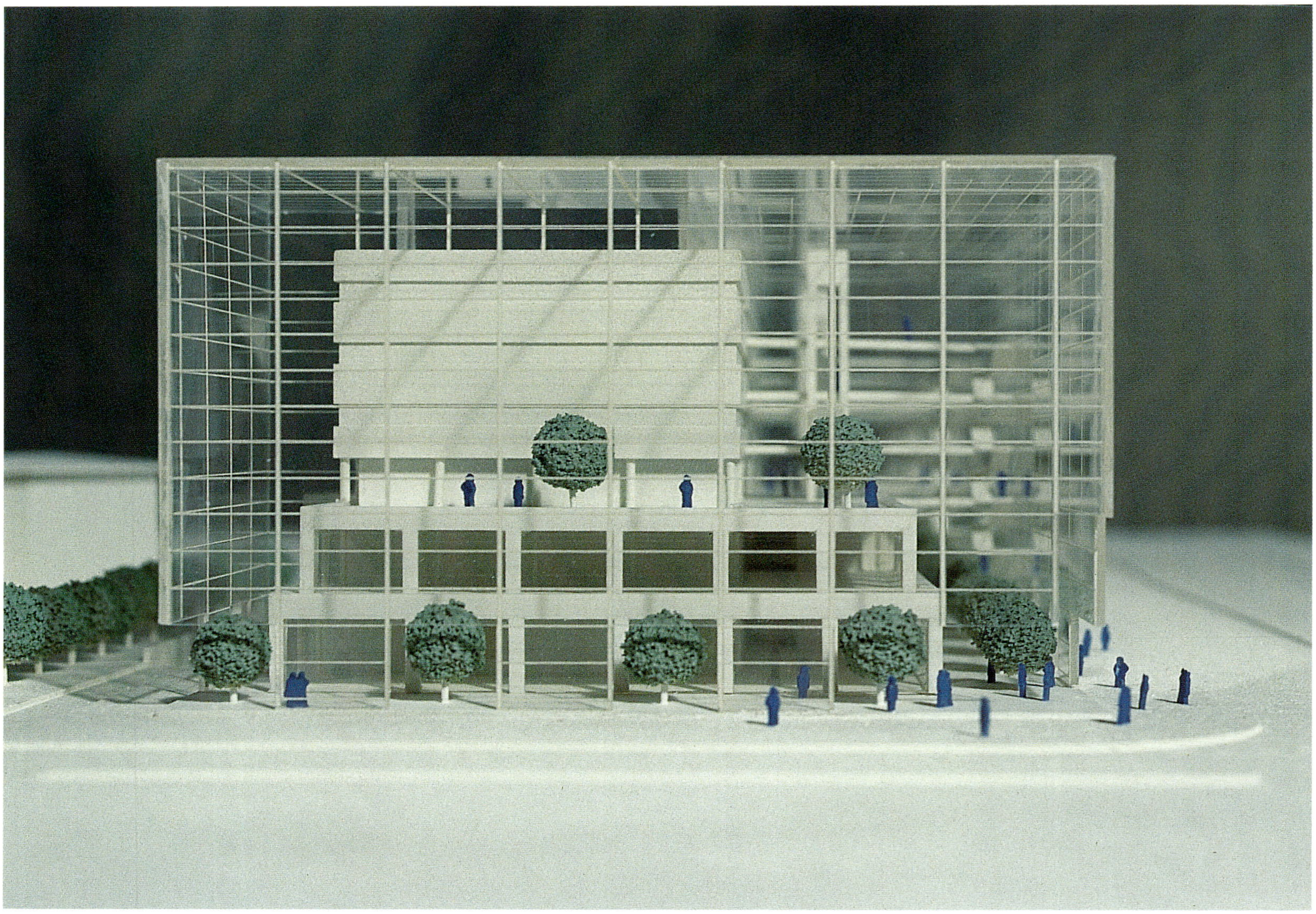

HCH
Office Centre and Shopping Mall
Büro-und Einkaufszentrum

An elongated block runs along the length of the lozenge-shaped plot along Hansastrasse in the Hohenschönhausen district of Berlin. The main street running out of town and Malchower Weg at right angles to this to some extent define the "public" part of the extensive building project on an industrial wasteland. Residential streets lie to the south and along the back of the plot. These are to be shielded again traffic noise and granted a certain never previously enjoyed privacy.

A block with a length of 250 metres forms the heart of the complex. Yet this dominates only half the total length. The massive two-storey block largely disappears under a glazed hall the height of the building. This extends and opens its "core" outwards. The hall forms part of a semi-public square astride the two streets with through traffic. The complex has been planned as a shopping and services centre.

The two lower levels are earmarked for sales areas. Above these four floors of offices are planned, these being distinctly set back (by 10 metres). This creates a green open space of distinctly private character.

The side of the plot facing the dwellings further south will be used as an open green space planted with trees.

This planning sets an architectural standard for the whole area of the crossing, for within the foreseeable future this district is to undergo radical change in town planning terms. The planning presented here approaches and introduces a form of mutual consideration of a kind which encourages hopes of steep qualitative improvement generally.

Ein langgestreckter Baukörper folgt der Längsseite des rautenförmigen Grundstücks entlang der Hansastraße in Berlin-Hohenschönhausen. Die stadtauswärts führende Hauptstraße und der rechtwinklig abbiegende Malchower Weg beschreiben gewissermaßen den „öffentlichen" Teil der geplanten umfangreichen Bebauung einer Industriebrache. Zur südlichen Rückseite liegen Wohnstraßen. Sie sollen vor Straßenlärm geschützt werden und zugleich eine gewisse „Privatheit" erhalten, die ihnen zuvor nicht zu eigen war.

Die Baukörper, der eine Kantenlänge von 250 m hat, ist der Kern des Komplexes. Er dominiert aber nur knapp die Hälfte der gesamten Länge. Der zweigeschossige massive Baukörper verschwindet zu einem großen Teil unter einer gebäudehohen gläsernen Halle. Sie erweitert und öffnet den „Kern" nach außen. Zu beiden Straßenseiten mit Durchgangsverkehr ist die Halle Teil eines halböffentlichen Platzes. Der Komplex ist als Dienstleistungs- und Shoppingcenter geplant.

Die unteren zwei Ebenen sind für Verkaufsflächen vorgesehen. Darüber sind vier Stockwerke mit Büroflächen geplant, die deutlich um 10 m zurückgesetzt sind. Dadurch entsteht eine Grün- und Freifläche mit spürbar privatem Charakter.

Zur südlich gelegenen Wohnbebauung wird das Grundstück begrünt und mit Bäumen bepflanzt.

Diese Planung setzt für den gesamten Kreuzungsbereich einen architektonischen Maßstab, denn in absehbarer Zeit wird dieser Bereich städtebaulich radikal verändert werden. Mit der vorgelegten Planung ist eine Form gegenseitiger Rücksichtnahme angesprochen und eingeleitet, die eine hohe qualitative Verbesserung gesamthaft erwarten läßt.

From bottom up: plans of the ground floor, second and fourth floor.
Von unten nach oben: Grundriß des Erdgeschosses, des zweiten und vierten Geschosses.

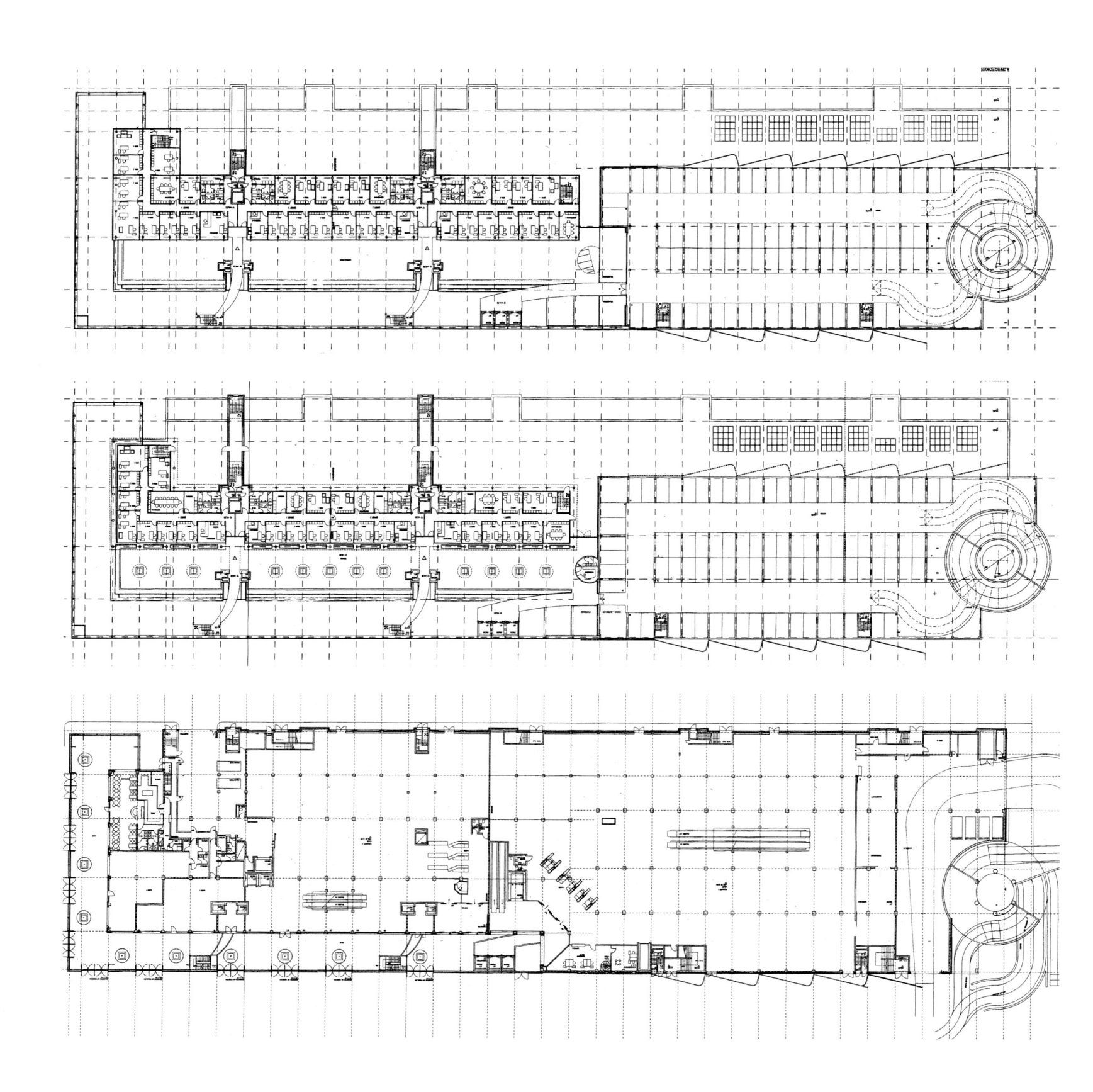

Aerial view of the model.
Luftbild des Modells.

Cross sections of the shopping-administration centre covering six floors. The first two are full of shops while the top four are used as office space.
Querschnitte des 6-geschossigen Fachmarkt- und Dienstleistungszentrums. Die ersten zwei Geschosse sind reine Verkaufsflächen, wobei die oberen vier als Bürogeschosse ausgebildet werden.

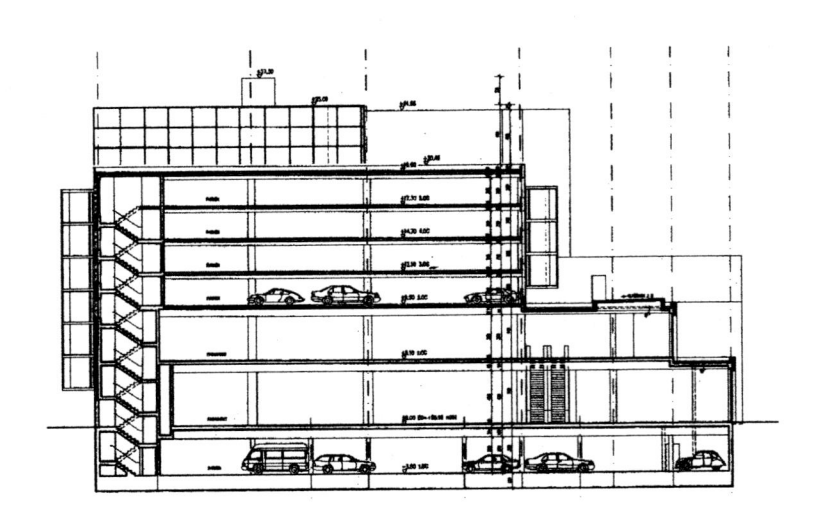

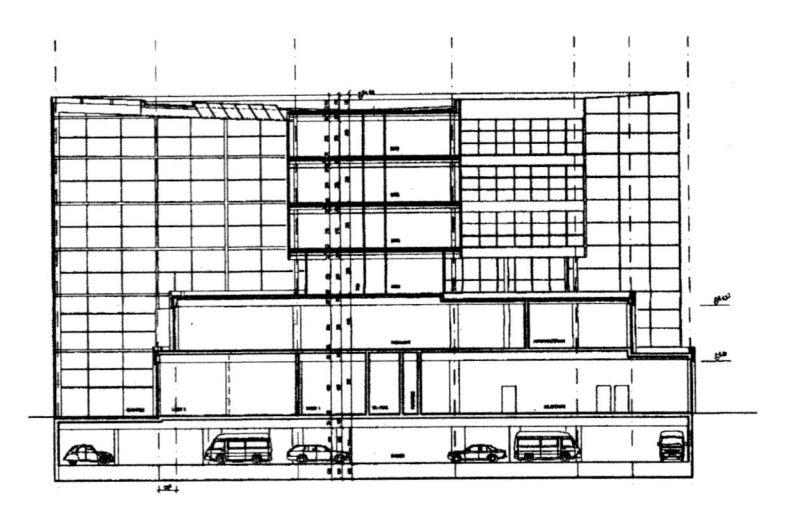

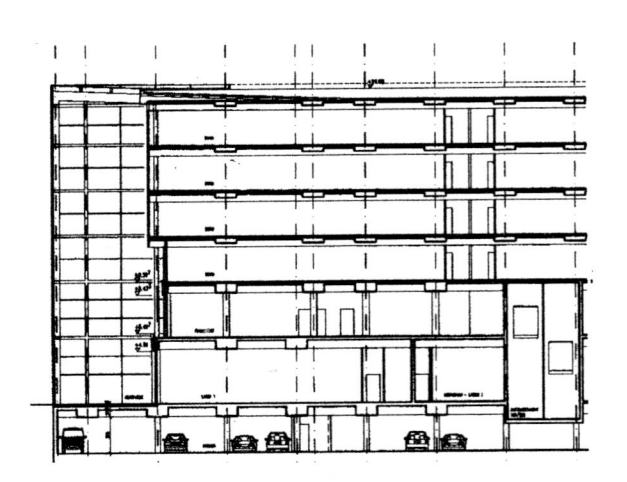

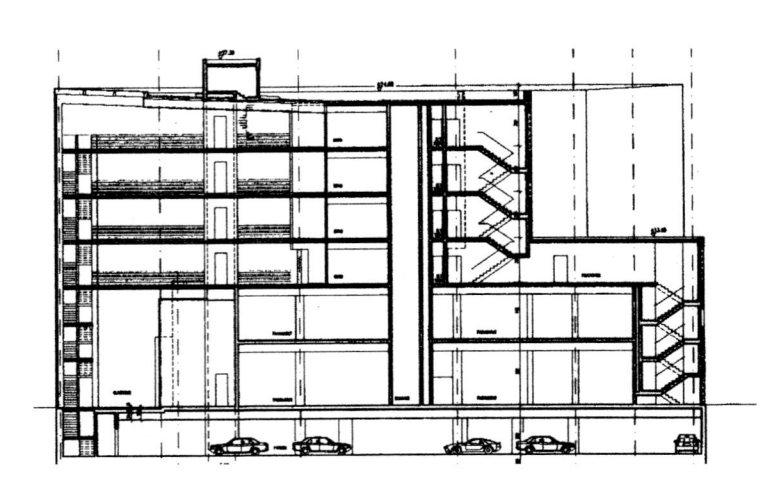

Views of the model. The building features a contrasting combination of a stone unit and transparent glass shell around the north part of the centre.
Gesamtansicht des Modells. Das Gebäude lebt aus der Dualität von monolitischem, kubischen Äußeren, der nach Süden gerichteten steinernen Lochfassade mit einem gläsernen, filigranen und hochtransparenten Inneren des nach Norden ausgerichteten Hallenkörpers, der den Block 3-seitig umhüllt.

SOPHIENSTRASSE

GIPSSTRASSE

ROSENTHALER STRASSE

RO 30
Commercial Complex with Retail, Offices and Apartments
Büro-, Geschäfts- und Apartmentkomplex

The site for the planned project as a whole is situated in the centre of the capital Berlin (in district Mitte), west of Alexanderplatz. The area comprises the top of a long plot stretching from Rosenthaler Strasse north-west between Sophienstrasse and Gipsstrasse. The project is confined on its west side by existing old buildings.

On Rosenthaler Strasse the building formerly occupied by the Wertheimer department store has been retained. This is of outstanding historic importance and is notable for its striking arched arcades. It will be used as a services and trading centre. On the former coal yard at the store, four separate pavilions, transparent and filigree, are planned for use as bistros and shops.

Existing buildings preclude the complex from being given one uniform character. The interior courtyards so typical for Berlin force one to think in terms offering no scope for a building standing alone. Instead, the aim must be to discover new forms of architectural networking.

The project tries to upgrade the inner courtyards by treating these as parts of a separate realm of experience. Without exception, they are given a semi-public character. Making green spaces and planting these is one of the possibilities. Such spaces alternate with two expanses of water dominating the courtyards to the Rosenthaler Strasse and the same size as these. Large parts of the yards, moreover, are protected from the weather by glass roofs. This creates not only a balanced interior climate of pleasant temperature but also an oasis suitable for relaxation. The extreme building density is relieved by these park segments. The second, inner part of the complex features a distinctive design for the courtyards, with projecting and recessed segments of a circle within the new buildings conveying the impression of Baroque sensuousness. Here a proximity is created that enables people to look one another in the "eyes", i.e., the windows, though having to blink in doing so, with the sun enjoying relatively direct access to the fronts of the back courtyards. Here too, the facades start to vibrate with life and one can indeed speak of a hidden "paradise garden" rather than a dismal backyard.

Das Baugrundstück für das geplante Gesamtprojekt liegt im Zentrum der Bundeshauptstadt Berlin (Bezirk Mitte), westlich vom Alexanderplatz. Das Areal bildet den Kopfteil eines langgestreckten Grundstücks, das sich von der Rosenthaler Straße nordwestlich zwischen der Sophien- und der Gipsstraße erstreckt. Das Projekt wird im Westen durch vorhandenen Altbaubestand begrenzt.

An der Rosenthaler Straße ist das Gebäude des ehemaligen Kaufhauses Wertheim erhalten. Es nimmt eine herausragende historische Stellung ein und ist durch ausgeprägte Bogenarkaden charakterisiert. Es wird als Dienstleistungs- und Gewerbezentrum genutzt. Auf dem ehemaligen Kohlenhof des Kaufhauses sind vier einzelne transparente und filigrane Pavillons für Laden- und Bistronutzung geplant.

Der Komplex kann auf Grund der vorhandenen Bausubstanz keine einheitliche Prägung erfahren. Die für Berlin typischen Innenhöfe erzwingen ein Denken, in dem der Solitär keine Chance hat. Es geht statt dessen um neue Formen einer architektonischen Vernetzung.

Das Projekt versucht die Innenhöfe aufzuwerten, indem es sie als Teile eines eigenständigen Erlebnisraumes behandelt. Sie bekommen allesamt einen halböffentlichen Charakter. Begrünung und Bepflanzung der Flächen sind dabei eine der Möglichkeiten. Sie alternieren mit zwei innenhof-großen Wasserflächen, die die Innenhöfe zur Rosenthaler Straße dominieren. Zudem werden weite Teile der Innenhöfe mit Glasdächern vor Witterungseinflüssen geschützt. Das schafft zum einen ein wohltemperiertes, ausgeglichenes Binnenklima und zum anderen eine Entspannung vermittelnde Oase. Die extrem dichte Bebauung wird durch diese Parksegmente aufgelockert. Eine eigenwillige Innenhofgestaltung findet sich im zweiten, inneren Teil der Grundstücksbebauung: vorkragende und zurückspringende Kreissegmente innerhalb der neuen Gebäude vermitteln den Eindruck einer barocken Sinnlichkeit. Hier wird Nähe damit hergestellt, daß man sich in die „Augen", also die Fenster, sehen kann und daß man blinzeln muß, denn die Sonne hat wieder einen relativ direkten Zugriff auf die Hinterhof-Fronten. Da beginnen dann auch die Fassaden wieder lebendig zu vibrieren und man kann eher von einem versteckten „Paradiesgärtlein" reden als von einem tristen Hinterhof.

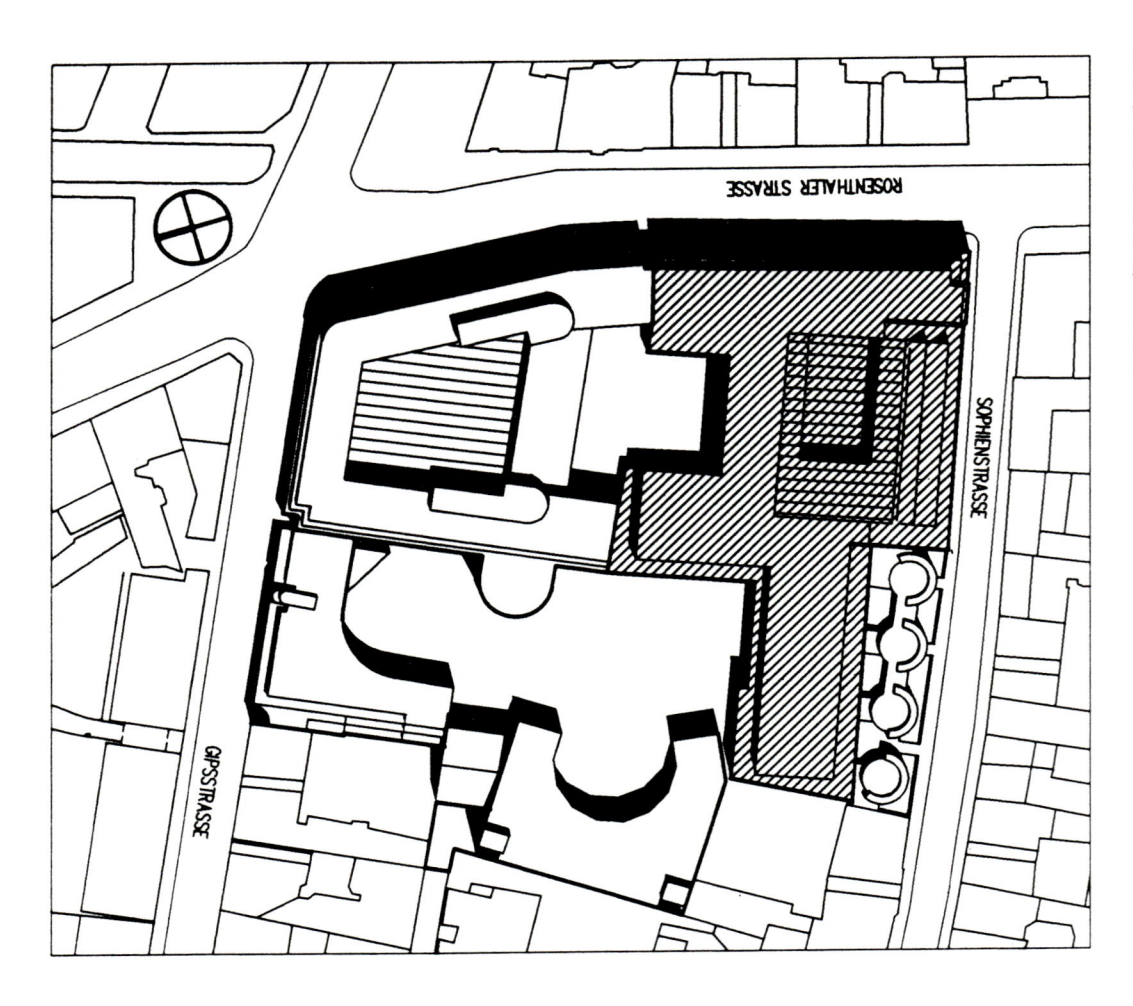

Site plan. Below: the model, seen from the west of the mixed used project of apartments, offices and shops in the city centre of Berlin.
Lageplan. Unten: das Modell vom Westen gesehen. Das Projekt umfaßt Apartments, Büros und Ladenzonen im Zentrum der Hauptstadt Berlin.

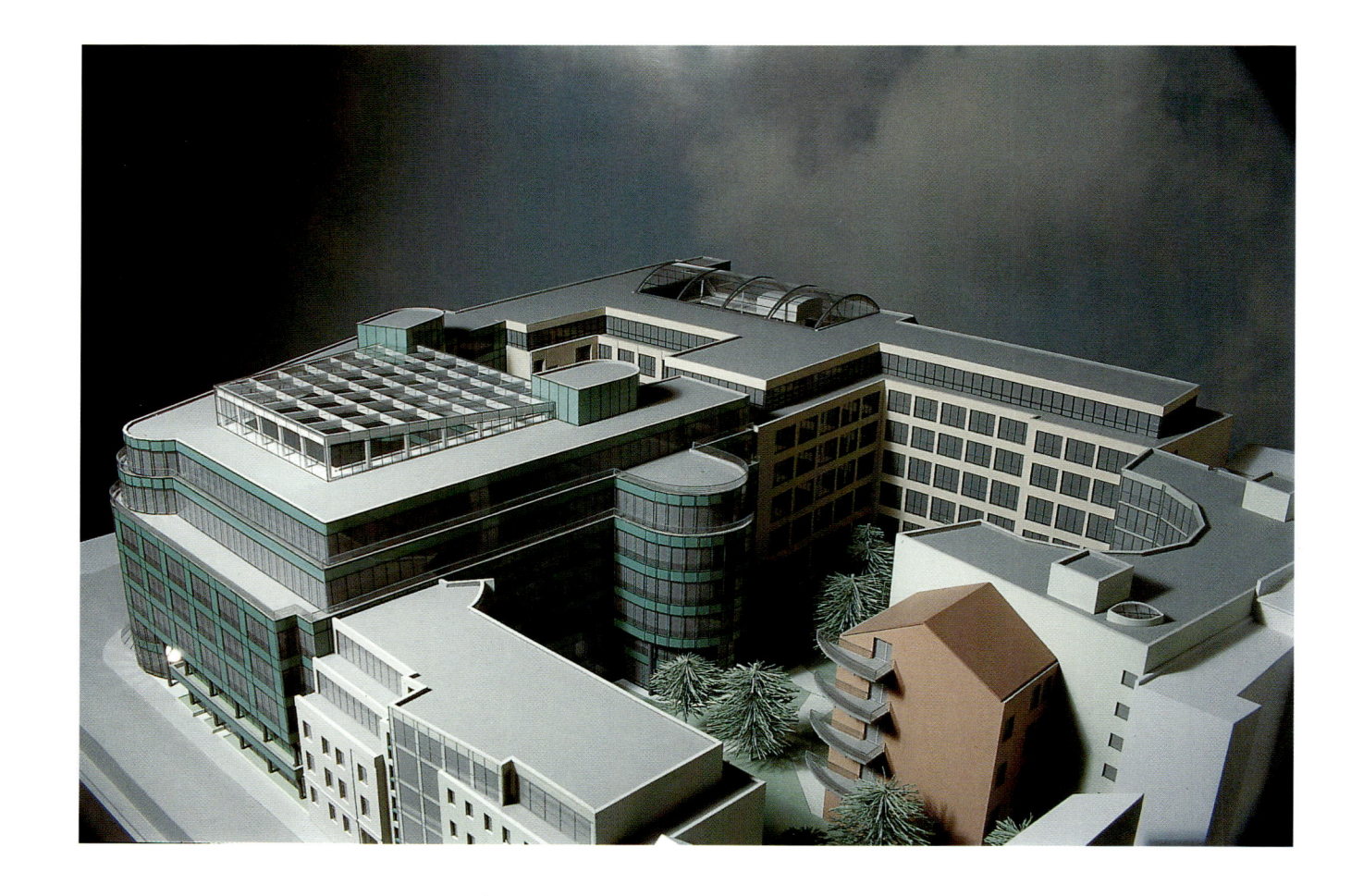

Detail of the semi-public courtyard inside the complex.
Detail des halböffentlichen Innenhofs des Komplexes.

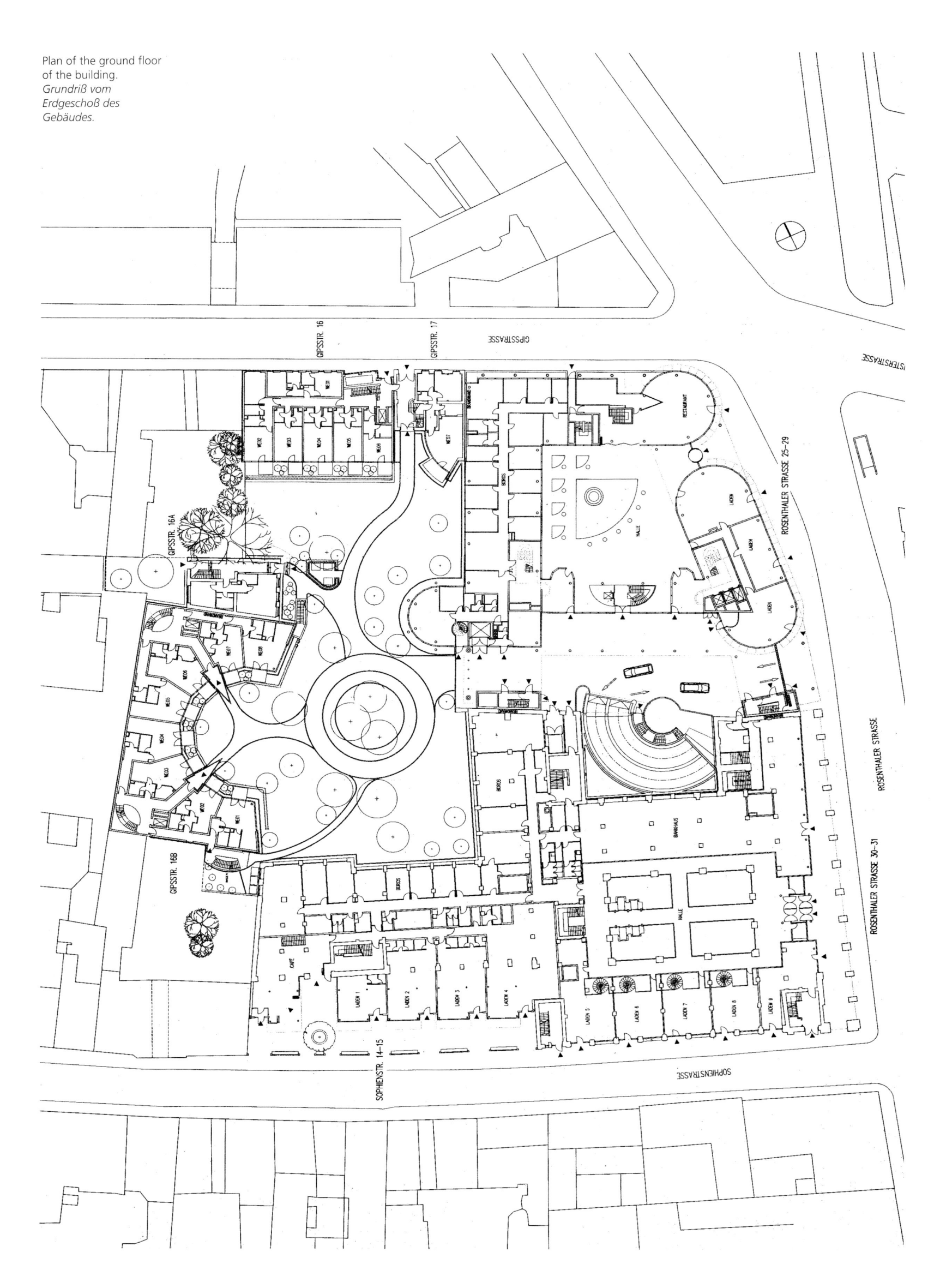

Plan of the ground floor of the building.
Grundriß vom Erdgeschoß des Gebäudes.

Views of the model. The complex fits into the Berlin cityscape as a multi-purpose complex combining private-public functions around a large central courtyard.
Ansichten des Modells. Der Komplex fügt sich in der deutschen Metropole mit einem Mehrzweckcharakter ein, bestehend aus privaten und öffentlichen Einrichtungen, die um verschiedene Innenhöfe gelegt sind.

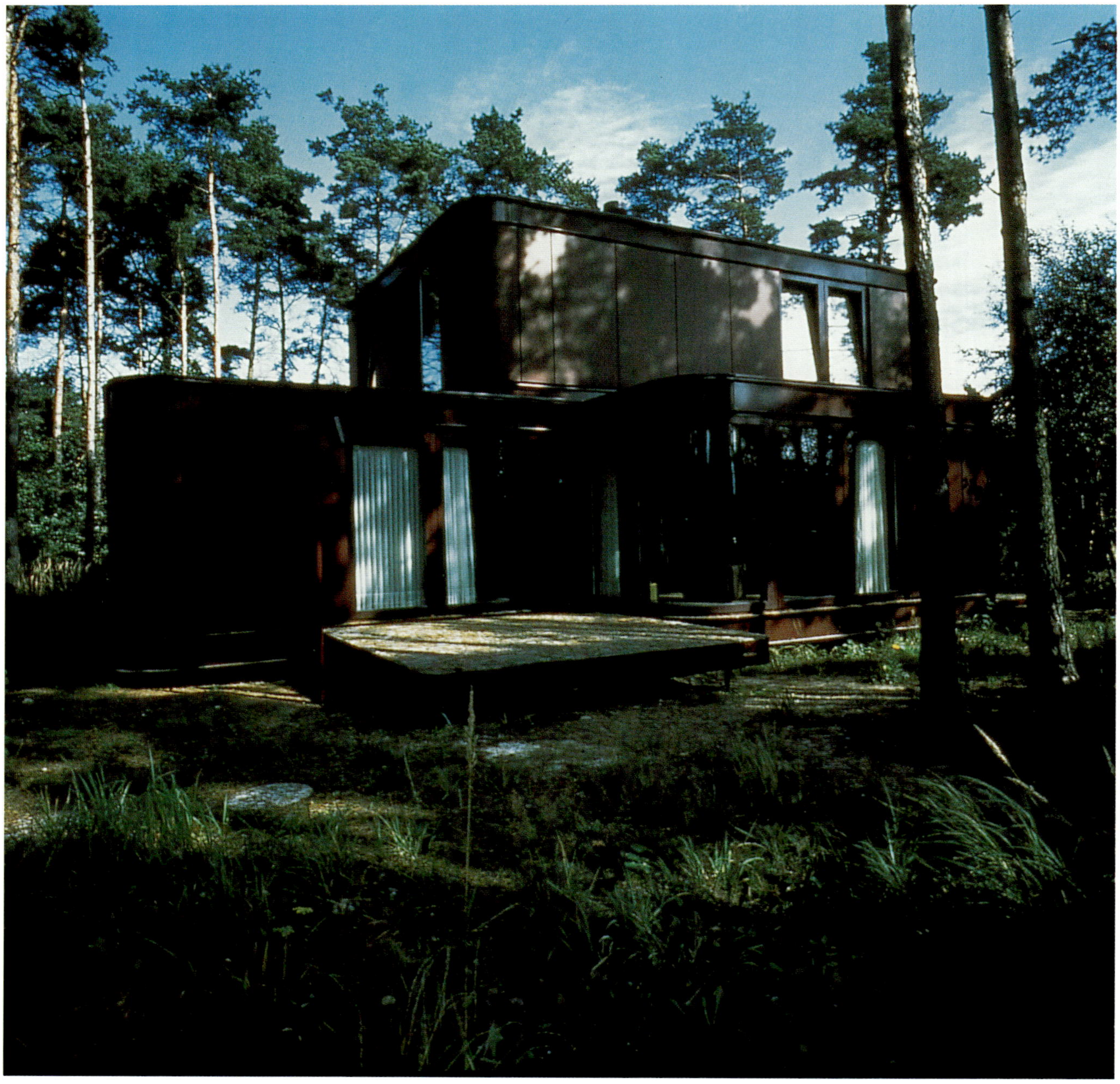

HAUS WULF
One-Family-House
Einfamilienhaus

The house has been set into a thickly wooded plot as a foreign body - and a deliberate pointer to human building activity. In common with the client, the architects wished to avoid helping themselves to nature. Rather the idea was that nature and civilization should encounter each other self-confidently and independently while commencing a mutual dialogue.

Very simple shapes were chosen for the dwelling house: the ground plan comprises four rounded triangles of slightly varying size. These are sympathetic shapes reminiscent of metal baking tins of the kind gladly used for keeping small bits and pieces. The roundings and the anodized aluminium facade - in which the windows seem to be cut like peepholes - convey a feeling of sheltered comfort. The offset triangles in each of the rooms mean that one always feels slightly outdoors, since parts of the facade of the house can be seen when looking out of the windows. So the protective character of the building is repeatedly experienced through the visual impression.

The living area is concentrated into a small space and stands in the desired contrast to burgeoning nature.

The structure as built avoids the house becoming a cave on account of excessive size (whether desired or undesired). Respectful co-existence was attempted and has also been achieved for the long term.

Das Haus ist in das dicht bewachsene Waldgrundstück als ein Fremdkörper hineingesetzt worden, als ein bewußter Hinweis auf menschliches Bauen. Die Architekten wollten - im Sinne des Bauherrn - kein Andienern an die Natur. Natur und Kultur sollten sich selbstbewußt und selbständig gegenüberstehen und dennoch einen Dialog miteinander aufnehmen.

Für das Wohnhaus sind sehr einfache Formen gewählt worden: vier abgerundete Rechtecke von leicht variierender Größe bilden den Grundriß. Es sind anheimelnde Formen, die an metallene Gebäckschachteln erinnern, die gern zum Aufbewahren von Kleinteilen benutzt worden sind. Schutz und Wohlgefühl vermitteln die Rundungen und die eloxierte Aluminiumfassade, in die die Fenster wie Ausgucke hineingeschnitten zu sein scheinen.

Man ist durch die versetzten Rechtecke in jedem der Zimmer immer auch ein wenig draußen, weil man Fassadenteile des Hauses beim Blick aus den Fenstern sieht. So erfährt man den Schutzcharakter des Hauses immer wieder auch über den visuellen Eindruck.

Das Wohnen ist auf wenig Raum konzentriert und steht in einem gewollten Kontrast zu der sich ausbreitenden Natur.

Mit der durchgeführten Konstruktion ist vermieden worden, daß das Haus durch (gewollte oder ungewollte) Überwucherung zur Höhle wird. Ein respektvolles Nebeneinander war angestrebt und ist auch langfristig erreicht worden.

Right and opposite page: the terrace extending out towards the wood over the south-west corner. Below, from left to right, plans of the basement, ground floor, and first floor.
*Rechts und auf der Seite nebenan: die Terrasse, die in den Wald nach Südwesten auskragt.
Unten, von links nach rechts: Grundriß des Kellergeschosses, des Erd- und ersten Obergeschosses.*

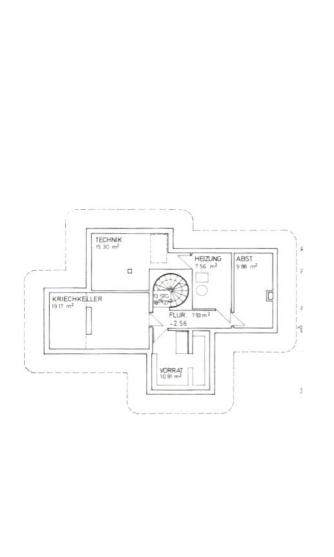

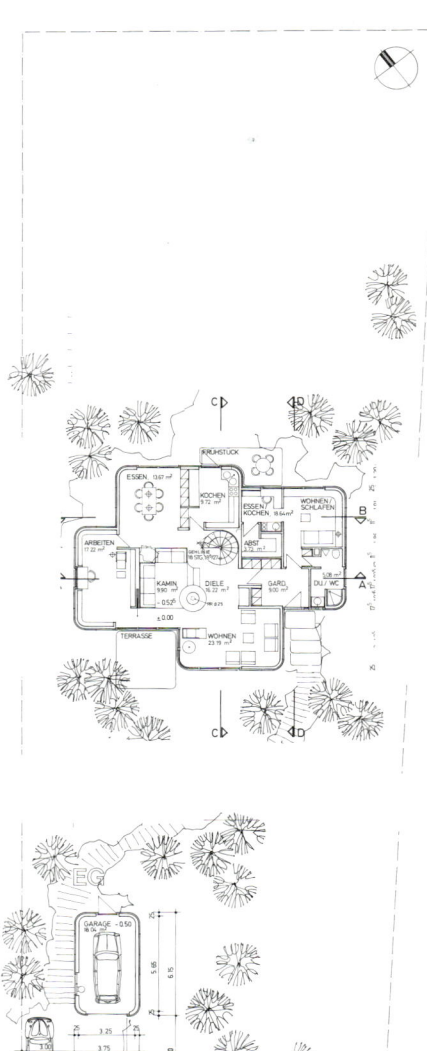

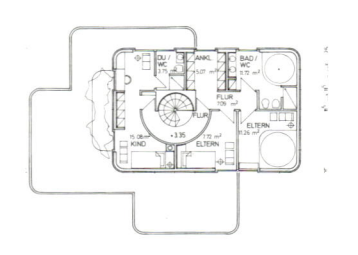

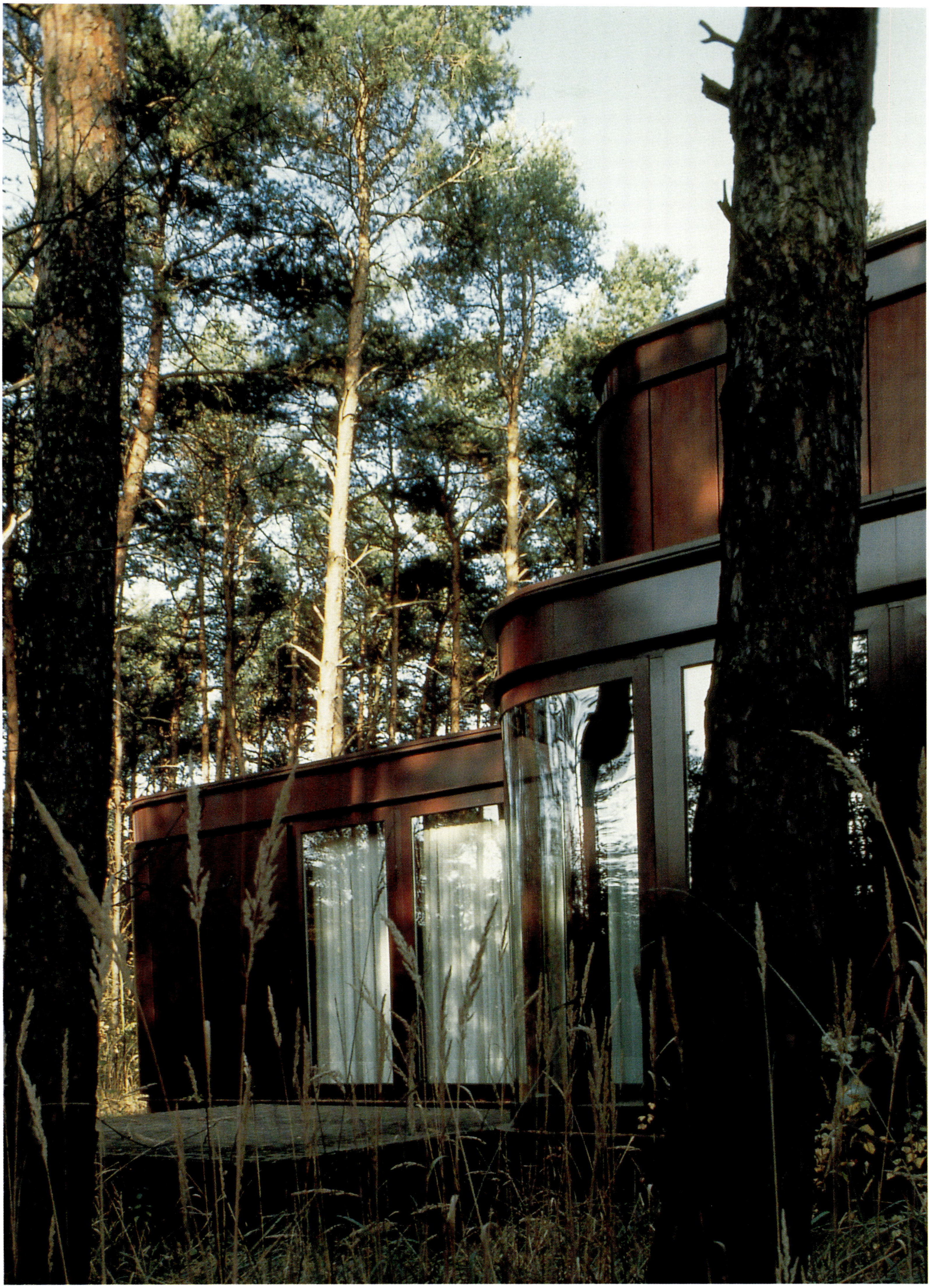

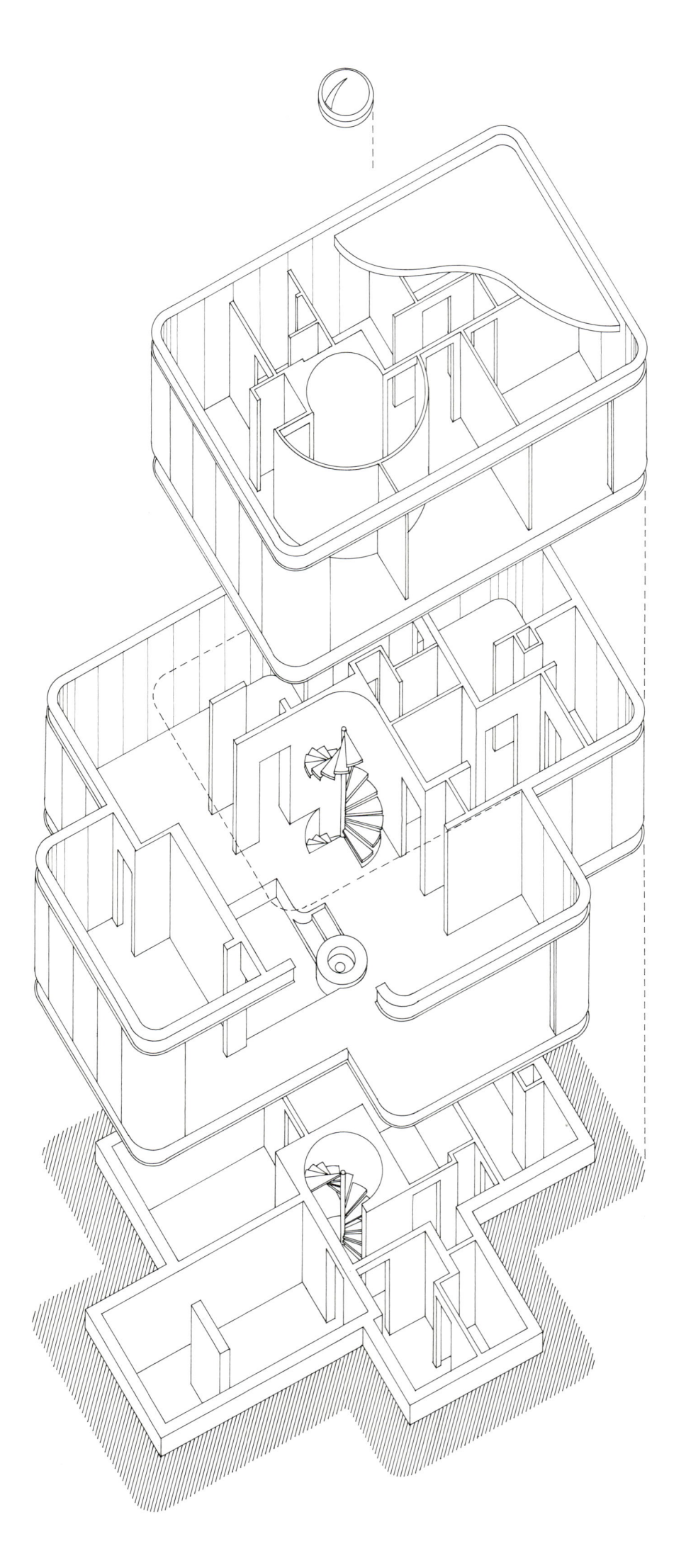

Axonometric blow-up.
Opposite page, top:
sections. Below: detail
of the north-east corner.
*Isometrische
Explosionsperspektive.
Auf der Seite nebenan,
oben: Schnitte. Unten:
Detail der Nord-Ost-
Fassade.*

144

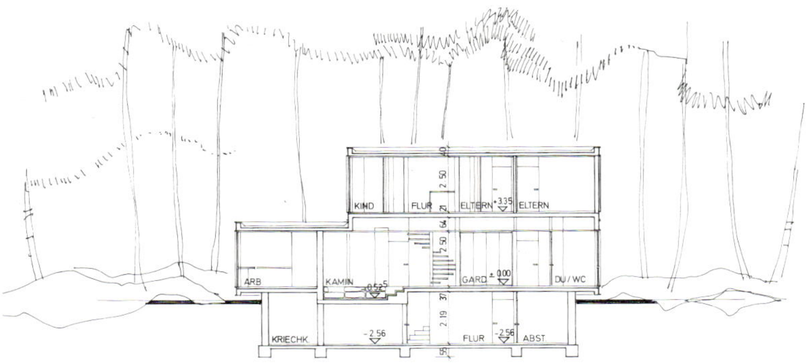

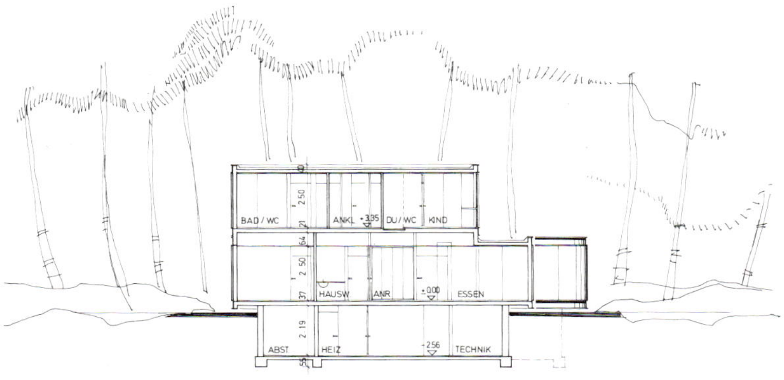

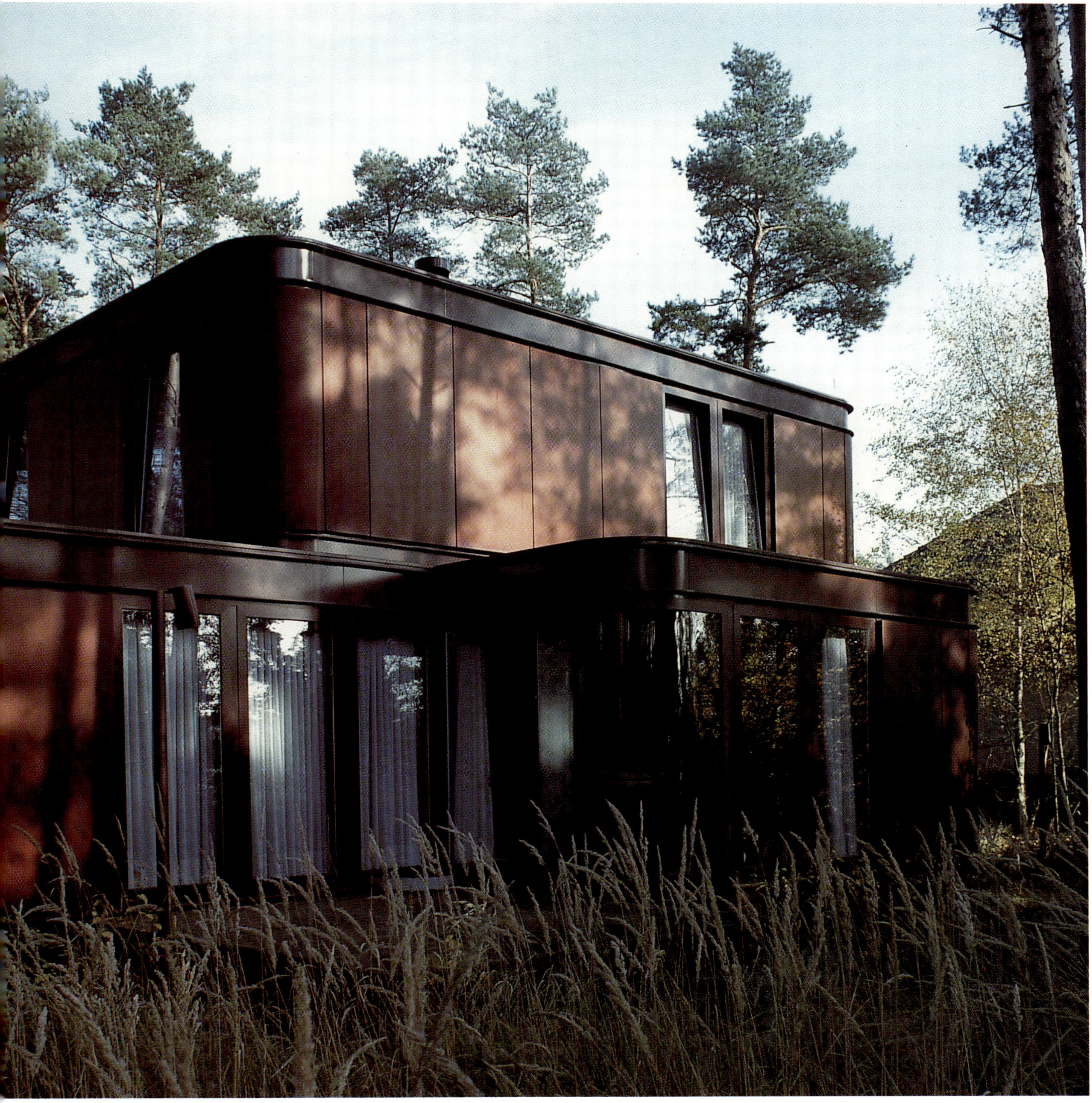

Details of the outside facades of the house clad with reddish-coloured anodized aluminium panels contrasting with the green of the surrounding trees.

Details der äußeren Fassade des Hauses. Eine eloxierte Alumiumfassade wurde vorgehängt, die in ihrer rötlichen Farbgebung besonders reizvoll zu den über die Jahreszeiten wechselnden Grünfarben des Waldes im Kontrast steht.

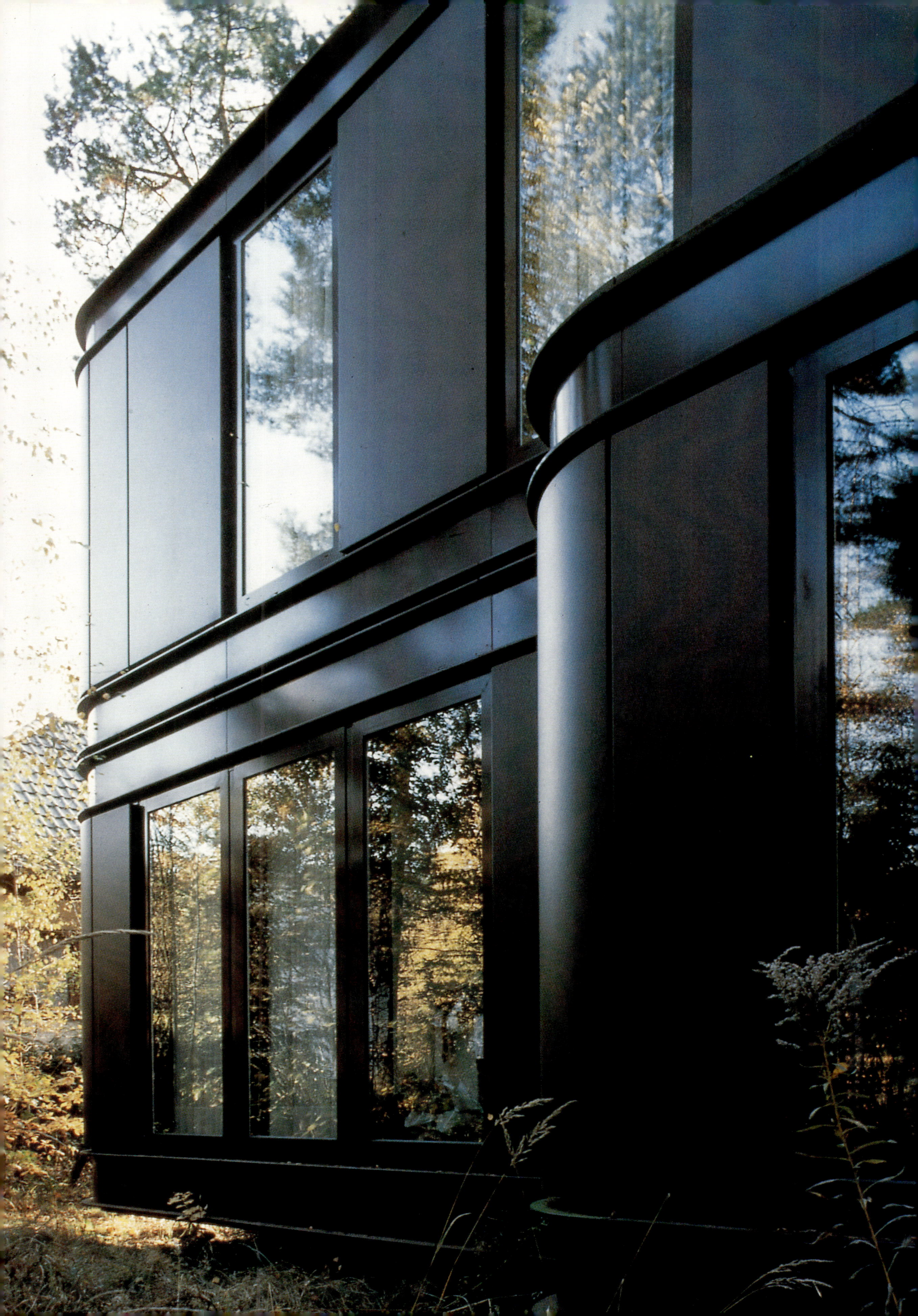

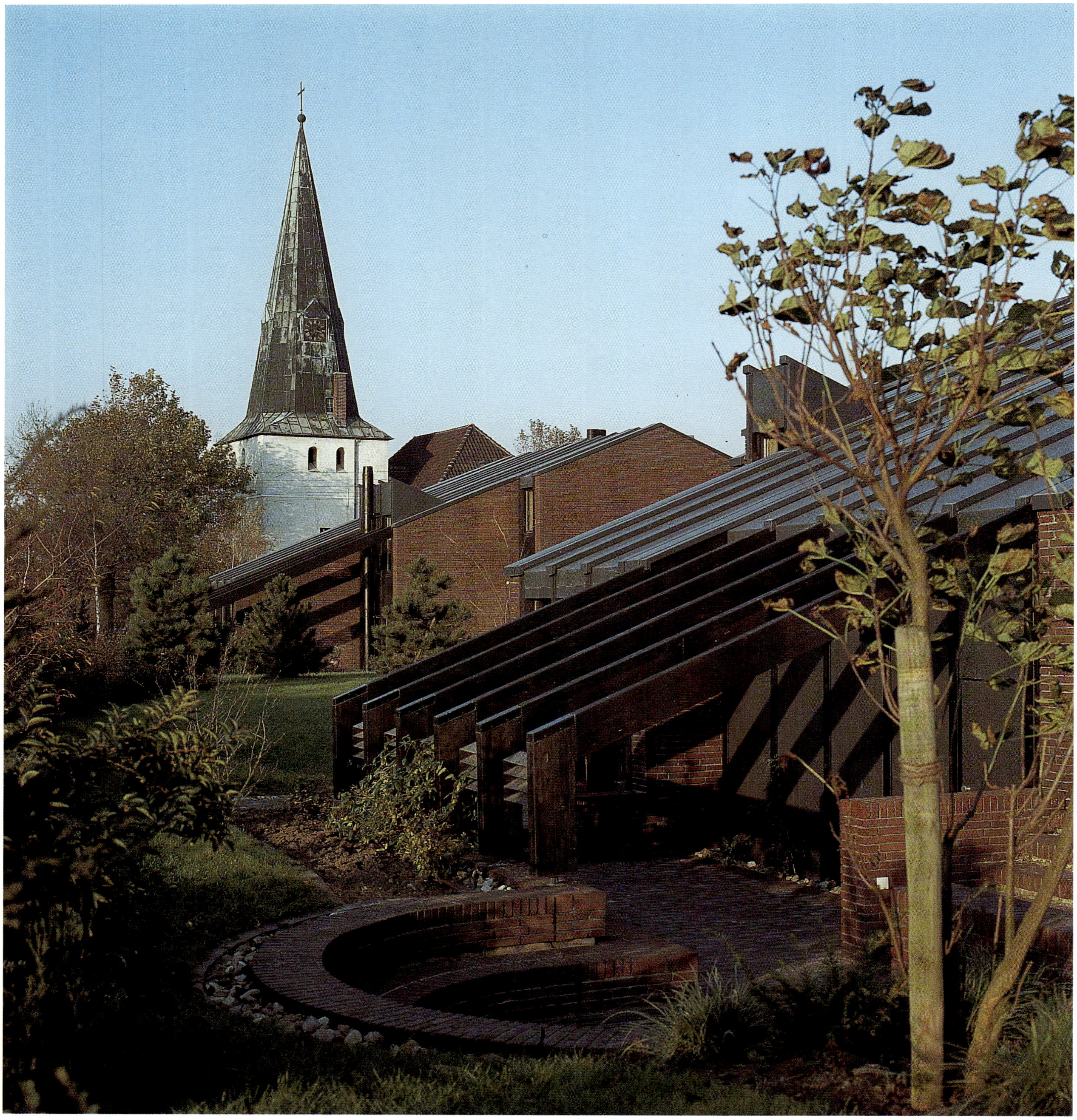

HEMME-HOF
House-Ensemble
Wohnhausgruppe

Openness and compactness have become elements of the atmosphere in this ensemble of buildings. These are the cornerstones within which an exciting individuality in building and accommodation has been developed. Here we have the openness of common usage of open spaces offset by the compactness of the separate dwelling houses. These houses do not set out to be transparent. The basic structural pattern of glued trusses makes the technical thinking very clear, but also points the immense flexibility and variability these incorporate.

The separate accommodation blocks have strongly structured ground plans differing in nuances yet not in principle. The facades blend into the surrounding scenery and thus avoid the impression of wishing to defy nature. Instead, one discerns a tendency here to surrender to the expansiveness associated with any landscape in agricultural use.

Offenheit und Geschlossenheit sind zu atmosphärischen Elementen in dieser Ensemble-Bebauung geworden. Sie sind die Eckpfeiler, innerhalb derer sich eine spannungsreiche Individualität in Bauen und Wohnen entwickelt. Da ist die Offenheit des gemeinsamen Nutzens der Freiflächen und da ist die Geschlossenheit der einzelnen Wohnhäuser. Die Häuser sind nicht auf Transparenz angelegt. Das konstruktive Grundmuster der Leimbinder macht das technische Denken sehr deutlich, verweist aber zugleich auch auf die darin liegende große Flexibilität und Variabilität.

Die einzelnen Wohnbauten haben stark strukturierte Grundrisse, die sich in Nuancen, aber nicht im Prinzip unterscheiden. Die Fassaden schieben sich in die umgebende Landschaft hinein und vermeiden somit den Eindruck, als wollten sie der Natur trotzen. Man spürt viel eher die Tendenz, sich auf die Weitläufigkeit einzulassen, die man mit bäuerlich genutzter Landschaft verbindet.

Site plan of the five-unit residential complex.
Lageplan des Wohnkomplexes, der aus fünf Einfamilienhäusern besteht.

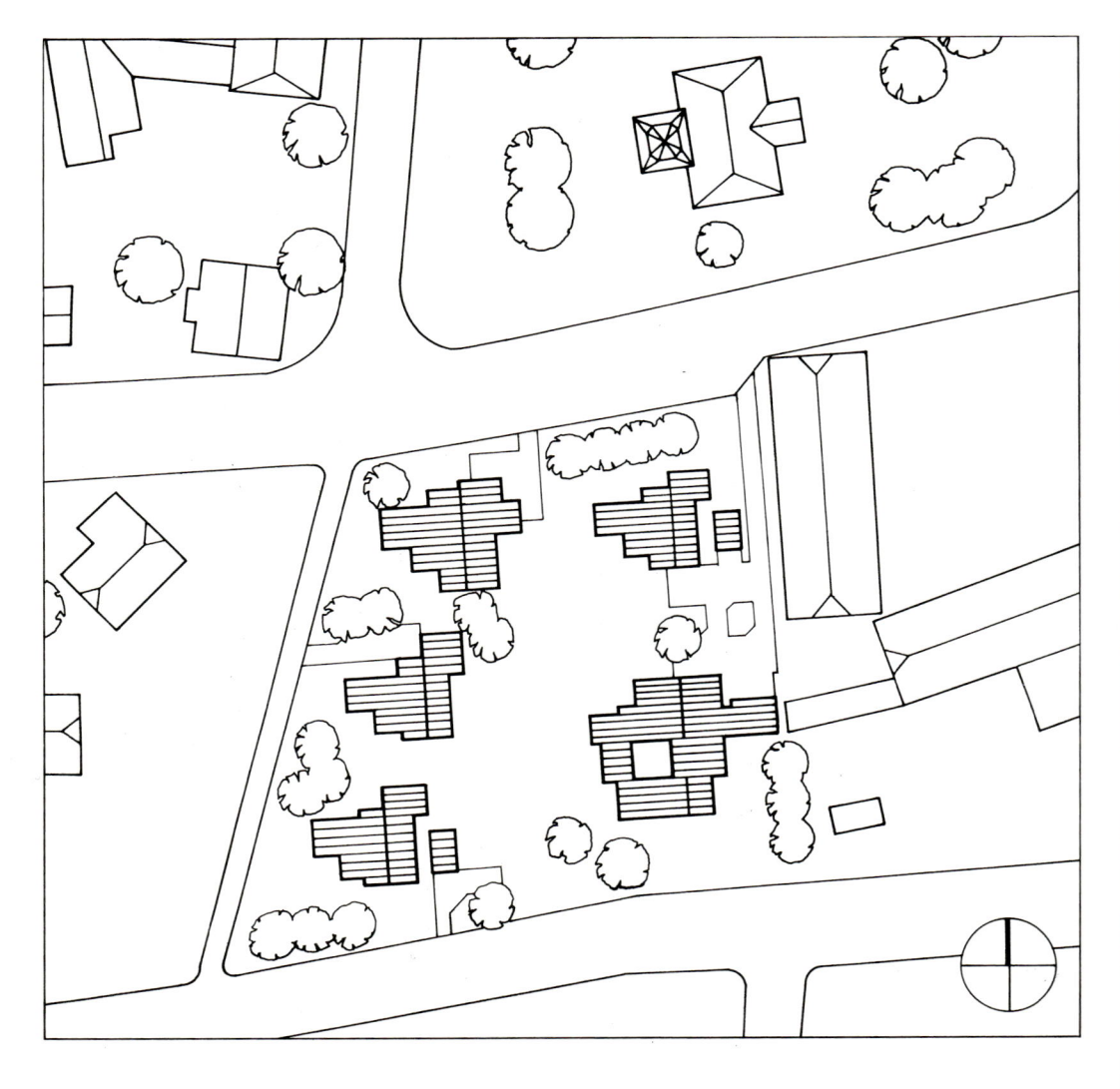

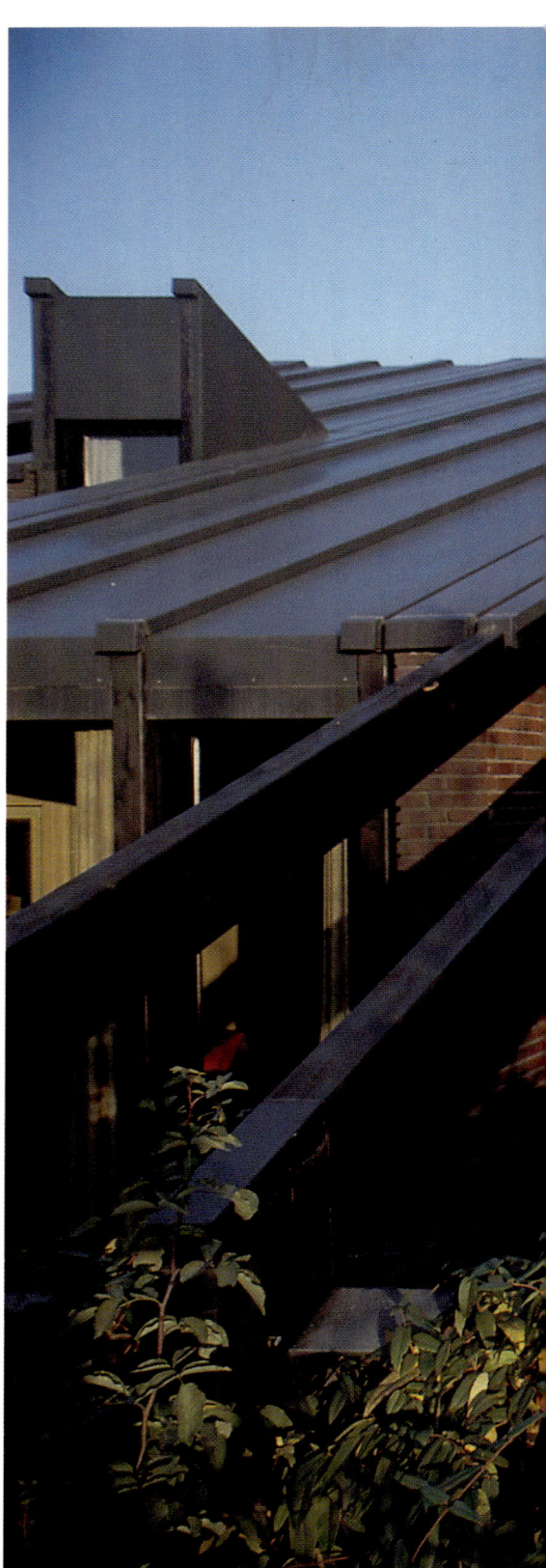

Details of the roofs made of prefabricated materials constructed out of special sandwich metal sheets with a Tedlar coating and exposed laminated wooden beams.

Details der Dachabdeckung, die mit vorgefertigten Materialien gebaut sind und die aus einem speziell angefertigten Sandwich-Blech mit Tedlar-Beschichtung und sichtbaren Trägern aus Leimbinderholz bestehen.

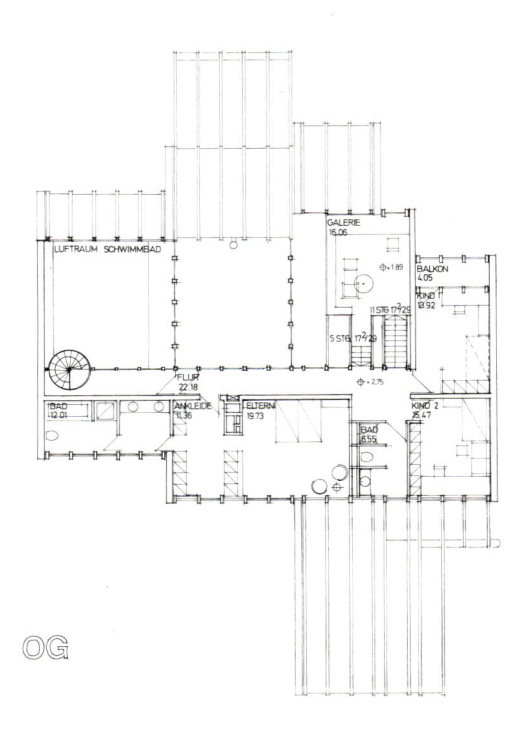

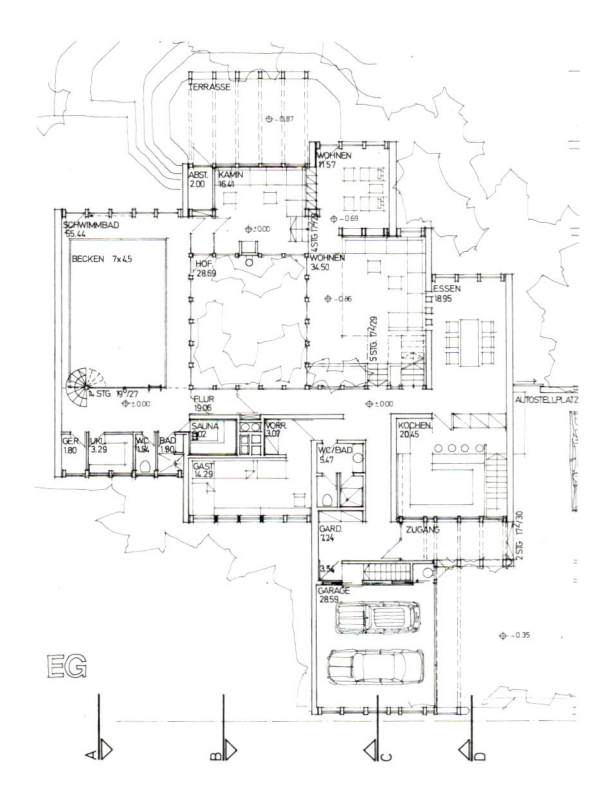

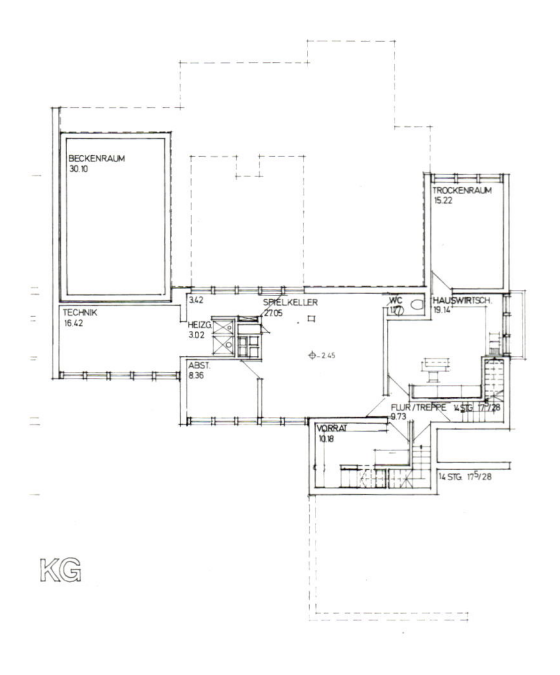

Left, from bottom up: plans of the basement, ground floor and first floor.
Below: partial view of the courtyard in one of the buildings.
*Links, von unten nach oben: Grundriß des Kellergeschosses, des Erd- und ersten Obergeschosses.
Unten: Blick in einen der Innenhöfe.*

Left: partial view of the ground-floor lounge, visually connected to the outside courtyard by wide glass windows. Below: the stairs leading up to the top floor, where the bedrooms and other private quarters are located.
Links: Einsicht in das Wohnzimmer im Erdgeschoß. Dieser Bereich ist visuell mit dem Hof dank großer Fenster verbunden. Unten: die Treppe zu den oberen Geschossen, wo die Schlafzimmer und andere private Zimmer gelegen sind.

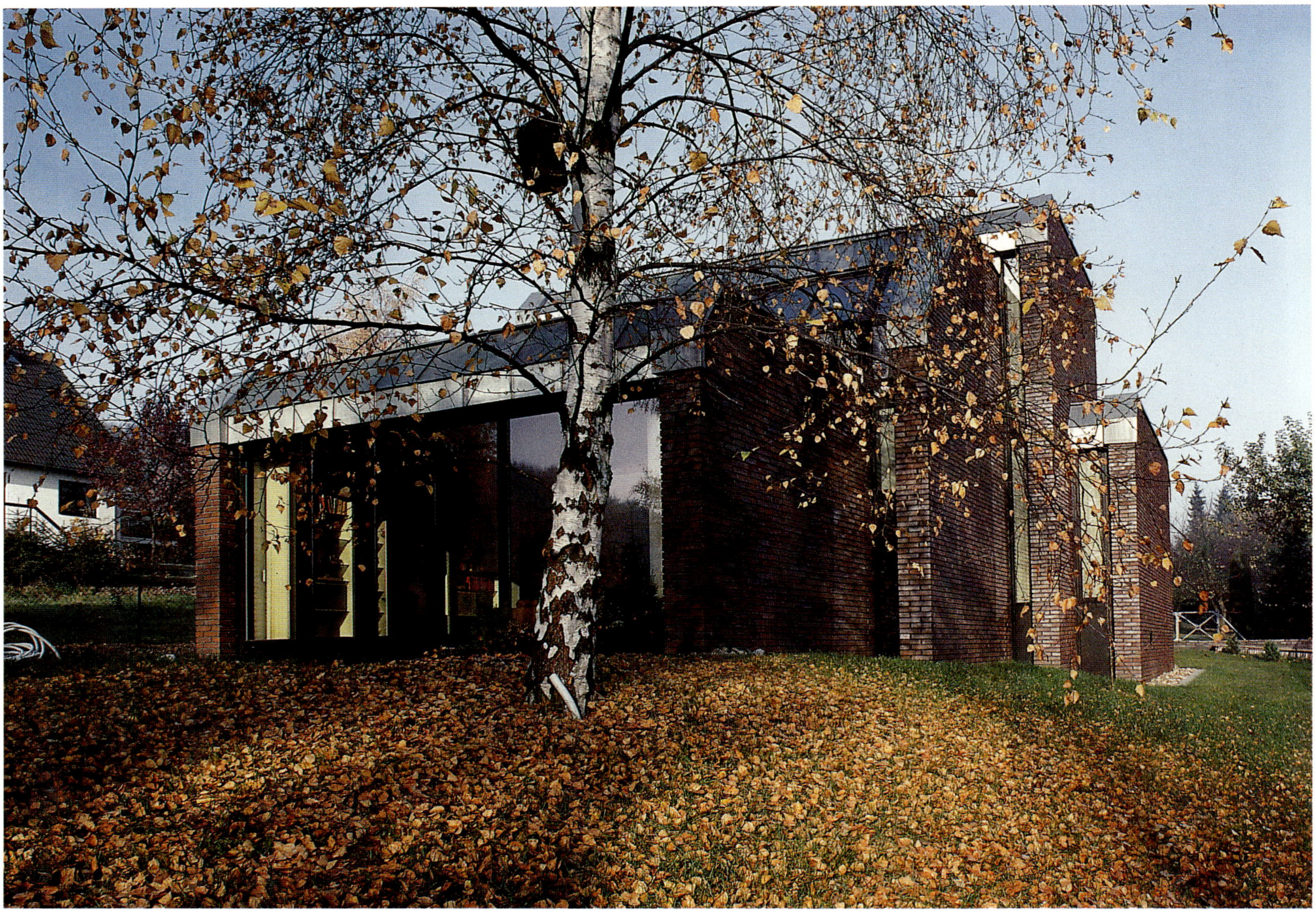

HAUS KÖRNER
One-Family-House
Einfamilienhaus

"The idea was to structure and arrange a very small living area in such a way as to provide stimulating accommodation and living conditions for a married couple without children, but with varied leisure and professional interests.

A wish was also expressed that the need for maintenance of the open spaces should be reduced to a minimum, all the more so since the plot consists of a long, narrow piece of land parallel to the run of the slope. Sheer walls of traditional construction and sintered blue-red brick were laid on an east-west axis. The interim zones consisted of prefabricated wood-glass elements with sheet zinc cladding. The indoor living areas are constructed as open living and sleeping areas, often of different heights, so that only the sanitary and kitchen zones are enclosed." (completed 1977)

This free-standing dwelling house avoids having an identical silhouette on all sides. Instead it presents an individual and distinct appearance on each side. Only along its length, to north and south, is there a load-bearing wall acting as a screen. Yet this does not represent any effort at enclosure since the two "walls" are constructed of several panels in telescopic sequence. The block opens up to the surrounding landscape to west and east with room-high windows. If the cellar is included, there are four distinctly different levels. So the side silhouettes also display the shape of a terraced hillock. The separate spaces are clearly separated and are completed by a flat roof in the form of a hipped roof.

The diversity of the exterior appearance reflects the multifarious possibilities for using the interior.

„Eine sehr kleine Wohnfläche sollte so interessant strukturiert und gestaltet werden, daß ein Ehepaar ohne Kinder, jedoch mit differenzierten Freizeit- und Berufsinteressen, anregende Wohn- und Lebensverhältnisse erhalten sollte. Gleichzeitig bestand der Wunsch, die Außenanlagen möglichst wenig unterhalten zu müssen, zumal das Grundstück ein sehr langes, schmales, parallel zum Hangablauf liegendes Gelände darstellt. Es wurden ostwestlich ausgerichtete Wandscheiben aus blaurot gesintertem Backstein in traditioneller Bauweise gesetzt. Dabei wurden die Zwischenzonen als Holz-Glas-Fertigelemente mit Zinkblechverkleidung erstellt. Die inneren Wohnbereiche sind als offene, mehrfach höhenversetzte Wohn- und Schlafbereiche ausgebildet, so daß nur die Sanitär- und Küchenbereiche geschlossene Zonen ergeben." (Ausführung 1977)

Das freistehende Wohnhaus vermeidet eine allseits gleiche Silhouette. Statt dessen bietet es von jeder Seite eine individuelle und eigenständige Erscheinung. Nur in der Längsausdehnung, zur nördlichen und südlichen Seite, gibt es ein abschirmendes und tragendes Mauerwerk. Dabei wurde keine Geschlossenheit angestrebt, denn die beiden „Wände" bauen sich aus mehreren Wandscheiben zusammen, die teleskopartig aufeinander folgen. Nach Westen und Osten öffnet sich der Baukörper zur umgebenden Landschaft mit raumhohen Fenstern. Unter Einschluß des Kellergeschosses gibt es vier deutlich unterschiedene Ebenen. Die seitlichen Silhouetten zeigen deshalb auch eine terrassierte Hügelform. Die einzelnen Räume behalten einen deutlichen Solitärcharakter und werden mit jeweils einem Flachdach (in Form eines gedrückten Walmdaches) abgeschlossen.

Die Vielfalt der äußeren Erscheinung spiegelt die vielfältigen Nutzungsmöglichkeiten des Innenraumes wider.

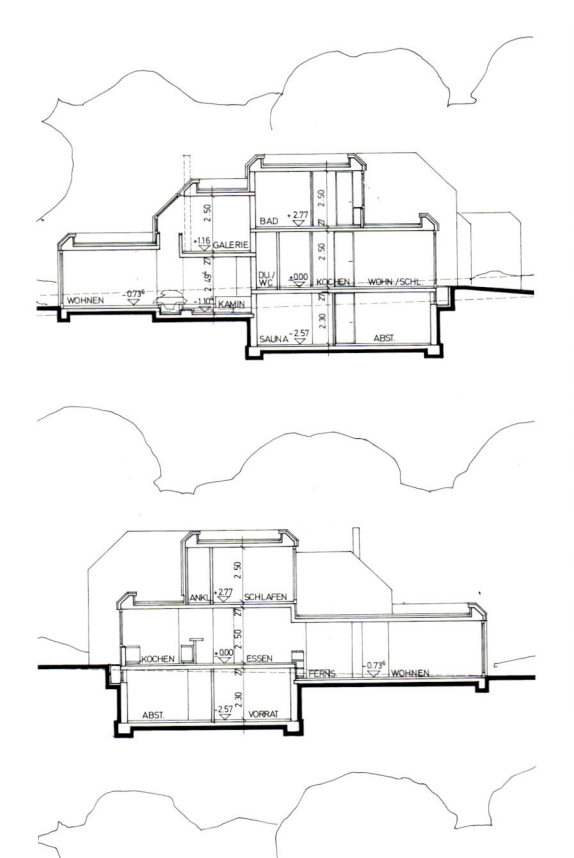

Above: the east facade of the single-family unit.
Below, from left to right: plans of the basement, ground floor and first floor.
Left, from bottom up: several sections.
Opposite page: detail of the facade, made of sintered bricks in the traditional way.

*Oben: die Ostfassade des Einfamilienhauses.
Unten, von links nach rechts: Grundriß des Kellergeschosses, des Erd- und ersten Obergeschosses.
Links, von unten nach oben: diverse Schnitte.
Auf der Seite gegenüber: Details der Wandscheiben, die aus gesinterten Klinkersteinen in traditioneller Bauweise erstellt wurden.*

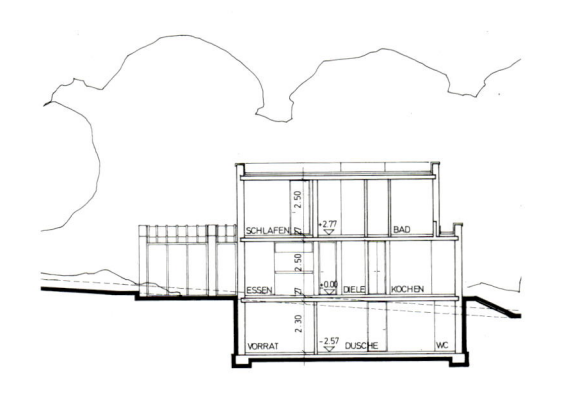

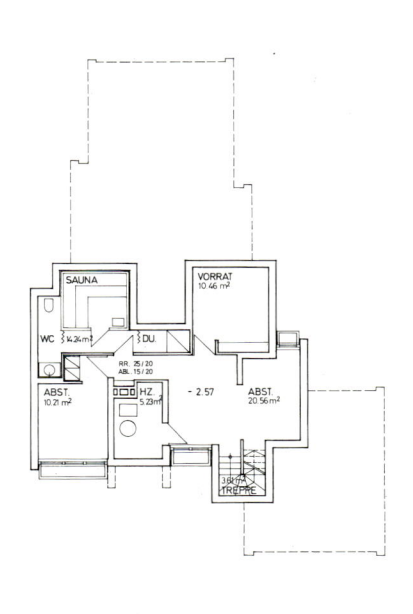

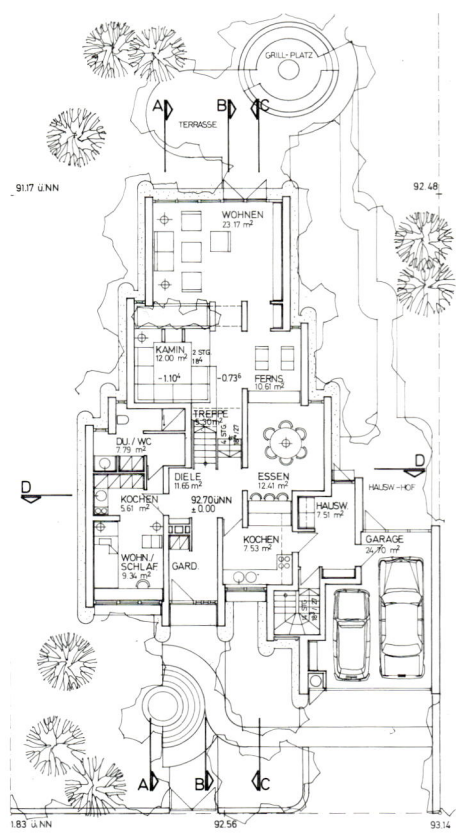

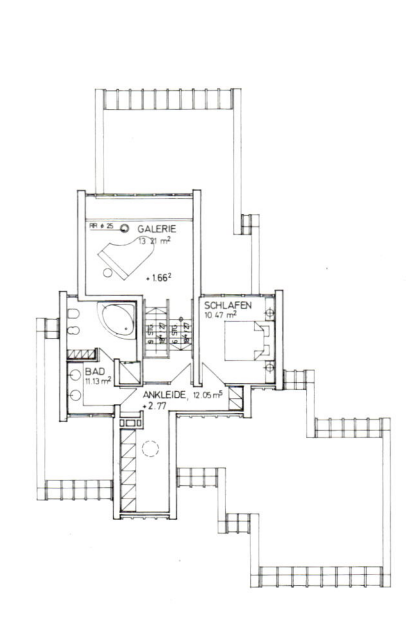

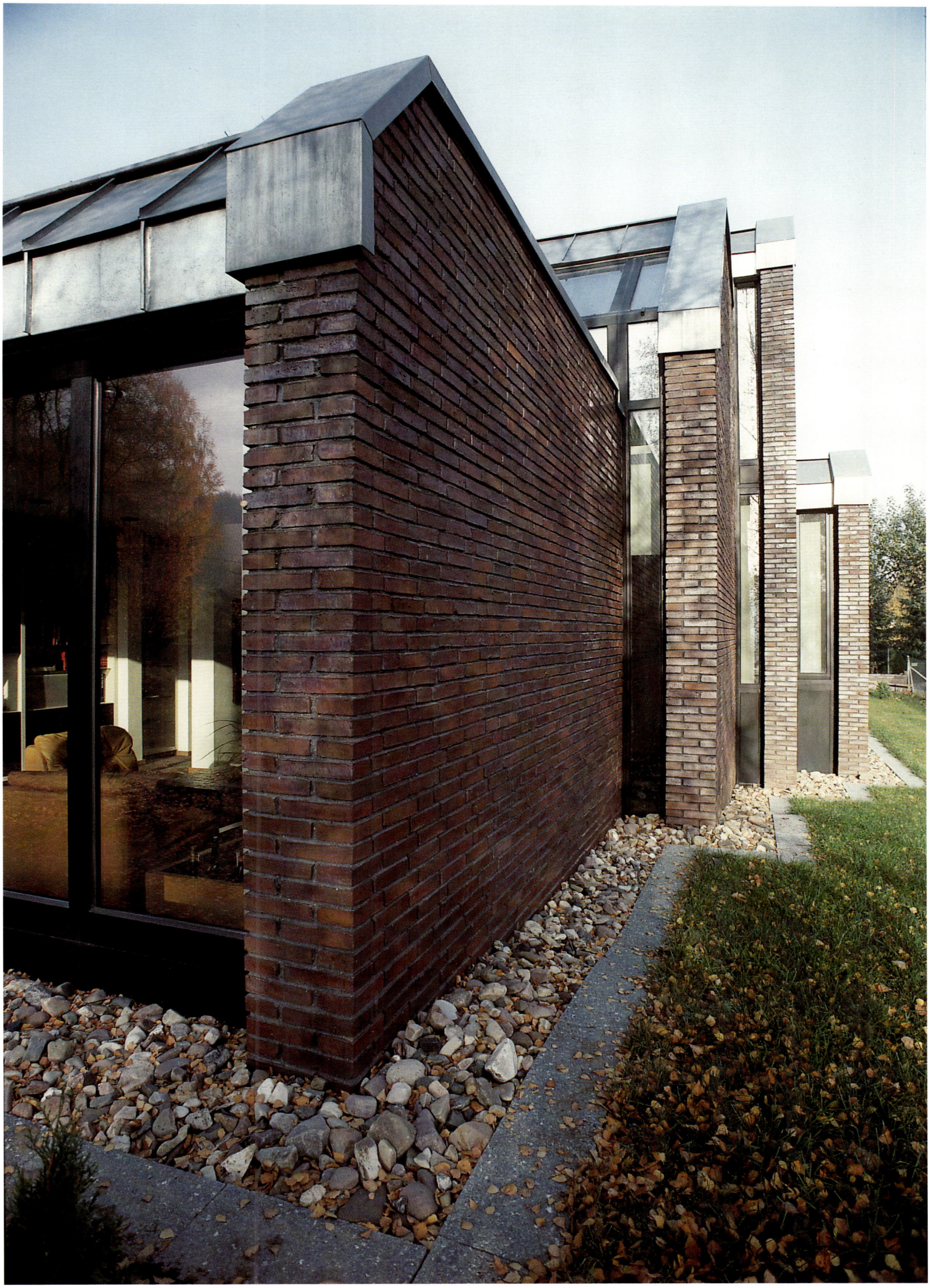

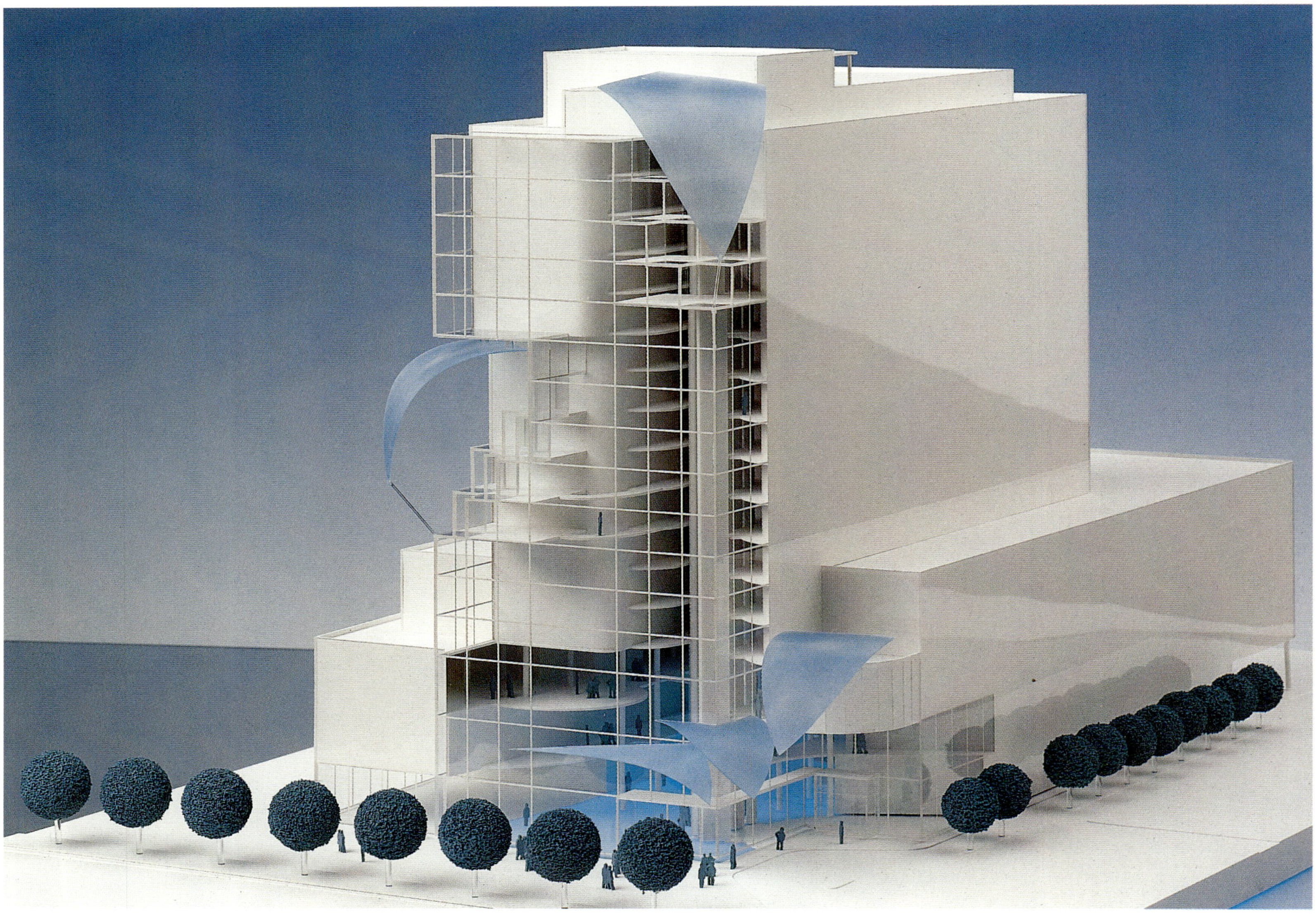

PLOT 176
Hotel and Shopping Mall
Hotel- und Einkaufspassage

The building rises 16 storeys above ground level, three more lie underground. A block with a slender frontage to Rigga Road extends well back into the plot and is of considerable volume.

The purpose of the complex consists of a café, restaurants, a dance hall, conference rooms and a hotel. The entrance area for the mall is laid out as a visible link running the entire height of the building. A transparency flooded with light guarantees an open atmosphere by day and by night without imposing a disquieting lack of privacy.

The mall area draws the exterior like some measured vacuum through the curtain facade with its reflective solar glass plus a central hall three storeys high. A very extensive green area in the middle of the block replaces the outside environment with an atmosphere of wellbeing. An air circulation system backed by air conditioning creates a natural climate and an optimal atmosphere in the mall and in other public floors of the building. Various sun awnings are attached to the facade and function as eye-catching providers of shade.

The project was designed as a skeleton structure of reinforced concrete of conventional construction and with the customary span lengths. The apartment and hotel floors are envisaged as being of reinforced concrete bulkhead construction.

Sechzehn Stockwerke hoch erhebt sich das Gebäude über die Straßenebene, drei Ebenen liegen unter der Erde. Der zur Straßenfront der Rigga Road hin schlanke Baukörper erstreckt sich deutlich in die Tiefe des Grundstücks und zeigt ein beachtliches Volumen.

Eine Shopping Mall mit Café, Restaurants, Ballsaal und Konferenzräumen und ein Hotel sind die Nutzer des Komplexes. Der Eingangsbereich für die Mall ist als gebäudehohe sichtbare Verbindung gestaltet. Lichtdurchflutete Transparenz gewährt am Tage wie in der Nacht eine atmosphärische Offenheit, ohne eine störende Durchsichtigkeit zu offerieren.

Der Mall-Bereich zieht durch die Vorhangfassade mit Sonnenschutzreflexionsglas und durch eine drei Stockwerk hohe zentrale Halle nach Außen wie ein dosiertes Vakuum nach Innen. Ein sehr umfangreicher Grünbereich in der Mitte des Baukörpers transformiert die äußere Umwelt in eine Atmosphäre des Wohlbefindens. Ein von Klimaanlagen unterstütztes Zirkulationssystem bildet eine natürliche Thermik und ein optimales Raumklima in der Mall wie in den anderen Nutzungsgeschossen des Gebäudes.

An der Fassade sind verschiedene Sonnensegel angebracht, die Blickfang wie Schattenspender zugleich sind.

Das Projekt ist als Stahlbeton-Skelettbau konzipiert in konventioneller Bauweise und in den dabei konstruktiv üblichen Spannweiten. Apartment- und Hotelgeschosse sind in Stahlbetonschotterbauweise vorgesehen.

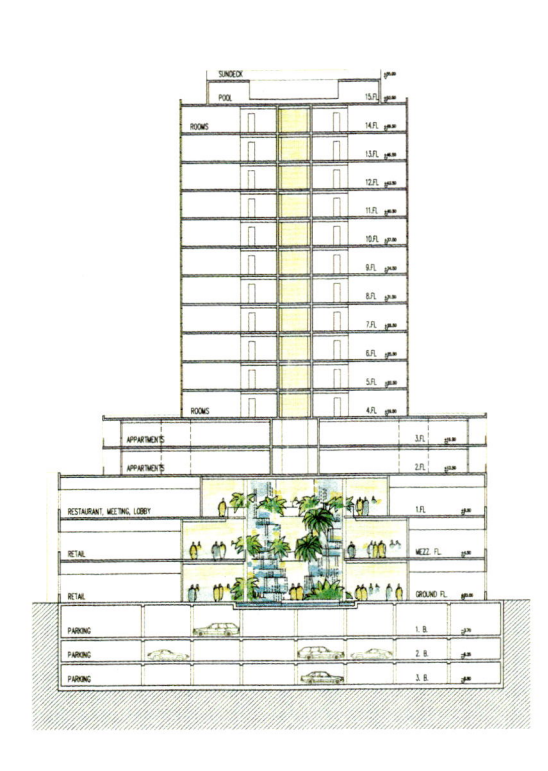

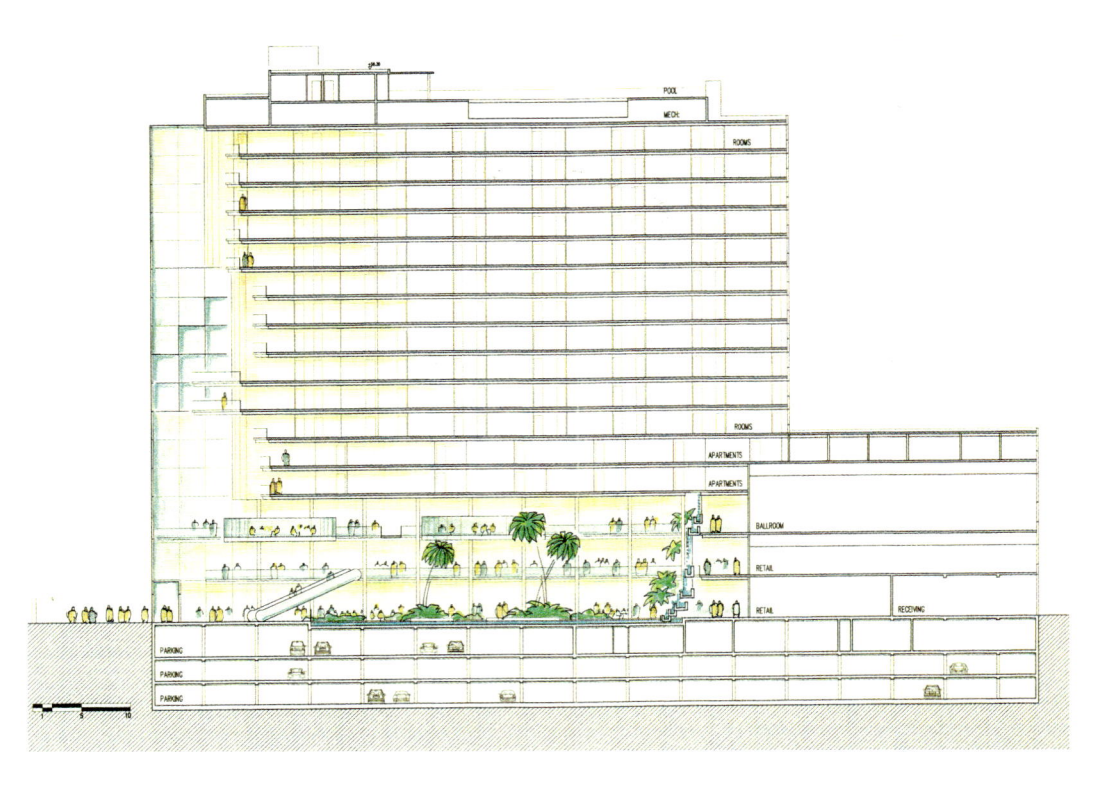

Above, left, cross section and, right, longitudinal section. Below: views of the model.
Oben links: Querschnitt und rechts: Längsschnitt. Unten: Ansichten des Modells.

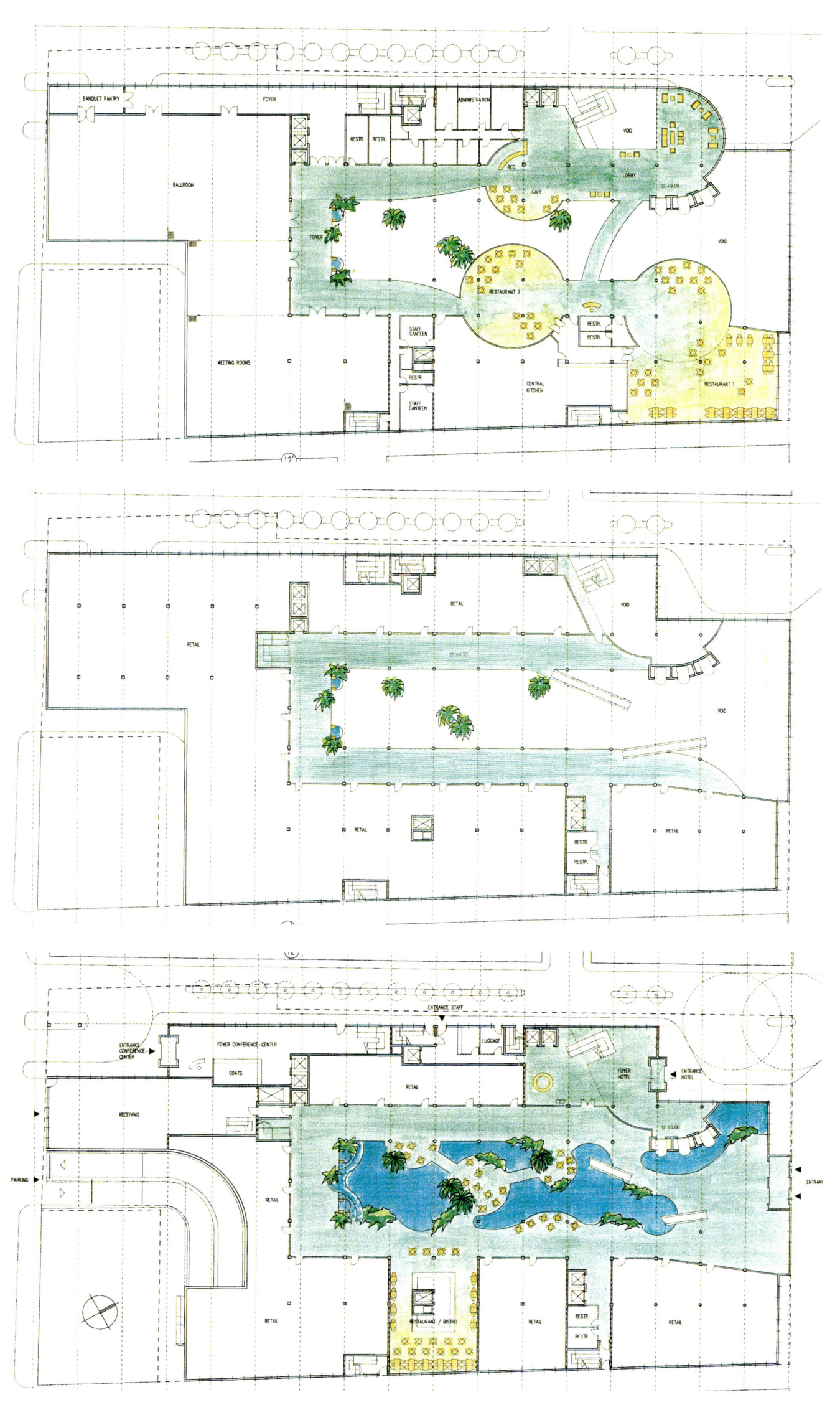

From bottom up: plans of the ground floor, mezzanine and hotel level.
Von unten nach oben: Grundrisse des Erdgeschosses, des Mezzanins und der Hotelebene.

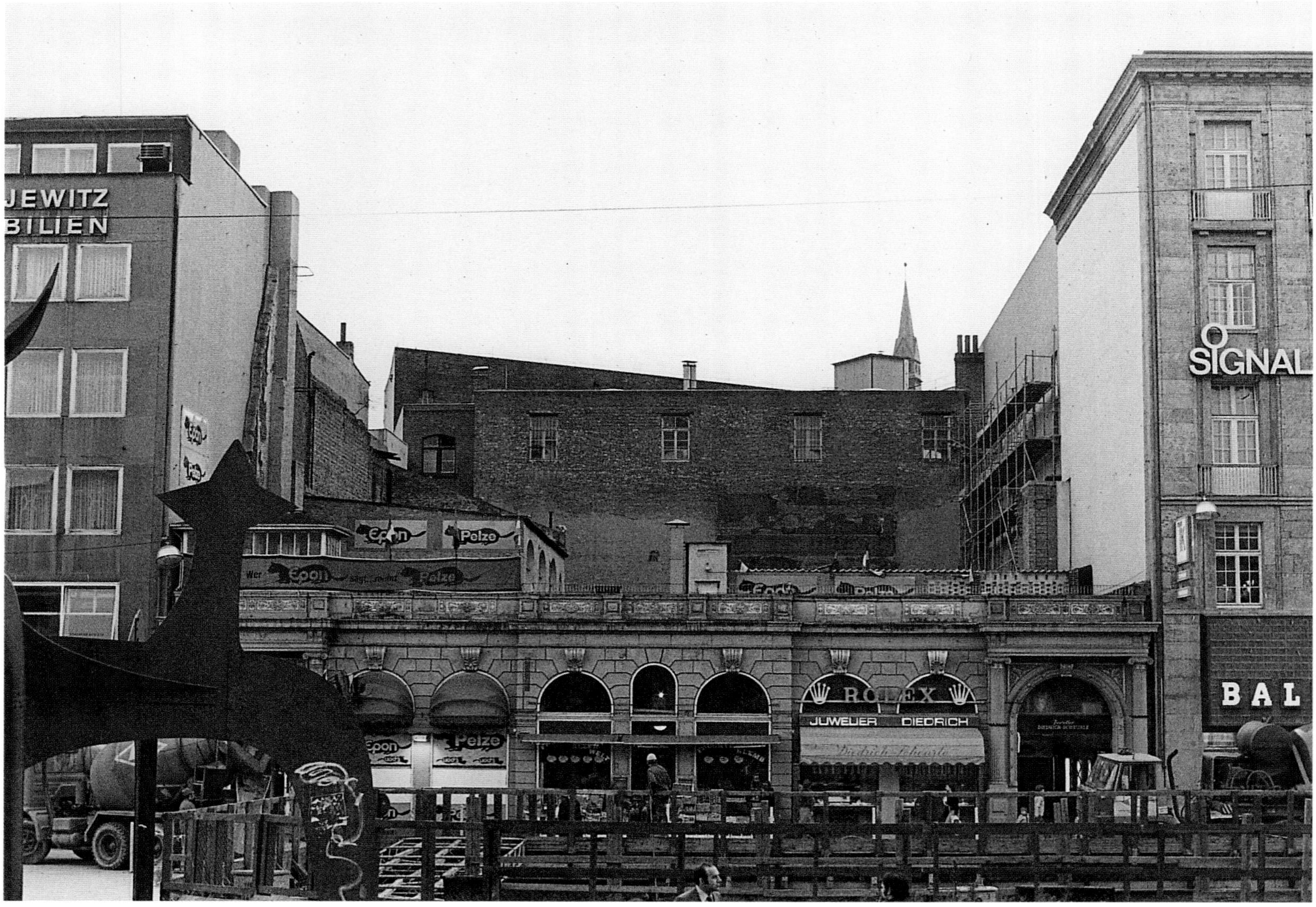
JEWITZ
BILIEN
SIGNAL
Pelze
JUWELIER DIEDRICH
BAL

G 38
Commercial Building
Büro- und Geschäftshaus

"The project consists of an in-filling in the vicinity of Hanover's most elegant shopping street, immediately opposite the main entrance of the opera house, adjacent to the square in front of it. The emphasis in the planning was on creating elegant two-storey shops units backing on to a sandstone arcade of historical value, which being listed has to be preserved, plus office premises for rent on the opposite side.

The complex consists of a front building, 15 metres deep and closing the gap, plus a building at the back of identical breadth and depth, bordering on a back courtyard. Under this is an extensive underground car park." (erected 1977)

Georgstraße is the main street in downtown Hanover. This borders what used to be the old city and marks the course of the former fortifications. Georgstraße was originally built in the first half of the 19th century. Most of the buildings here were destroyed in the Second World War. In the 1950s and 1960s five-storey and six-storey shops were built here, some of these incorporating a few remains of earlier building.

A listed historic building, the remains of the facade at Georgstraße 38 originate from 1873/74 and comprise one of the very few Neo-Renaissance survivals in Hanover.

The facade has been extended into an arcade passage. This has enabled spacious shop window fronts, appropriate to the period, to be inserted. The long-established Opernkonditorei café has been transferred from the ground floor to the first floor. That has been taken as the opportunity to let the facade step back to provide a kind of terrace and to lead it back to the general frontage in the next storey.

This creates the impression of a base running horizontally and akin to a viaduct. Above this rises a vertically structured facade. This makes the robust three-storey office block running diagonally amazingly light. The whole building seems divided into two, with one part earthbound and the other floating. Nevertheless, the smaller and seemingly lighter part is definitely anchored to the ground. The appearance of the whole thus gains volume. A plastic object has been created here, not some facade of a depth impossible to discern.

The entrance area reflects the plasticity and volume of the whole building. The slightly rounded shapes convey a determined feeling for space. The reflecting wall facings, while fundamentally banishing all constraints, amazingly enough actually enhance this effect.

„Das Projekt umfaßt eine Baulückenschließung im Bereich der elegantesten Einkaufsstraße Hannovers, unmittelbar gegenüber dem Haupteingang des Opernhauses, angrenzend an den Opernplatz. Schwerpunkt der Planung ist die Schaffung von zweigeschossigen eleganten Landeneinheiten, rückwärtig einer historisch wertvollen Sandsteinarkade, die unter Denkmalschutz steht und erhalten werden mußte, sowie darüber liegenden Büroräumen zur Vermietung. Der Gebäudekomplex besteht aus einem die Baulücke schließenden Frontgebäude mit einer Tiefe von 15 Metern und, angrenzend an einen rückwärtigen Innenhof, einem Hinterhaus von gleicher Breite und Tiefe. Darunter befindet sich eine großflächige Tiefgarage." (errichtet 1977)

Die Georgstraße ist die Hauptstraße der hannoverschen Innenstadt. Sie zieht sich um die ehemalige Altstadt und markiert den Verlauf der ehemaligen Festungswälle. Die Georgstraße ist erst in der ersten Hälfte des 19. Jahrhunderts bebaut worden. Der größte Teil der Bebauung ist während des Zweiten Weltkrieges zerstört worden. In den 1950-60er Jahren sind fünf- und sechsgeschossige Geschäftshäuser errichtet worden, zum Teil mit wenigen Resten alter Bebauung.

Der denkmalgeschützte Fassadenrest der Georgstraße 38 stammt aus den Jahren 1873/74 und gehört zu den wenigen Relikten der Neorenaissance in Hannover.

Die Fassade ist zum Arkadengang erweitert worden. Das ermöglichte es, dahinter großzügige und der Zeit angemessene Schaufensterfronten zu legen. Ein traditionsreiches Café (Opernkonditorei) wurde aus dem Erdgeschoß in das erste Obergeschoß verlagert. Das wurde zum Anlaß genommen, die Fassade für eine Art Terrasse zurückspringen zu lassen und im nächsten Stockwerk wieder zur allgemeinen Fluchtlinie vorzuführen. So ergibt sich der Eindruck einer horizontal verlaufenden Basis mit Viaduktcharakter. Darüber steigt dann eine vertikal strukturierte Fassade auf. Sie gibt dem mächtigen, quergelegten Körper von drei Bürogeschossen eine erstaunliche Leichtigkeit. Das gesamte Gebäude wirkt wie zweigeteilt, mit einem bodenständigen und einem schwebenden Teil. Wobei der kleinere und scheinbar leichtere Teil deutlich bodenverhaftet ist. Das Ganze gewinnt dadurch optisch an Volumen. Hier ist ein plastisches Objekt erstellt worden und nicht eine Fassade mit unsichtbarer Tiefe.

Der Eingangsbereich spiegelt Plastizität und Volumen im objekthaften Sinne wider. Die leicht gerundeten Formen vermitteln ein dezidiertes Raumgefühl. Die spiegelnden Wandverkleidungen erhöhen erstaunlicherweise diesen Eindruck, obwohl sie im Grunde jegliche Begrenzung aufheben.

From bottom up: plans of the ground floor, first floor and second floor.
Opposite page: the facade of the new building whose sandblasted concrete lesenes take up the rhythm of the existing colonnade.
*Von unten nach oben: Grundriß des Erdgeschosses, des ersten und zweiten Geschosses.
Auf der Seite gegenüber: die Fassade des neuen Gebäudes, die mit ihren vertikalen, sandgestrahlten Lisenen den Rhythmus der bestehenden Arkade wieder aufnimmt.*

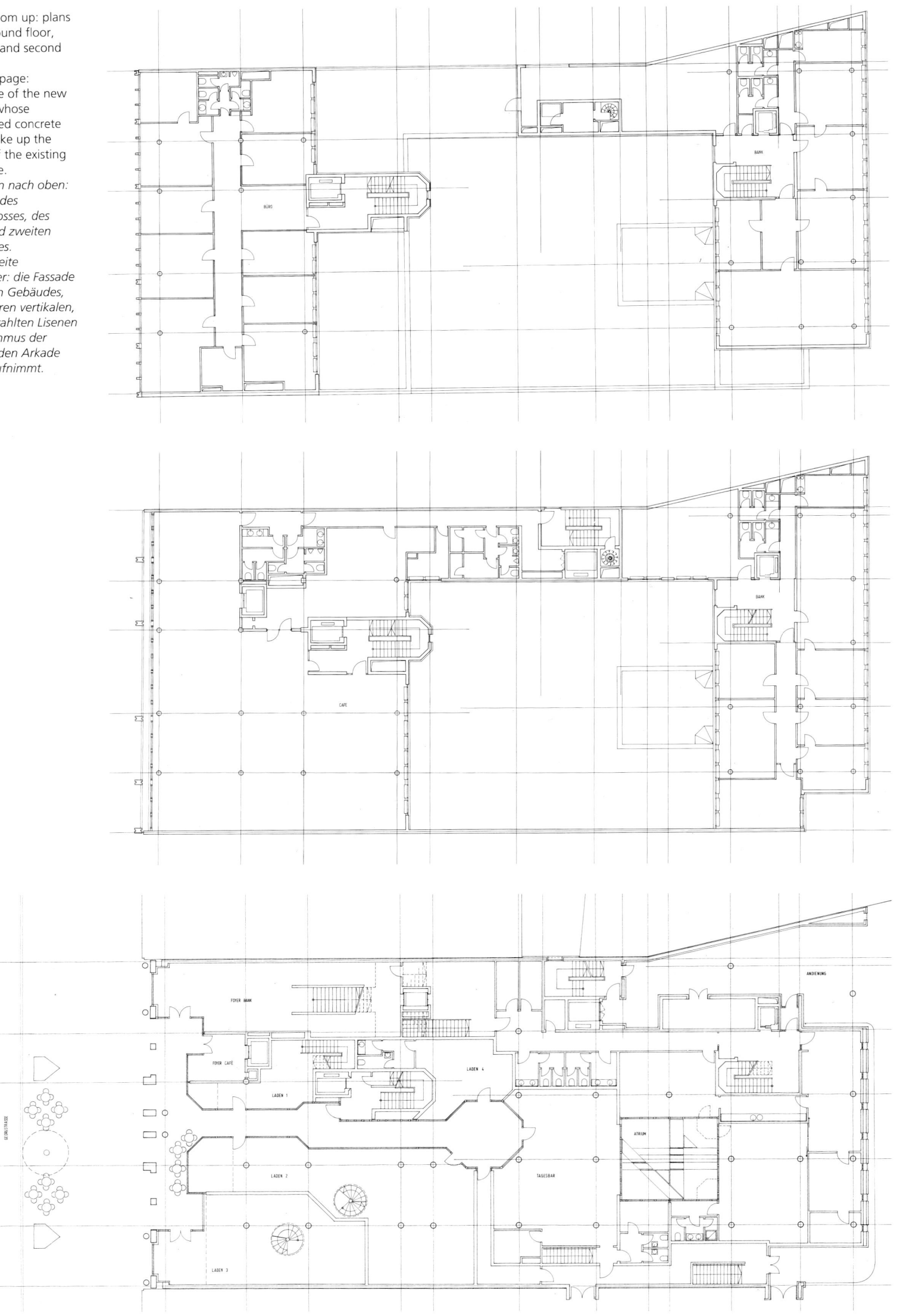

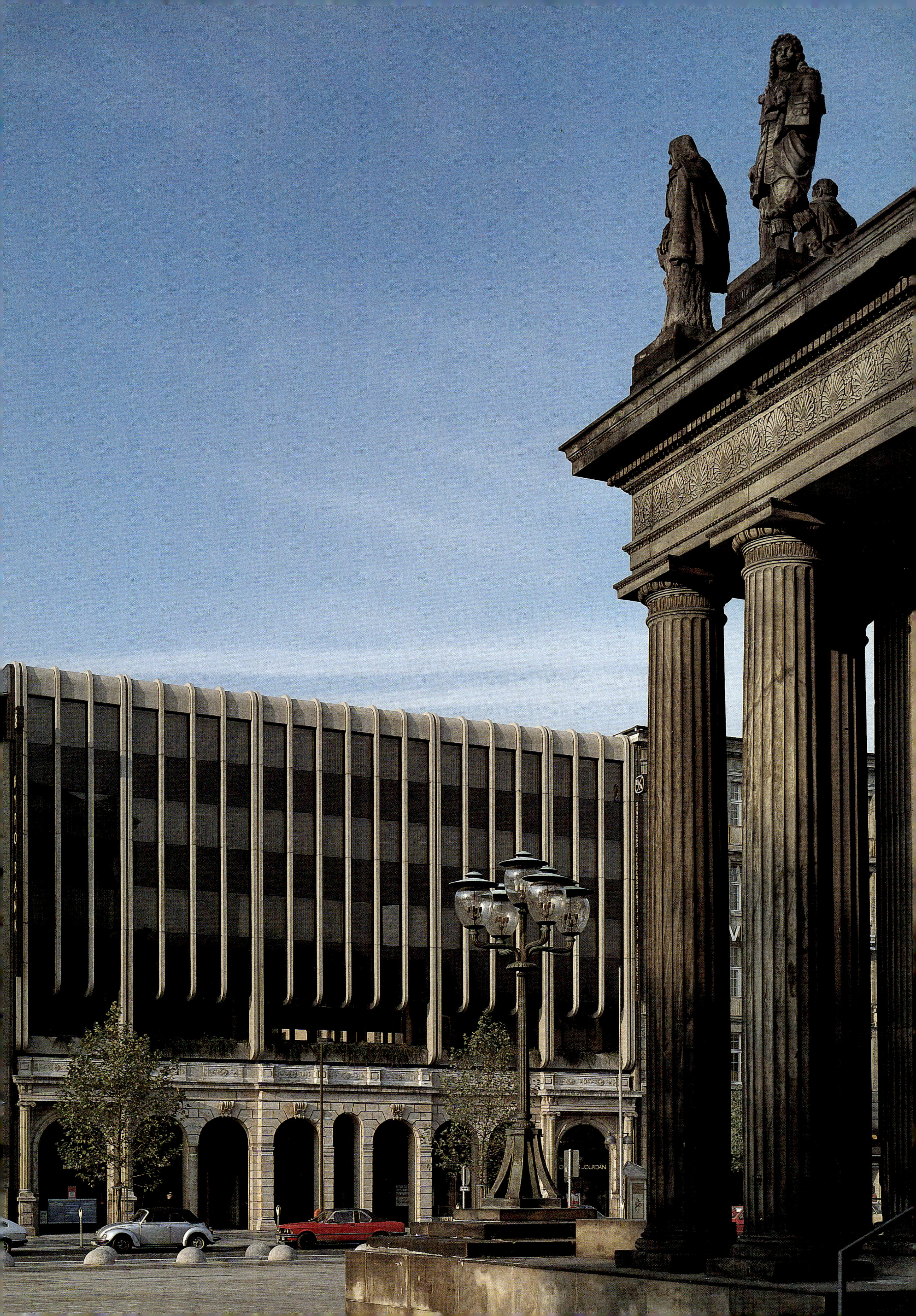

Details of the new building's entrance lobby.
Details der Eingangshalle des neuen Gebäudes.

167

Partial view of the ground floor, where the shops are located.
Ansicht des Erdgeschosses und der Ladenzone.

Details of the new building's elegant interior decoration.
Details der eleganten Innenausstattung des neuen Gebäudes.

169

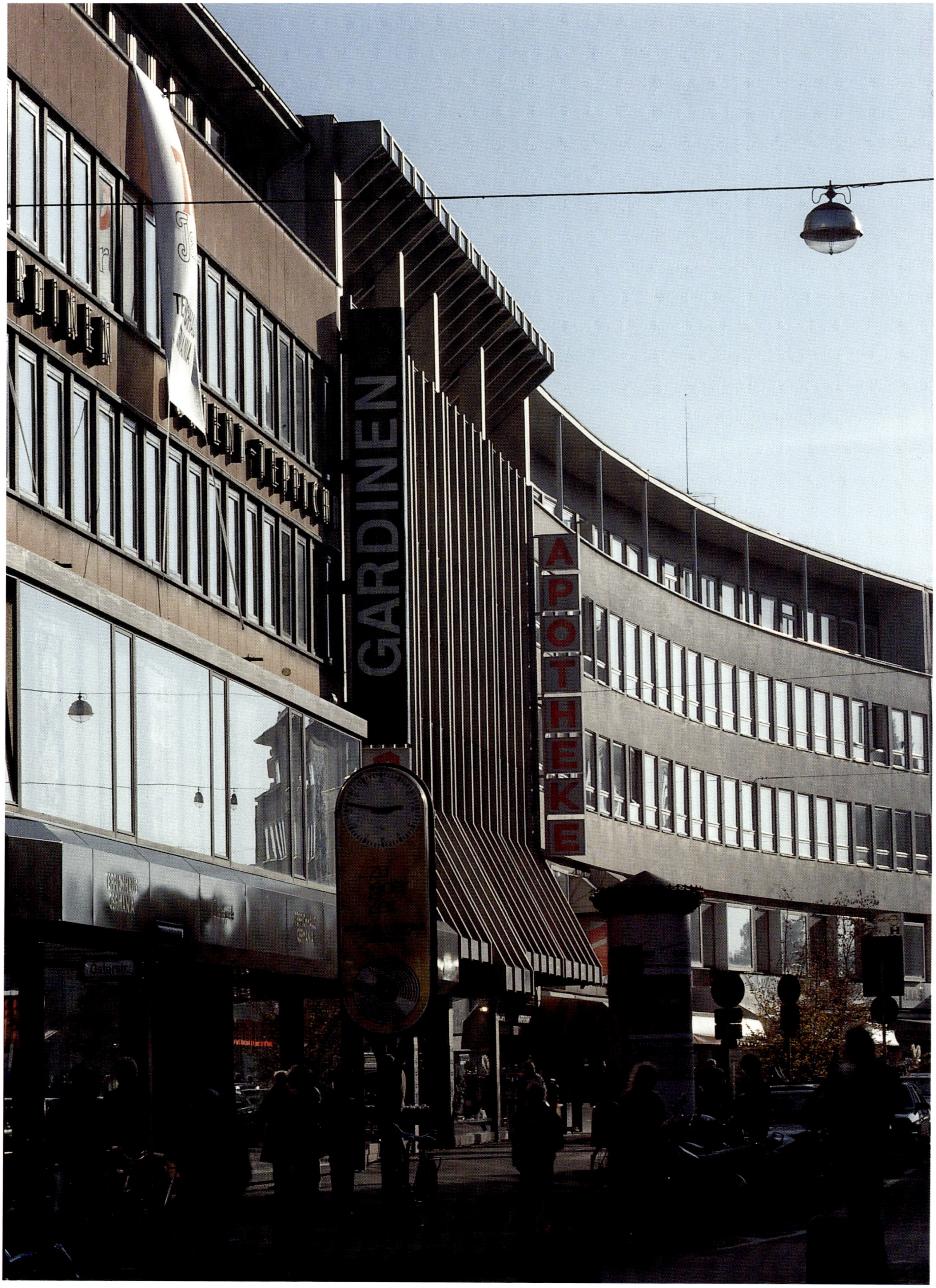

GARDINEN
APOTHEKE

KS 23-25
Commercial Building
Büro- und Geschäftshaus

Karmarschstrasse presents a picture of the economic and architectural upswing of the 1950s and 1960s. Originally driven into the existing old city at the end of the 19th century, the street was widened and given a uniform appearance in the wake of the post-war redevelopment of the city centre. Horizontal rows of windows, shop sun-blinds and top storeys set back from the street produce a vista which is not just uniform but also plain monotonous.

A medical centre was inserted into the street picture, more or less as a building to stand alone. Yet this was only to some extent the true situation, since a single storey building was already in existence and had to be used. Usage of the four-storeys atop this was determined by simple structures, which allowed the whole emphasis of the design to concentrate on the facade.

This repeats the structure of the neighbouring building while concealing this in an all-glass facade so that it is not immediately apparent. In addition, the facade is structured vertically by means of conspicuous slats. Looking along the whole length of the street, then this facade is an irritant. Below, the slats culminate in stiff awnings. As a gently ironic commentary, they also incorporate the former shop window awnings fitted to all facades. In reflection, the fourth, receding storey is also decked out with trompe l'oeuil awnings, also to be understood as an ironic gesture.

The ribs emphasizing the vertical element afford the building a pleasant, independent volume which certainly sets it apart from the flatness of the other facades.

Die Karmarschstraße zeichnet ein Bild des wirtschaftlichen und architektonischen Aufbaus der 50er und 60er Jahre. Die erst zum Ende des 19. Jahrhunderts in die gewachsene Altstadt geschlagene Straße wurde im Zuge der innerstädtischen Neugestaltung nach dem Kriege verbreitert und stilistisch einheitlich gestaltet. Horizontal verlaufende Fensterbänder, Geschäftsmarkisen und zurückspringende Dachgeschosse ergeben ein Straßenbild, das sowohl einheitlich als auch eintönig ist.

In dieses Straßenbild ist der Bau des Ärztezentrums als eine Art Solitär hineingesetzt worden. Allerdings trifft das die Situation nur bedingt, denn es war bereits eine Erdgeschoß-Bebauung vorhanden, die auch genutzt werden mußte. Die Nutzung der darauf aufbauenden vier Geschosse war mit einfachen Strukturen festgelegt. Der Schwerpunkt des Entwurfs konnte sich somit ausschließlich auf die Fassadengestaltung erstrecken.

Die Fassade nimmt die Struktur der Fensterbänder der benachbarten Gebäude auf, versteckt sie allerdings in einer Ganzglasfassade, so daß sie nicht gleich einsichtig sind. Zudem wird die Fassade durch aufragende Lamellen in der Vertikalen deutlich strukturiert. Die Fassade ist eine Irritation, wenn man den gesamten Straßenverlauf ins Auge faßt. Unten laufen die Lamellen in steinerne Markisen aus. Sie nehmen (als ein sanft ironischer Kommentar) die an allen Fassaden zusätzlich angebrachten Schaufenstermarkisen auf. Spiegelbildlich ist das zurückspringende vierte Obergeschoß ebenfalls mit optischen Markisen versehen - auch gleichermaßen ironisch zu verstehen.

Die die Vertikale betonenden Rippen geben dem Bau ein wohltuend eigenständiges Volumen, das sich gegen die Flächigkeit der übrigen Fassaden deutlich abhebt.

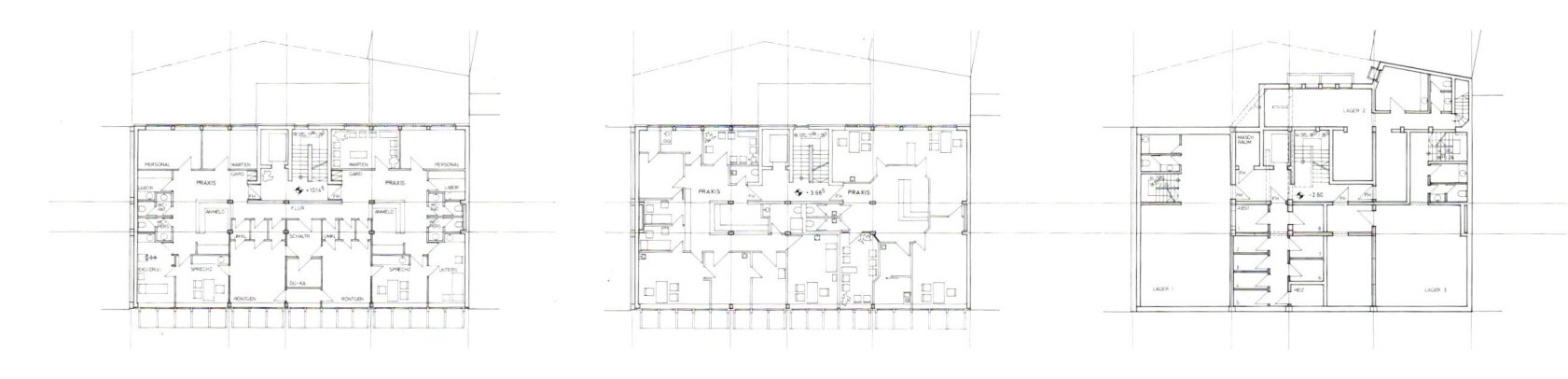

Details of the facade of the Medical Centre filling the first to fourth floors of an existing construction grid.
Top of page, from left to right: plans of the basement, ground to fourth floor.

Details der Fassade des Ärztezentrums, das auf einem bestehenden Gebäude im Erdgeschoß 4-geschossig errichtet wurde und den Rhythmus der existierenden Konstruktion aufnimmt. Oben, von links nach rechts: Grundrisse des Kellergeschosses sowie des Erdgeschosses bis zum 4. Obergeschoß.

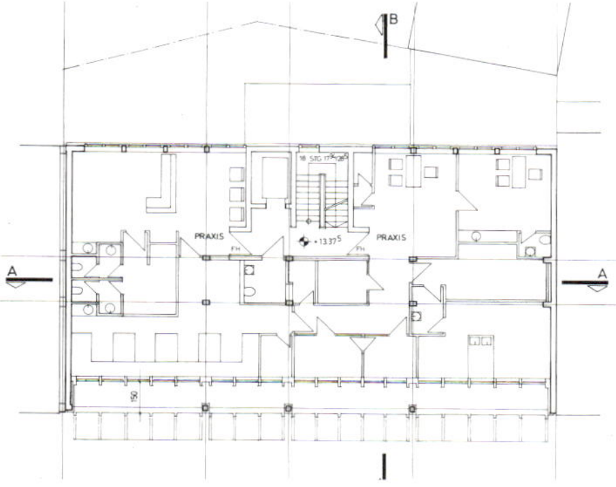
B
A
PRAXIS
PRAXIS
A

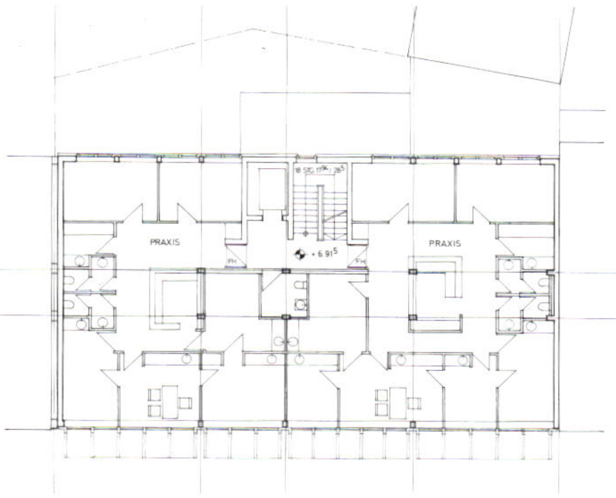
PRAXIS
PRAXIS

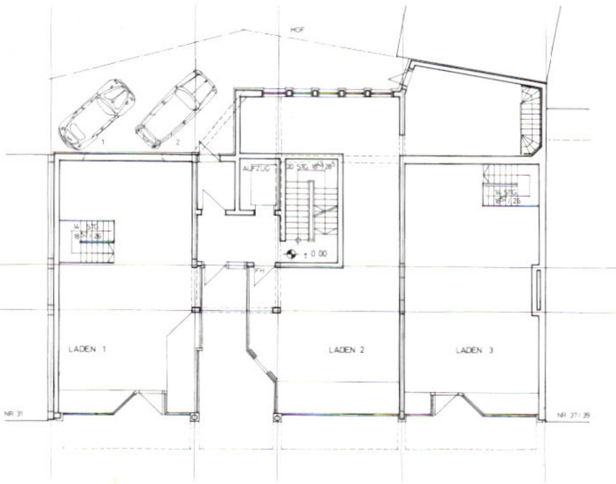
LADEN 1
LADEN 2
LADEN 3

APOTHEKE
P 200m Park-Garage
SPAHN-OPTIK
KISKE
Kiske

The glass facade is designed as a rhythmic contrast to the flat facades of the adjacent buildings.
Die Glasfassade wird als Zentralpunkt der Rundung innerhalb des gesamten Straßenzuges gesehen und bildet somit einen kontrastvollen Höhepunkt innerhalb der übrigen schlichten und nahezu langweiligen Fassadengestaltungen der straßenbegleitenden Gebäude.

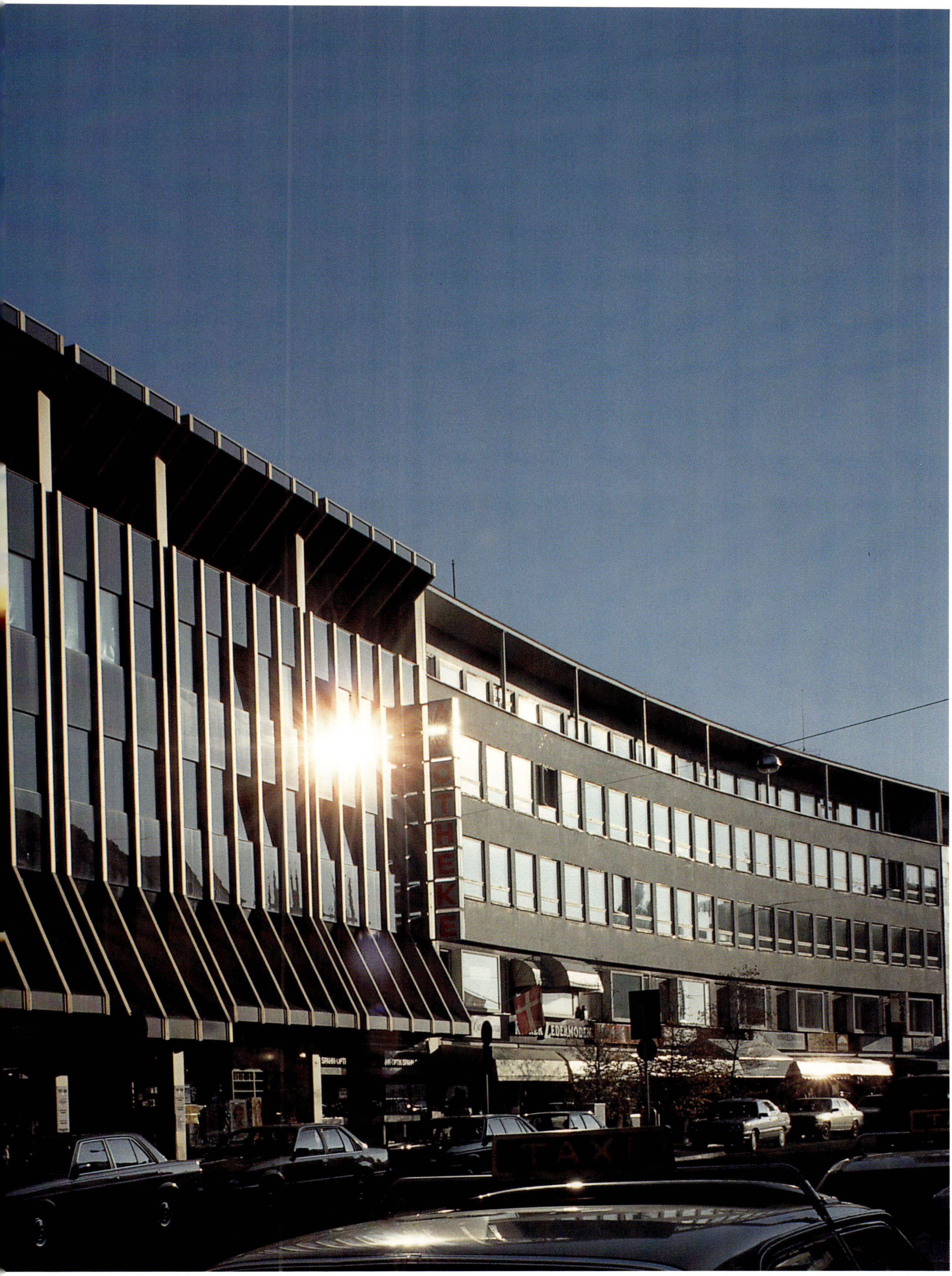

Roland
4
Notar
Wachter
Winterhoff
Rechtsanwälte
Dr. Wolter & Partner mbH
Hartmut Genee
Zahnarzt

LS 4
Commercial Building
Büro- und Geschäftshaus

To the right of the "Galerie Luise" shopping arcade a former hotel from pre-war days has been revamped to match the appearance of the gallery. Despite the poor quality of the building, complete demolition of Luisenstrasse 4 was not permissible. The height of the storeys was hydraulically adjusted and they were furnished with a front facade compatible with, yet utterly distinct from, the adjacent "Galerie Luise".

Polished natural stone was selected for both facades, but differing in panel size and the intensity of its red tone.

Heights of floors and sizes of windows differ. Square windows were chosen for the Luisenstrasse 4 building so as to offset the narrow, emphatically vertical windows of the "Galerie" with ones of a more serene character. The mezzanine heights of the shopping areas also differ, those of Galerie Luise being very slightly higher. The facade is centrally positioned, with a central main entrance and on each side of this a shop entrance between two display windows. In the area of the mezzanine floor the window fronts are set back. The facade above this and the majority of the window fronts at the back of the shops admit additional light and provide an unexpectedly bright space.

The shop level is optically linked with the first office floor above by narrow, vertical "glass fingers". The top two floors are closely linked in the same manner.

The two facades of "related" design contribute a discreet elegance to the street as a whole. Without stealing the limelight, they are noticeably smarter than the other house fronts. They possess a certain "gentle allure".

Rechts neben der Ladenpassage „Galerie Luise" ist ein ehemaliges Hotel aus der Vorkriegszeit umgestaltet und dem Erscheinungsbild der Galerie angepaßt worden. Das Gebäude Luisenstraße 4 durfte trotz schlechter Bausubstanz nicht vollständig abgerissen werden. Die Geschoßhöhen wurden hydraulisch verändert und mit einer Frontfassade versehen, die sich sowohl der benachbarten „Galerie Luise" angleicht als auch deutlich von ihr abweicht.

Für beide Fassaden wurde geschliffener Naturstein gewählt, der sich in der Plattengröße und in der Intensität der rötlichen Farbigkeit unterscheidet.

Die Geschoßhöhen und Fenstergrößen sind unterschiedlich. Für das Gebäude Luisenstraße 4 wurden quadratische Fenster gewählt, die den schmalen, vertikal aufstrebenden Fenstern der „Galerie" einen ruhigen Charakter entgegensetzen. Auch die Mezzaninhöhen der Ladenbereiche sind unterschiedlich. Im Gebäude der „Galerie Luise" liegen sie um Nuancen höher.

Die Fassade ist mittig angelegt, mit einem zentralen Haupteingang und rechts und links jeweils einem Geschäftseingang zwischen zwei Schaufenstern. Im Bereich des Mezzanin-Obergeschosses sind die Fensterfronten zurückgesetzt. Die darüber liegende Fassade und der größere Teil der Schaufensterfronten kragen vor. Fensterfronten auf der Rückseite der Ladenlokale lassen zusätzlich Licht ein und ergeben einen unerwartet hellen Raum.

Die Ladenebene ist durch schmale senkrechte „Glasfinger" mit dem darüber liegenden ersten Bürogeschoß optisch verbunden. Auf gleiche Weise gehen die letzten beiden Stockwerke eine enge Verbindung ein.

Die beiden „verwandtschaftlich" gestalteten Fassaden bringen eine zurückhaltende Eleganz in die gesamte Straßenzeile. Sie sind deutlich schicker als die übrigen Fronten, ohne sich allerdings in den Vordergrund zu spielen. Sie haben eine gewisse „sanfte Attraktivität".

From the bottom up: plans of the ground floor, the mezzanine, first, third and fourth floor.
Von unten nach oben: Grundrisse des Erdgeschosses sowie des Mezzanins, des 1. des 3. und 4. Geschosses einschließlich der Dachaufsicht.

Two pictures of the former hotel dating back to the thirties, which has now been converted.
Zwei Bilder des ehemaligen Hotels, das aus der Vorkriegszeit stammte und das vollständig umgebaut wurde.

The new entrance from
the Luisenstraße.
Below: sections.
*Der neue Eingang von
der Luisenstraße.
Unten: Schnitte.*

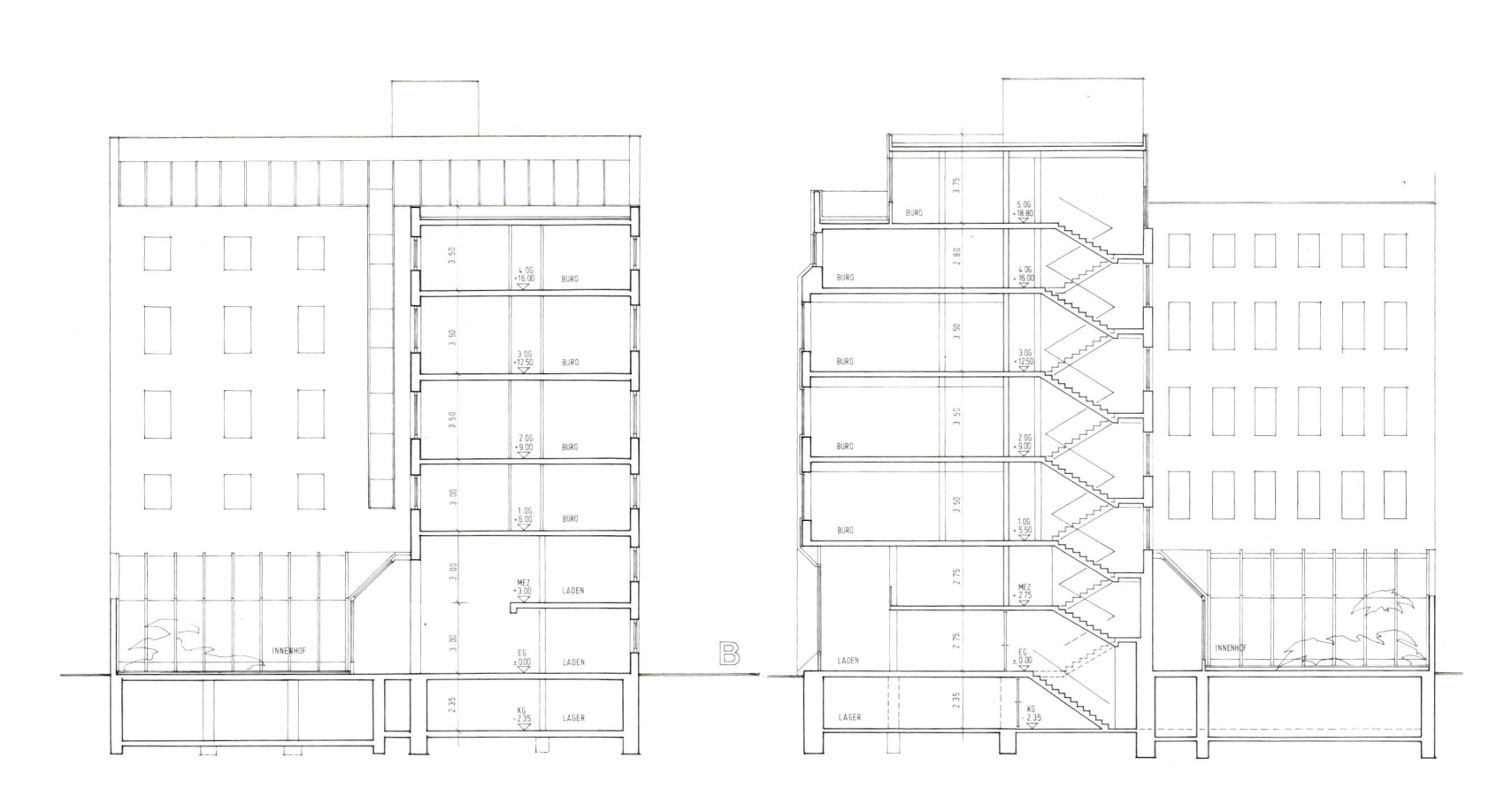

Detail of the new facade, attached onto the existing facade in harmony with the patterns of old facades nearby.
Detail der neuen Fassade, die vor die bestehende gehängt wurde und die sich einfügt in die bestehenden historischen Fassaden der Nachbarschaft.

Perspective views of the building Luisentraße 4. The buildings with inset windows on the ground floor and first floor create a new shopping arcade.
Gesamtansicht des Gebäudes Luisenstraße 4. Das Gebäude mit den zurückgesetzten Fenstern des Erdgeschosses und des Mezzanins schaffen den Eindruck einer neuen Ladengalerie.

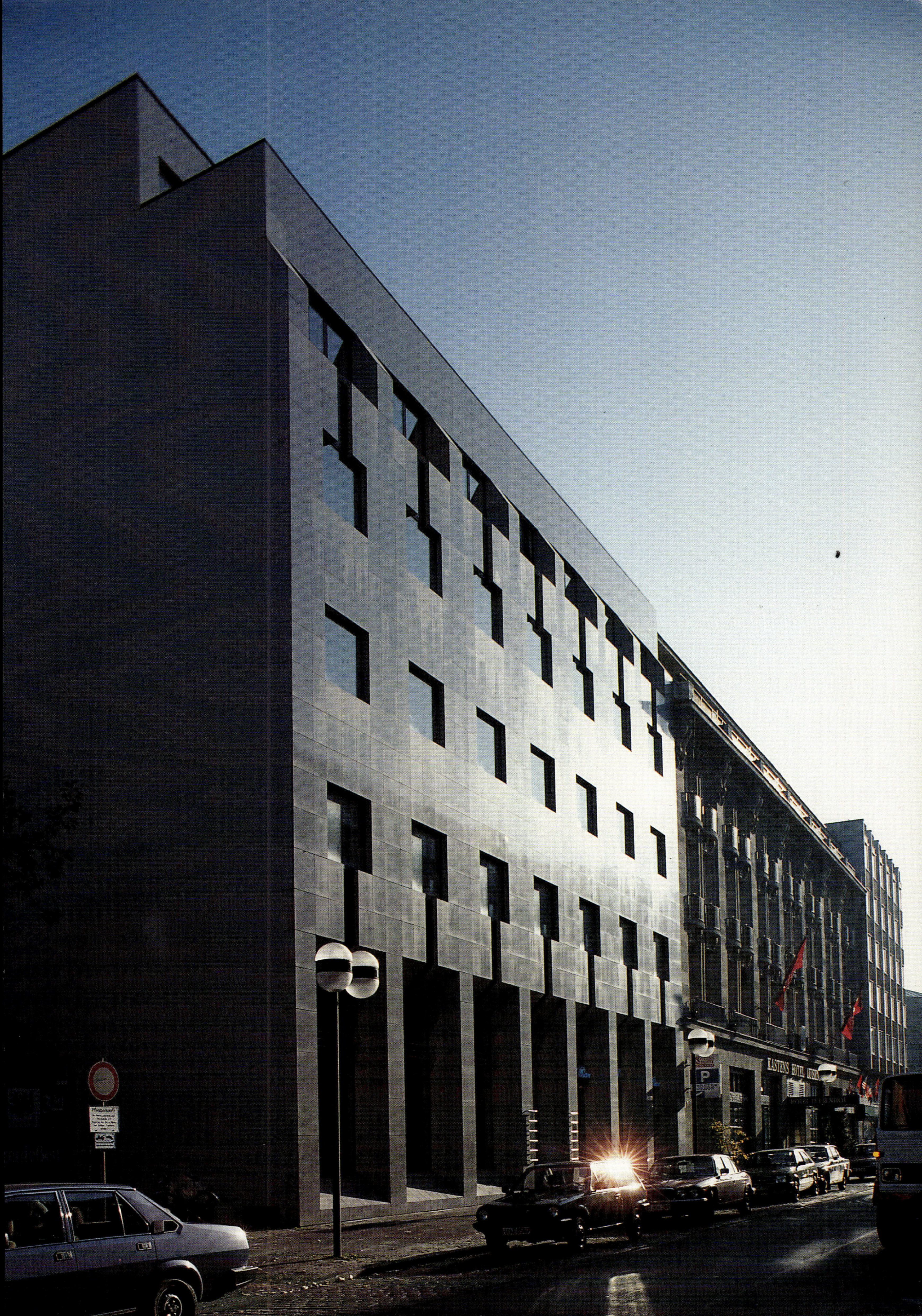
P
KASTENS HOTEL

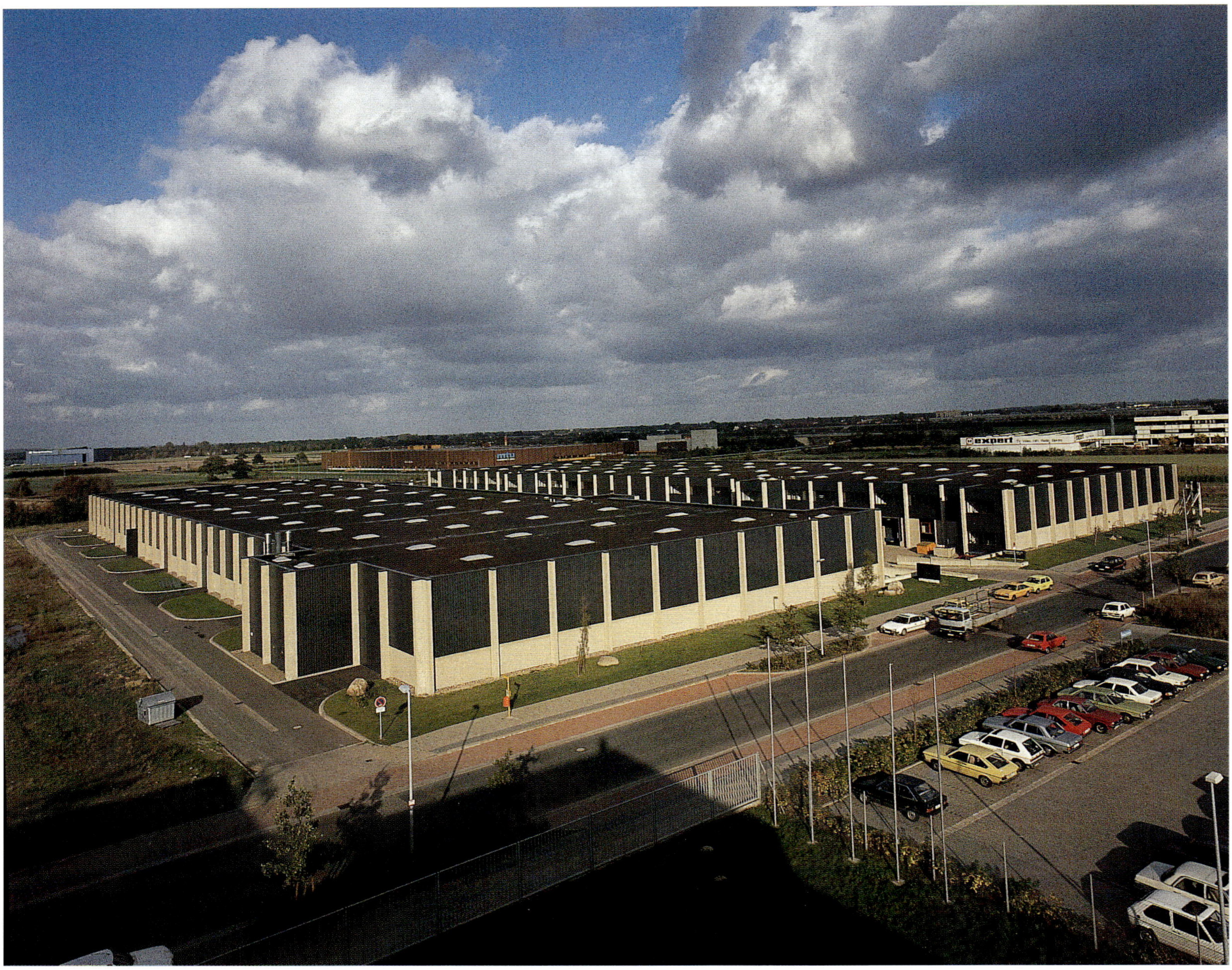

AGID
Freight Centre
Frachtzentrum

Freight centres are of their nature boring buildings. Effectiveness is far more important than allure. Yet this one manages to combine both elements.

Two seven-aisle storage and cargo-handling sheds run on either side of a central strip. These are constructed of prefabricated industrial system building elements. Prefabricated reinforced concrete supports are visibly distinct from the facades. These form a grid along the frontages at intervals of 5 metres. Up to a height of 2.50 metres the intervals are also filled by prefabricated concrete elements. Above this and up to the full height of the building - approximately 8 metres - is a tinplate facade lined by an aerated cement shell.

The entire plot is defined by a standard grid. Yet the effect is not monotonous, for the separate supports and the facade materials with alternating light and heavy, dark and bright effects, combined with the windows, doors and freight portals, by no means suggest a relentlessly even rhythm.

The client for this extensive freight and storage terminal immediately adjacent to Hanover-Langenhagen Airport has specialized in constructing storage and freight centres all around the world. These are leased in varying sizes to air freight carriers and industrial companies.

Frachtzentren sind gemeinhin langweilige Bauten. Effektivität ist weitaus wichtiger als Attraktivität. Hier ist es aber gelungen, beide Elemente zu kombinieren.

Zwei siebenschiffige Lager- und Umschlaghallen verlaufen beidseitig eines Mittelstreifens. Sie sind aus industriell gefertigten Systembauteilen zusammengesetzt. Stahlbetonfertigteilstützen sind sichtbar vor der Fassade belassen. Sie rastern die jeweiligen Stirnseiten im Abstand von je 5 m. Bis auf die Höhe von 2,50 m sind die Zwischenräume mit ebenfalls vorgefertigten Betonteilen geschlossen. Darüber folgt bis zur Gebäudehöhe von etwa 8 m eine Blechfassade mit innenliegender Gasbetonschale.

Das gesamte Areal wird von einem einheitlichen Raster geprägt. Eintönigkeit kommt dennoch nicht auf, denn die vorgestellten Stützen und die leicht und schwer, dunkel und hell wirkenden Fassadenmaterialien ergeben im Zusammenspiel mit Fenstern, Türen und Frachttoren einen nicht immer gleichmäßigen Rhythmus.

Der Auftraggeber dieses großflächigen Fracht- und Lagerterminals in unmittelbarer Nähe des Flughafens Hannover-Langenhagen hat sich weltweit auf die Errichtung von Lager- und Frachtzentren spezialisiert. Sie werden in variablen Großeinheiten an Luftfrachtgesellschaften und Industrieunternehmen vermietet.

Left and opposite page: details of the outside facades of the two buildings used for warehouse and distribution purposes for firms operating near Hanover Airport.
Bottom of page: ground floor plan.
Below: first floor plan.

*Links und auf der Seite gegenüber: Fassadendetails der beiden Baukörper, die als Lager- und Frachtzentrum benutzt werden für Firmen, die am hannoverschen Flughafen arbeiten.
Unten: Grundriß des Erdgeschosses.
Unten: Grundriß des ersten Obergeschosses.*

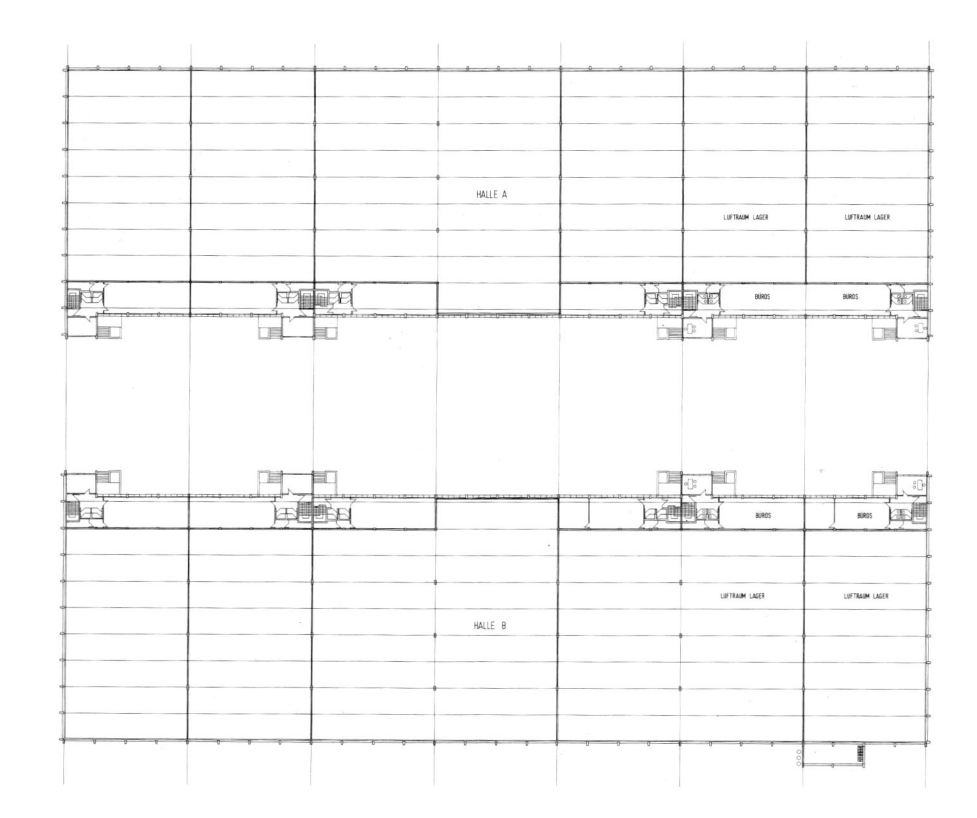

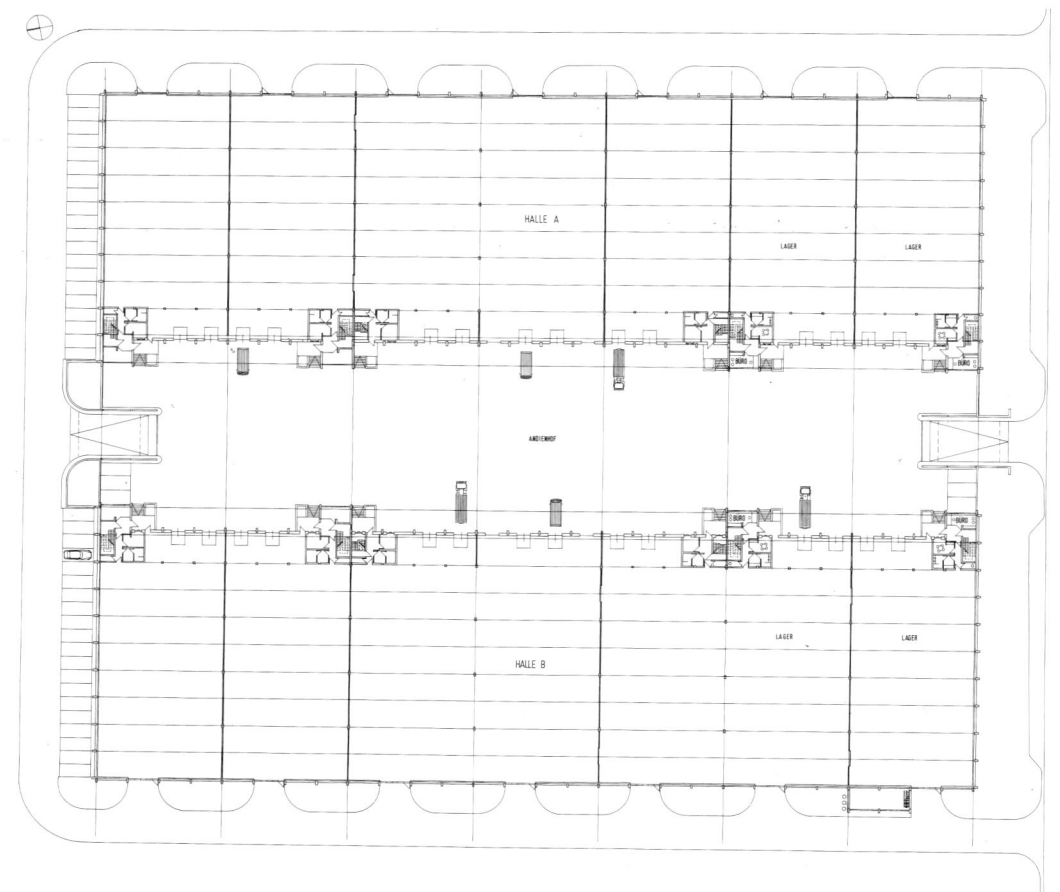

GEWERBEPARK AGID LTD.
Bayernstrasse 14-16

Cross section.
Below and opposite page: perspective views of the two bays. The facades feature is a series of sandblasted columns arranged in a grid of 5.00 m on the face side and 5.625 m on the long side.
*Querschnitt.
Unten und auf der gegenüberliegenden Seite: Ansichten der beiden Hallen. Die Fassaden erhalten einen Rhythmus durch sandgestrahlte Stahlbetonfertigteilstützen, die sichtbar vor der Fassade in einem Stützenraster von 5,0 m auf der Stirnseite und 5,625 m auf der Längsseite gerichtet sind.*

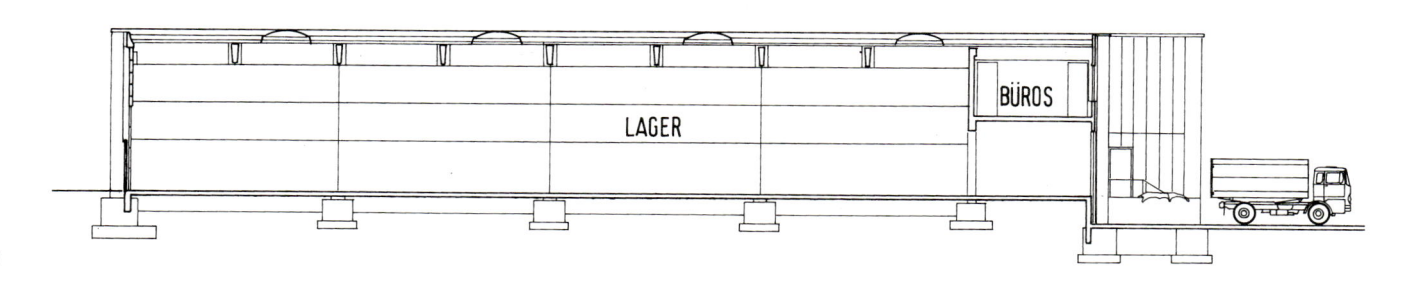

BÜROS LAGER

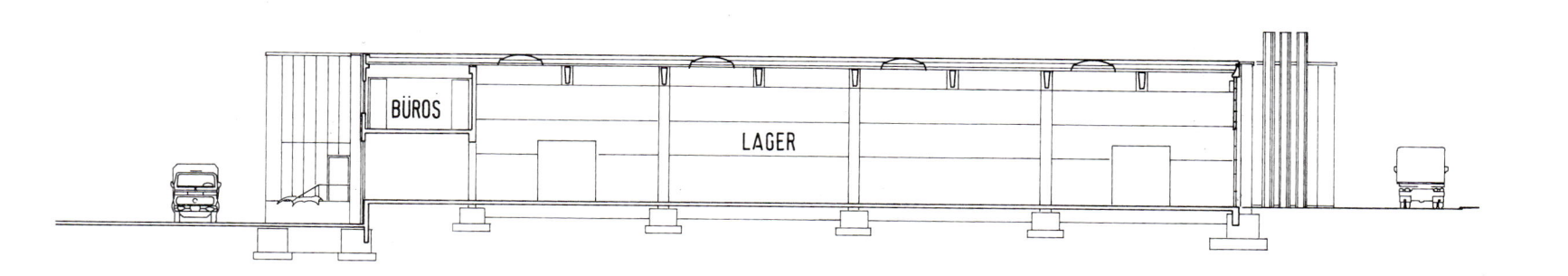

189

Overall views of the area. The buildings so far built are just the first stage of a more extensive project which, when it is completed, will cover a total surface area of over 30,000 square metres.
Unterschiedliche Ansichten des Komplexes. Der hier gezeigte Gebäudeabschnitt stellt den ersten Bauabschnitt einer Gesamtanlage dar, die nach ihrer Fertigstellung mehr als 30.000 m2 Nutzfläche haben wird.

Gieseke
Gieseke
Gieseke
Gieseke
GEWERBEPARK AGID LTD.
Bayernstrasse 14-16

Employees and architects SE & Partner
Mitarbeiter Büro SE & Partner

Akgün, Baldt, Baumert, Bayer, Bieber, Boeker, Bohling, Bolz, Brockmann, Brodersen, Brunke, Busche, Carl, Christov, Eckl, Fitschen, Frank-Harder, Franzkowiak, Gebauer, Gerhards, Gläser, Gökham, Grewecke, Hagel, Höcker, Hoffmann, Hübner, Hundt, Inoue, Isensee, Job, Juraschek, Jürges, Käbberich, Kahlert, Kalkanli, Kanaan, Kaubisch, Kaygusuz, Khabazian, Klawikowski, Klein, Klinger, Kohlstedt, Koslowski, Kraus, Kroos, Kruppa, Ladehof, Leinert, Lindenberg, Lorang, Lorenz, Lucas, Ludwig, Maaß, Marhenke, Meschede, Mohler, Mohsenyar, Monien, Müller, Neumann, Nihat, Obimpeh, Ottlik, Overberg, Özbek, Pemöller, Pfingsthorn, Pinar, Przybyla, Püttcher, Ramm, Reinecke, Rolf, Rommel, Ronski, Rosterg, Sauerhammer, Sauthof, Schäffler, Schepping, Schmidt, Schöyen, Schrader, Schubert, Schulz, Seemann, Selek, Spieler, Stange, Steingräber, Steinmetz, Störmer, Taskin, Teichert, Thanisch, Thies, Thonke, Trebitz, van de Loo, Veddeler, Voeske, von Altrock, von Ditfurth, Wegener, Wilke, Wolf, Yazdanfar, Yazdanpanah, Zhai, Zinowsky, Zirke

List of works
Liste der Werke

1977
HAUS GOTTSCHALK
Private residence, Ilsede, Lower Saxony
Privates Wohnhaus, Ilsede Niedersachsen

NRÜ
Grammar-school with media-library, Neustadt a. R., Lower Saxony
Gymnasium mit Mediothek, Neustadt am Rübenberge, Niedersachsen

GEORGSTRASSE 38
Commercial and office building with banking branch and restaurant, Hanover, Lower Saxony
Büro- und Geschäftshaus mit Bankniederlassung und Restaurant, Hannover, Niedersachsen

HAUS SCHWETJE
Private residence, Sehnde, Lower Saxony
Privates Wohnhaus, Sehnde, Niedersachsen

HAUS WINKENBACH
Private residence, Sehnde, Lower Saxony
Privates Wohnhaus, Sehnde, Niedersachsen

BEBAUUNG HEMME-HOF
Housing complex, Sehnde, Lower Saxony
Wohnhausgruppe, Sehnde, Niedersachsen

WOHNHAUS GOLIBERZUCH
Private residence, Ilsede, Lower Saxony
Privates Wohnhaus, Ilsede, Niedersachsen

HAUS MERTENS
Private residence, Alfeld, Lower Saxony
Privates Wohnhaus, Alfeld, Niedersachsen

HAUS DR. WULF
Private residence, Ehlershausen, Lower Saxony
Privates Wohnhaus, Ehlershausen, Niedersachsen

HAUS BEHRENS
Private residence, Wennigsen, Lower Saxony
Privates Wohnhaus, Wennigsen, Niedersachsen

HAUS KÖRNER
Private residence, Gehrden, Lower Saxony
Privates Wohnhaus, Gehrden, Niedersachsen

1978
LADEHOLZSTRASSE
Residential building with medical practice, Sehnde, Lower Saxony
Wohnhaus mit Arztpraxen, Sehnde, Niedersachsen

OSTERSTRASSE
Commercial and office building, Hanover, Lower Saxony
Büro- und Geschäftshaus, Hannover, Niedersachsen

HAUS BARTELS
Private residence, Lehrte, Lower Saxony
Privates Wohnhaus, Lehrte, Niedersachsen

KARMARSCHSTRASSE 23-25
Commercial and medical centre, Hanover, Lower Saxony
Geschäfts- und Ärztezentrum, Hannover, Niedersachsen

BAYERISCHE HYPOTHEKEN- UND WECHSELBANK, GEORGSTRASSE 38
Banking branch, Hanover, Lower Saxony
Bankniederlassung, Hannover, Niedersachsen

LÜNEBEST
Production and distribution centre, Lüneburg, Lower Saxony
Produktions- und Vertriebszentrum, Lüneburg, Niedersachsen

1979
ALEX
Shopping mall with office building, Celle, Lower Saxony
Ladenpassage mit Büroflächen, Celle, Niedersachsen

AGID
Distribution and warehouse-centre Hanover-Airport, Lower Saxony
Lager- und Industriekomplex Flughafen, Hannover, Niedersachsen

1980
FRIEDRICH-WILHELM-STRASSE
Office, hotel and shopping complex, Braunschweig, Lower Saxony
Büro, Hotel- und Geschäftskomplex, Braunschweig, Niedersachsen

PRAXIS DR. BERNDT
Dental practice, Hanover, Lower Saxony
Zahnarztpraxis, Hannover, Niedersachsen

1981
PROJEKT GOSLAR
Parking building with commercial space, Goslar, Lower Saxony
Parkhaus mit Gewerbeflächen, Goslar, Niedersachsen

KARMARSCHSTRASSE 23
Alteration and refurnishment of a shopping-mall with office-tower, Hanover, Lower Saxony
(Kröpke-Center) Umbau Geschäfts- und Bürozentrum, Hannover, Niedersachsen

ROONSTRASSE
Hotel and residential complex, Bad Salzuflen, Lower Saxony
Hotel- und Wohnzentrum, Bad Salzuflen, Niedersachsen

HAUS LIEBERMANNSTRASSE
Apartment house Hanover, Lower Saxony
Privates Apartmenthaus, Hannover, Niedersachsen

HAUS AM MARKT
Office, hotel and commercial complex, Langenhagen, Lower Saxony
Büro, Hotel -und Geschäftskomplex, Langenhagen, Niedersachsen

HOTEL AM NOBELRING
Office, hotel and commercial complex, Hanover, Lower Saxony
Büro-, Hotel- und Geschäftszentrum, Hannover, Niedersachsen

COMPETITION: EXPANSION OF THE TOWNHALL
Wilhelmshaven, Lower Saxony
WBW WILHELMSHAVEN
Rathaus und Geschäftszentrum, Wilhelmshaven, Niedersachsen

GRAND HYATT PRINZENSTRASSE
Hotel and commercial complex, Hanover, Lower Saxony
Hotel- und Geschäftskomplex Hannover, Niedersachsen

COMPETITION: GERMAN LIBRARY
Frankfurt am Main, Hessian
WBW DEUTSCHE BIBLIOTHEK
Frankfurt am Main, Hessen

LUISENSTRASSE 4
Commercial and office building, Hanover, Lower Saxony
Geschäfts- und Bürohaus, Hannover, Niedersachsen

PROJEKT BRANDES
Gardening and sales centre, Langenhagen, Lower Saxony
Gärtnerei und Verkaufszentrum, Langenhagen, Niedersachsen

PROJEKT BERGEN
Hotel and commercial centre, Bergen, Lower Saxony
Hotel- und Geschäftszentrum, Bergen, Niedersachsen

1982
GERTRUDENSTRASSE
Commercial and office building, Hamburg
Büro- und Geschäftshaus, Hamburg

ALTER FLUGHAFEN 16B
Office building, Hanover, Lower Saxony
Bürogebäude, Hannover, Niedersachsen

PROJEKT WIESENAU
Distribution and commercial park, Hanover, Lower Saxony
Lager- und Gewerbepark, Hannover, Niedersachsen

PROJEKT NICOLAISTRASSE
Commercial and residential complex, Hanover, Lower Saxony

Geschäfts- und Wohnkomplex, Hannover,
Niedersachsen

COMPETITION: BERGEN
Townhall and administration, Bergen,
Lower Saxony
WETTBEWERB BERGEN
Stadthalle und Stadtverwaltung, Bergen, Niedersachsen

PROJEKT LÜBECKERSTRASSE I
Trading and warehouse centre, Laatzen,
Lower Saxony
Gewerbe- und Lagerzentrum, Laatzen, Niedersachsen

PROJEKT LÜBECKERSTRASSE II
Trading and warehouse centre, Laatzen,
Lower Saxony
Gewerbe- und Lagerzentrum, Laatzen, Niedersachsen

PROJEKT HAMBURGER/KIELER STRASSE
Trading and warehouse centre, Laatzen, Lower
Saxony
Gewerbe- und Lagerzentrum, Laatzen,
Niedersachsen

PROJEKT HÖLTYSTRASSE
Apartment house, Hanover, Lower Saxony
Apartmenthaus, Hannover, Niedersachsen

BOCO
Laundry Hanover, Lower Saxony
Großwäscherei Hannover, Niedersachsen

PROJEKT JUNGFERNSTIEG 50
Office and commercial building, Hamburg
Büro- und Geschäftshaus, Hamburg

PROJEKT DIAHREN
Private residence, Diahren, Lower Saxony
Privates Wohnhaus, Diahren, Niedersachsen

COMPETITION: MANNHEIM National museum
for technique and work
Mannheim, Baden-Württemberg
WETTBEWERB MANNHEIM LANDESMUSEUM
FÜR TECHNIK & ARBEIT
Mannheim, Baden-Württemberg

WEVER & CO.
Warehouse centre and administration, Airport
Hanover, Lower Saxony
Lagerzentrum mit Verwaltung, Flughafen Hannover,
Niedersachsen

HILDESHEIMER STR. 5
Office and commercial centre, Hanover,
Lower Saxony
Büro- und Geschäftshaus, Hannover, Niedersachsen

KÖNIGSTR. 55
Office and commercial centre, Hanover,
Lower Saxony
Büro- und Geschäftshaus, Hannover, Niedersachsen

SALLSTRASSE
Office and commercial centre, Hanover,
Lower Saxony
Büro- und Geschäftshaus, Hannover, Niedersachsen

CENTRE OF NEIGHBORHOOD
AND URBAN DISTRICT
Hanover, Lower Saxony
NACHBARSCHAFTS- UND
STADTTEILZENTRUM
Hannover, Niedersachsen

PROJEKT HÖLTJE
Printing-press and administration, Hanover,
Lower Saxony
Druckerei und Verwaltung, Hannover, Niedersachsen

„BUNTE WELT" GOSERIEDE
Performance centre with restaurant and
administration, Hanover, Lower Saxony
Veranstaltungszentrum mit Restaurant
und Verwaltung, Hannover, Niedersachsen

WEENDER HOF
Residential and commercial building, Göttingen,
Lower Saxony
Wohn- und Geschäftshaus, Göttingen, Niedersachsen

WARMBÜCHENSTRASSE
Apartment building, Hanover, Lower Saxony
Apartmenthaus, Hannover, Niedersachsen

NORCON
Office building, Hanover, Lower Saxony
Bürohaus Hannover, Niedersachsen

POSTKAMP 10
Office and residential complex, Hanover,
Lower Saxony
Geschäfts- und Wohnkomplex Hannover, Niedersachsen

PAUL HARTMANN AG
Distribution centre and warehouse, Bietigheim,
Baden-Württemberg
Auslieferungslager, Bietigheim, Baden-Württemberg

GRAND HYATT INTERNATIONAL HOTEL
Hanover, Lower Saxony
Hannover, Niedersachsen

ROSSKAMPSTRASSE 32
Apartment house, Hanover, Lower Saxony
Apartmenthaus Hannover, Niedersachsen

COMPETITION: "The Peak"
Hongkong
WBW „The Peak"
Hongkong

COURT HOUSE
with administration, Nordheim, Lower Saxony
AMTSGERICHT
mit Verwaltung, Nordheim, Niedersachsen

1983
BOSCH-SIEMENS
Distribution and administration centre, Hanover,
Lower Saxony
Vertriebs- und Verwaltungszentrum, Hannover,
Niedersachsen

HILDESHEIMER STR. 5/AEGI
Office and commercial centre, Hanover,
Lower Saxony
Büro- und Geschäftszentrum, Hannover, Niedersachsen

WBW OPERA BASTILLE
Opera house, Paris, France
Opernhaus, Paris, Frankreich

COMPETITION: WASTE RECYCLING CENTRE
Frankfurt, Hessian
WBW MÜLLVERBRENNUNGSANLAGE
Frankfurt, Hessen

COMPETITION: COURT HOUSE WOLFSBURG
Court with administration, Wolfsburg, Lower
Saxony
WBW AMTSGERICHT WOLFSBURG
Amtsgericht mit Verwaltung, Wolfsburg,
Niedersachsen

COMPETITION: REGIONAL PARLIAMENT
HANOVER
Hanover, Lower Saxony
WBW LANDTAG HANNOVER
Hannover, Niedersachsen

HELSTOFER STR. 1
Distribution centre for dental products
and administration, Hanover, Lower Saxony
Dentallager mit Verwaltung, Hannover,
Niedersachsen

COMPETITION: HAMBURG DOM
Hamburg
WBW HAMBURG DOM
Hamburg

COMPETITION: MESSEPAVILLON KRUPP
Fair pavilion, Hanover, Lower Saxony
WBW MESSEPAVILLON KRUPP
Messepavillon, Hannover, Niedersachsen

AOK BURGDORF
Office building and administration Burgdorf,
Lower Saxony
Bürogebäude und Verwaltung Burgdorf,
Niedersachsen

EXPANSION BOSCH-SIEMENS
Distribution centre, Hanover, Lower Saxony
ERWEITERUNG BOSCH-SIEMENS
Vertriebszentrum, Hannover, Niedersachsen

UOP
Administration and distribution centre, Hanover,
Lower Saxony

Verwaltungs- und Versandzentrum,
Hannover, Niedersachsen

MAZ
Office and exhibition complex, Hanover, Lower Saxony
Büro- und Ausstellungskomplex, Hannover, Niedersachsen

OMUK
Television and radio centre, Hanover, Lower Saxony
Fernseh- und Rundfunkzentrum, Hannover, Niedersachsen

HAUS DR. BEHRENS
Medical and private residence, Wennigsen, Lower Saxony
Ärzte- und Wohnhaus, Wennigsen, Niedersachsen

1984
HANOVER FAIR
Restaurant and bar, Hanover, Lower Saxony
MESSE HANNOVER
Restaurant und Bar, Hannover, Niedersachsen

WOHLENBERGSTRASSE
Office and commercial complex, Hanover, Lower Saxony
Büro- und Geschäftshaus, Hannover, Niedersachsen

PORSCHESTR. 74
Office and commercial complex, Wolfsburg, Lower Saxony
Büro- und Geschäftshaus Wolfsburg, Niedersachsen

M + S
Textile factory, Hanover, Lower Saxony
Textilwerk Linden, Hannover

NOBELRING-CENTER
Office and commercial complex, Hanover, Lower Saxony
Büro- und Geschäftshaus, Hannover, Niedersachsen

GUSTAV-ADOLF-STRASSE
Office and commercial building, Köln, Westphalia
Büro- und Geschäftshaus, Köln, Nordrhein-Westfalen

VAHRENWALDER STRASSE
Office building, Hanover, Lower Saxony
Bürohaus, Hannover, Niedersachsen

BRITISCHES ZENTRUM
Shopping mall with offices, Hanover, Lower Saxony
Geschäftspassage und Bürohäuser Hannover, Niedersachsen

MEDICAL PARK
Research and development park, Hanover, Lower Saxony
Forschungs- und Entwicklungspark Hannover, Niedersachsen

HAUS ERLBECK
Office and commercial building, Hanover, Lower Saxony
Büro- und Geschäftshaus, Hannover, Niedersachsen

COMPETITION: KRUPP PAVILION
Exhibition centre fair, Hanover, Lower Saxony
WBW KRUPP PAVILLON
Ausstellungszentrum Messe Hannover, Niedersachsen

COMPETITION: MUSEUM BONN
German Museum, Bonn, Westphalia
WBW MUSEUM BONN
Deutsches Museum, Bonn, Nordrhein-Westfalen

1985
WORKING MEN'S CLUB
Hanover-List, Lower Saxony
HANDWERKER- UND GEWERBEHOF
Hannover-List, Niedersachsen

COMPETITION: VECHTA
Town hall and administration centre, Vechta, Lower Saxony
WBW VECHTA
Rathaus- und Verwaltungszentrum, Vechta, Niedersachsen

COMPETITION: GOVERNMENT ADMINISTRATION
Hanover, Lower Saxony
WBW VERFÜGUNGSGEBÄUDE DER LANDESREGIERUNG
Hannover, Niedersachsen

JOACHIMSTRASSE 1
Office and commercial building, Hanover, Lower Saxony
Büro- und Geschäftshaus, Hannover, Niedersachsen

COMPETITION: NG-BANK
Banking and administration centre, Hanover, Lower Saxony
WBW NG-BANK
Bank- und Verwaltungszentrum, Hannover, Niedersachsen

1986
TOYOTA
Distribution and production centre, Hanover, Lower Saxony
Vertriebs- und Produktionszentrum, Hannover, Niedersachsen

COMPAQ
Computer development centre, Hanover, Lower Saxony
Computerentwicklungszentrum, Hannover, Niedersachsen

COMPETITION: GOETHEINSTITUT
Goetheinstitut with administration, Munich, Bavaria
WBW GOETHEINSTITUT
Goetheinstitut mit Verwaltung, München, Bayern

HFS
Army-training centre for helicopter pilots Bückeburg-Achum, Lower Saxony
Heeresfliegerwaffenschule Bückeburg-Achum, Niedersachsen

BIO-SCIENCE-CENTRE
Research centre Leiden, Holland
Forschungszentrum Leiden, Holland

GENERAL MOTORS
Motorproduction, Hanover, Lower Saxony
Motorenproduktion, Hannover, Niedersachsen

MEDICAL PARK HOTEL
Hotel, conference and commercial centre, Hanover, Lower Saxony
Hotel-, Konferenz- und Geschäftszentrum, Hannover, Niedersachsen

FIBH
Research institute, Hanover, Lower Saxony
Forschungsinstitut, Hannover, Niedersachsen

1987
FLACHGLAS AG
Office building, Gelsenkirchen, Westphalia
Bürozentrum, Gelsenkirchen, Nordrhein-Westfalen

COMPETITION: LABOR EXCHANGE WITH ADMINISTRATION
Oldenburg, Lower Saxony
WBW ARBEITSAMT MIT VERWALTUNG
Oldenburg, Niedersachsen

INVITRON
Research centre, Hanover, Lower Saxony
Genforschungszentrum, Hannover, Niedersachsen

COMPAQ M
European headquarters, Munich, Bavaria
Europäische Firmenzentrale, München, Bayern

GERMAN COMMERCIAL CENTRE
Exhibition and distribution centre, New Port Beach, California
Ausstellungs- und Vertriebszentrum, New Port Beach, California

UNISYS
Headquarters, Düsseldorf, Westphalia
Hauptverwaltung, Düsseldorf, Nordrhein-Westfalen

DIGITAL DEC
Headquarters, Braunschweig, Lower Saxony
Hauptverwaltung, Braunschweig, Niedersachsen

QUANTUM CENTRE
Office building, Arkon, Ohio
Bürohaus, Arkon, Ohio

MILES KALI CHEMIE
Laboratory centre, Hanover, Lower Saxony
Laborzentrum, Hannover, Niedersachsen

/M/A/I-COMPUTER
European headquarters, Frankfurt, Hessian
Europazentrale, Frankfurt, Hessen

BSV
Office building, Hanover, Lower Saxony
Bürozentrum, Hannover, Niedersachsen

1988
WVA WORLD CENTRE FOR VISUAL AUTOMATION
Princeton, New Jersey
Princton, New Jersey

LUISENSTRASSE 4
Office and commercial building, Hanover, Lower Saxony
Büro- und Geschäftshaus, Hannover, Niedersachsen

COMPETITION: HANOVER
Savings bank and administration, Hanover, Lower Saxony
WBW HANNOVER
Sparkassenschule und Verwaltung, Hannover, Niedersachsen

MEDICAL PARK CENTRE
Research park, Hanover, Lower Saxony
Forschungspark, Hannover, Niedersachsen

COMPETITION: HELVETIA INSURANCE
Insurance centre, Hanover, Lower Saxony
WBW HELVETIA VERSICHERUNGEN
Versicherungszentrum, Hannover, Niedersachsen

BAHCELI
Office and commercial centre, Izmir/Turkey
Büro- und Geschäftshaus, Izmir/Türkei

HAMBURGER ALLEE 26/30
Office and commercial centre, Hanover, Lower Saxony
Büro- und Geschäftshaus, Hannover, Niedersachsen

MEC, SISLI-TURKEY
Shopping mall and office building, Istanbul, Turkey
Ladenpassage und Bürohäuser, Istanbul, Türkei

HOTEL/ILICA/PASA LIMANI
Hotel and commercial centre, Çesme, Turkey
Hotel- und Geschäftszentrum, Çerme/Türkei

PITTLER
Headquarters, Frankfurt, Hessian
Firmenhauptverwaltung, Frankfurt, Hessen

1989
COMPETITION: BERLIN MUSEUM
Jewish museum, Berlin
WBW BERLIN MUSEUM
Jüdisches Museum, Berlin

JOACHIMSTRASSE 2
Office and commercial building, Hanover, Lower Saxony
Büro- und Geschäftshaus, Hannover, Niedersachsen

COMPETITION: FEDERAL COUNCIL
Bonn, Westphalia
WBW BUNDESRAT
Bonn, Nordrhein-Westfalen

COMPETITION: EUROPEAN PATENT-OFFICE
The Haag, Holland
WBW EUROPÄISCHES PATENTAMT
The Hague, Holland

WILKENBURGER STRASSE
Office building, Hanover, Lower Saxony
Bürohaus, Hannover, Niedersachsen

KARL-WIECHERT-ALLEE
Office building, Hanover, Lower Saxony
Bürohaus, Hannover, Niedersachsen

COMPETITION: GESAMTSCHULE RÖDINGHAUSEN
General school with sporting centre, Rödinghausen, Westphalia
WBW GESAMTSCHULE RÖDINGHAUSEN
Gesamtschule mit Sportzentrum, Rödinghausen, Nordrhein-Westfalen

MEDICAL PARK MOSCOW
Research centre, Moscow
Forschungszentrum, Moskau

EUROPEAN SPACE CENTRE DULLES INTERNATIONAL
Administration centre of the German space industry, Fairfax County, Virginia
Fairfax County, Verwaltungszentrum der Deutschen Raumfahrtindustrie, Virginia

COURTYARD-CENTRE
Hotel, commercial and office centre, Duisburg, Westphalia
Hotel-, Geschäfts- und Bürozentrum, Duisburg, Nordrhein-Westfalen

1990
/M/A/I
Office building, Frankfurt a. Main, Hessian
Bürohäuser, Frankfurt a. Main, Hessen

LA MIRADA METRO CENTRE
Office and commercial building, Los Angeles, California
Büro- und Geschäftshaus, Los Angeles, California

LUISENSTRASSE 8
Office building, Hanover, Lower Saxony
Geschäftshaus, Hannover, Niedersachsen

COMPETITION: LABOR EXCHANGE LOWER SAXONY-BREMEN
Hanover, Lower Saxony
WBW LANDESARBEITSAMT NIEDERSACHSEN-BREMEN
Hannover, Niedersachsen

ADMINISTRATION CENTRE
Hanover, Lower Saxony
VERWALTUNGSCENTER SELIGMANNALLEE 4
Verwaltungscentrum Hannover, Niedersachsen

NI 2 + NI 3
Office buildings, Frankfurt a. Main, Hessian
Bürogebäude, Frankfurt a. Main, Hessen

1991
ROSEMOUNT
Research centre, Alzenau, Hessian
Forschungszentrum, Alzenau, Hessen

OETTINGER
Commercial and production centre, Hanover, Lower Saxony
Gewerbe- und Fabrikationszentrum Hannover, Niedersachsen

LÖWENBASTION
Amusement park and restaurant, Hanover, Lower Saxony
Unterhaltungszentrum und Restaurant, Hannover, Niedersachsen

PROJEKT EUROPARK
Office and commercial centre, Duisburg, Westphalia
Büro- und Geschäftscenter, Duisburg, Nordrhein-Westfalen

PROJEKT HOTELCENTRE
Hotel and commercial centre, Köln, Westphalia
Hotel- und Geschäftscenter, Köln, Nordrhein-Westfalen

ROSENTHALER STRASSE 31 - 25
Office, commercial and private residence centre, Berlin-Mitte
Büro-, Wohn- und Geschäftscenter, Berlin-Mitte

STADTZENTRUM LEHRTE
Office and commercial centre, Lehrte,
Lower Saxony
Büro- und Geschäftszentrum, Lehrte, Niedersachsen

PROJEKT OSTERSTRASSE
Hotel- and commercial centre, Hanover, Lower Saxony
Hotel- und Geschäftscenter, Hannover, Niedersachsen

P. H. BRAUNS,
Sales and warehouse centre, Hanover, Lower Saxony
Verkaufs- und Lagercenter, Hannover, Niedersachsen

WERFTSTRASSE 1
Amusementpark with marina Hanover, Lower Saxony
Freizeitzentrum mit Jachthafen, Hannover, Niedersachsen

INVALIDENSTRASSE
Office and commercial building, Berlin-Mitte
Büro- und Geschäftshaus, Berlin-Mitte

BOA KRAUSENSTRASSE
Office and commercial building, Berlin-Mitte
Büro- und Geschäftszentrum, Berlin-Mitte

SÜDDEUTSCHE
Commercial and office centre with shopping mall, Konstanz/Bodensee, Baden-Württemberg
Geschäfts- und Bürozentrum mit Ladenpassage, Konstanz/Bodensee, Baden-Württemberg

UNI-CENTRE
Science and research park, Essen, Westphalia
Wissenschafts- und Entwicklungspark, Essen, Nordrhein-Westfalen

NEUSTRELITZ
Commercial and production park, Neustrelitz, Mecklenburg Vorpommern
Gewerbe- und Produktionspark, Neustrelitz, Mecklenburg Vorpommern

1992
OST-WEST-STRASSE 70
Office and administration centre, Hamburg
Büro- und Verwaltungszentrum, Hamburg

OETTINGER II
Office and production building, Empelde, Lower Saxony
Büro- und Fertigungsgebäude, Empelde, Niedersachsen

KTC
Technology center Kreuzberg, Berlin
Kreuzberger Technologiecentrum, Berlin

ESB
Savings bank, Burgdorf, Lower Saxony
Stadtsparkasse Burgdorf, Burgdorf, Niedersachsen

EISWERDER
Hotel- and training centre, Berlin
Hotel- und Schulungszentrum, Berlin

1993
RHENUS
Warehouse complex/ P & G Praha, Prague, Czechoslovakia
Lagerhallenkomplex / P & G Praha, Prag, Tschechei

BUG
Sailing club with hotel complex, Island Rügen, Mecklenburg-Vorpommern
Jachthafen mit Hotelkomplex, Insel Rügen, Mecklenburg-Vorpommern

COMPETITION: NÜRNBERG HEADQUARTERS
Nürnberger insurance company, Nürnberg, Bavaria
WBW NÜRNBERG HAUPTVERWALTUNG
Nürnberger Versicherung, Nürnberg; Bayern

COMPETITION: UNIVERSITY COTTBUS
General planning and construction library, Cottbus, Brandenburg
WBW UNIVERSITÄT COTTBUS
Generalplanung und Neubau Bibliothek, Cottbus, Brandenburg

COMPETITION: MAX-PLANCK-INSTITUT
Research institute with administration, Munich, Bavaria
WBW MAX-PLANCK-INSTITUT
Forschungsinstitut mit Verwaltung, München, Bayern

UFERPROMENADE CUVRYSTRASSE
Riverbank-Development with amusement facilities and shops, Berlin
Stegentwicklung mit Freizeit- und Geschäftseinrichtungen, Berlin

SPREESPEICHER OSTHAFEN
Office, commercial and exhibition centre, Osthafen, Berlin
Büro-, Geschäfts- und Ausstellungszentrum, Osthafen, Berlin

COMPETITION: MUSEUMSINSEL
Administration and cultural buildings, Berlin-Mitte
WBW MUSEUMSINSEL
Verwaltungs- und Kulturbauten, Berlin-Mitte

1994
HANSACENTER
Commercial, office and exhibition centre, Berlin
Geschäfts-, Büro, und Ausstellungszentrum, Berlin

COMPETITION: FEDERAL COUNCIL
Administration centre, Berlin-Mitte
WBW BUNDESPRÄSIDIALAMT
Verwaltungszentrum, Berlin-Mitte

COMPETITION: NORDHORN
Headquarters of the savings bank, Nordhorn, Lower-Saxony
WBW NORDHORN
Hauptverwaltung der Stadtsparkasse, Nordhorn, Niedersachsen

COMPETITION: AIRPORT LEIPZIG-HALLE
Leipzig, Saxony
WBW FLUGHAFEN LEIPZIG-HALLE
Leipzig, Sachsen

COMPETITION: SPEICHERSTADT POTSDAM
Central government, Potsdam, Brandenburg
WBW SPEICHERSTADT POTSDAM
Landesparlament, Potsdam, Brandenburg

COMPETITION: PÜNTKERS PATT
Hotel and commercial centre, Meppen, Lower Saxony
WBW PÜNTKERS PATT
Hotel- und Geschäftszentrum, Meppen, Niedersachsen

COMPETITION: BARNETSTRASSE
Educational and training establishment, Berlin
WBW BARNETSTRASSE
Bildungs- und Schulzentrum, Berlin

1995
COMPETITION: FELIX-NUSSBAUM-HAUS
Art museum, Osnabrück, Lower Saxony
WBW FELIX-NUSSBAUM-HAUS
Kunstmuseum, Osnabrück, Niedersachsen

COMPETITION: MAGDEBURG
Management of water and navigation, Magdeburg, Sachsen-Anhalt
WBW MAGDEBURG
Wasser- und Schiffahrtsdirektion, Magdeburg, Sachsen-Anhalt

COMPETITION: FRANKFURT-ODER
Grammar school, Frankfurt-Oder, Brandenburg
WBW FRANKFURT-ODER
Oberstufenschulzentrum, Frankfurt-Oder, Brandenburg

GERU
Commercial and production centre, Rudolfstrasse, Berlin-Friedrichshain
Gewerbe- und Produktionszentrum Rudolfstraße, Berlin-Friedrichshain

COMPETITION: LÜNEBURG
Downtown development Lüneburg, Lower Saxony
WBW LÜNEBURG
Platz- und Quartiersgestaltung, Lüneburg, Niedersachsen

COMPETITION: ERFURT
Main station with office and administration centre, Erfurt, Thurungia
WBW ERFURT
Hauptbahnhof mit Geschäfts- und Verwaltungszentrum, Erfurt, Thüringen

DB AG
Technical headquarters, Duisburg, Westphalia
Technisches Leitzentrum, Duisburg, Nordrhein-Westfalen

1996
COMPETITION: POTSDAM
Provincial administration and ministries, Potsdam, Brandenburg
WBW POTSDAM
Landesverwaltung und Ministerien, Potsdam- Brandenburg

CARREE (HEAG-PASSAGE)
Office and commercial centre with restaurants, shopping mall and theater, Darmstadt, Hessian
Büro- und Geschäftszentrum mit Restaurants und Kulturhalle, Darmstadt, Hessen

COMPETITION: LVA AUGSBURG
Federal insurance company, Schwaben, Augsburg, Bavaria
WBW LVA AUGSBURG
Landesversicherungsanstalt Schwaben, Augsburg, Bayern

COMPETITION: PAVILION
Great Garden Herrenhausen Restaurant and pavilion, Hanover, Lower Saxony
WBW PAVILLON GROSSER GARTEN
Restaurant und Pavillon, Hannover, Niedersachsen

1997
WBW BRÜHLSTRASSE
Office and apartment complex with church and parking place, Hanover, Lower Saxony
Büro- und Apartmentkomplex mit Kirche und Parkhaus, Hannover, Niedersachsen

COMPETITION: EXPO-PAVILION
German pavilion Expo 2000, Hanover, Lower Saxony
WBW EXPO-PAVILLON
Deutscher Pavillon Expo 2000, Hannover, Niedersachsen

COMPETITION: HTWS
Technical university Zittau, Görlitz, Brandenburg
WBW HTWS
Technische Hochschule Zittau, Görlitz, Brandenburg

RO 48
Commercial Building Berlin-Mitte
Geschäfts- und Wohnhaus, Berlin-Mitte

SPREEPARKHAUS
Central car park Berlin
Zentrales Parkhaus, Berlin

COMPETITION: RIGGA ROAD
Hotel and commercial centre, Dubai, UAE
WBW RIGGA ROAD
Hotel- und Geschäftszentrum, Dubai, UAE

EAP 8
Reconstruction of office and commercial building with banking centre, Hanover, Lower Saxony
Umbau Büro- und Geschäftshaus mit Bankzentrum, Hannover, Niedersachsen

COMPETITION: POST AG
Headquarters of the Post AG, Bonn, Westphalia
WBW Post AG
Generalvertretung der Post AG, Bonn, Nordrhein-Westfalen

1998
COMPETITION: UAE-Pavillon
Expo 2000 Hanover, Lower Saxony
WBW UAE
Pavillon Expo 2000 Hannover, Niedersachsen

COMPETITION: Service Centre Hanover of Volkswagen Commercial Vehicles,
Lower Saxony
WBW Kunden Center Hannover der VW AG Nutzfahrzeuge,
Niedersachsen

COMPETITION: city area around the train station, Erfurt,
Thurungia
WBW Bahnhofsumfeld in Erfurt,
Thüringen

COMPETITION: Budapester Square,
Stuttgart 21, Baden-Württemberg
WBW Budapester Platz,
Stuttgart 21, Baden-Württemberg

Biography

Klaus Schuwirth
Dipl.-Ing. Architekt
born 1947
Graduate engineer architect, senior-partner
management and architecture
geboren 1947
Dipl.-Ing. Architekt,
geschäftsführender Gesellschafter.

1969 - 1974
Studied at the Technical Universities
of Hanover, London and Paris
Studium der Architektur an der Technischen
Universität Hannover mit Studienaufenthalten
in London und Paris.

1974
Master's degree at the master class
of Prof. Spengelin, Hamburg and employee
at the institute of urban planning
Prof. Spengelin, Hamburg
Diplom bei Professor Spengelin, danach
Mitarbeit am Institut für Städtebau Hannover,
Professor Spengelin.

1975 - 1977
Employee at the architectural office of Wilke
& Partners, Hanover/Düsseldorf. Project
architect for Moscow International Airport
and Casablanca International Fair in Morocco
Mitarbeit im Büro Wilke & Partner,
Hannover/Düsseldorf.

since 1977
Partner in the architectural office SE &
Partners together with Dipl.-Ing. Erol Erman
seit 1977
Partner im Architekturbüro SE & Partner
zusammen mit Herrn Dipl.-Ing. Erol Erman.

Erol Erman
Dipl.-Ing. Architekt
born 1942 in Istanbul, Turkey
Graduate engineer architect, senior-partner
design and architecture
geboren 1942 in Istanbul, Türkey
Dipl.-Ing. Architekt,
geschäftsführender Gesellschafter.

1962 - 1967
Study at the D.G.S.A. Istanbul
with a master's degree
Architekturstudium an der D.G.S.A. Istanbul.

1968 - 1969
Employee at different architectural offices
in Istanbul, Paris and London.
Mitarbeit in verschiedenen Architekturbüros in
Istanbul, Paris und London.

1970 - 1977
Employee at the architectural office of Wilke
& Partners, Hanover/Düsseldorf, design
architect for Moscow International Airport
and Hanover International Airport,
International Airport Munich II, Casablanca
International Fair Morocco, Jakarta
International Fair, Indunija
Mitarbeit im Büro Wilke & Partner,
Hannover/Düsseldorf.

since 1977
Partner in the architectural office SE &
Partners together with Dipl.-Ing. Klaus
Schuwirth
seit 1977
Partner im Architekturbüro SE & Partner
zusammen mit Herrn Dipl.-Ing. Klaus
Schuwirth.